MIND IN ACTION

MIND IN ACTION

BEDE RUNDLE

CLARENDON PRESS · OXFORD
1997

Oxford University Press, Great Clarendon Street, Oxford OX2 6DP

Oxford New York

Athens Auckland Bangkok Bogota Bombay
Buenos Aires Calcutta Cape Town Dar es Salaam
Delhi Florence Hong Kong Istanbul Karachi
Kuala Lumpur Madras Madrid Melbourne
Mexico City Nairobi Paris Singapore
Taipei Tokyo Toronto Warsaw

and associated companies in
Berlin Ibadan

Oxford is a trade mark of Oxford University Press

Published in the United States
by Oxford University Press Inc., New York

British Library Cataloguing in Publication Data
Data available

Library of Congress Cataloging in Publication Data
Rundle, Bede.
Mind in action / Bede Rundle
Includes bibliographical references and index
1. Philosophy of mind   2. Act (Philosophy)   I. Title.
BD418.3.R86 1997   128'.4—dc21   97–18544
ISBN 0–19–823691–3

1 3 5 7 9 10 8 6 4 2

Typeset by Hope Services (Abingdon) Ltd.
Printed in Great Britain
on acid-free paper by
Biddles Ltd.,
Guildford & King's Lynn

For Ros

PREFACE

Can minds change the world? Those who believe that they might, with luck, *will* things to behave in certain ways have at best a dubious hypothesis to put to us, but there is nothing dubious about the familiar consideration that we act *because* of our beliefs, hopes, desires, fears, and so forth, and with this 'because' we seem to be acknowledging mental causes of physical happenings. Such a conception is the starting-point for much contemporary philosophy of mind and action, and it is a starting-point that to many appears unquestionable: if 'because' is not self-evidently causal in this use, at least there appear to be no alternative readings clamouring for our attention. True, if believing, hoping, wanting, and fearing are set alongside notions in which our everyday concept of cause is seen at its clearest, as with pushing, pulling, cutting, and twisting, we may have second thoughts about the causal potentialities of the former: it is difficult, with these, to see how the idea of one thing's acting upon another might be realized. However, another standpoint distinctive of current philosophy—a materialist view of the mind—is there to come to our aid. A Cartesian view of body and mind as separate substances nowadays finds little favour with philosophers; on the contrary, human beings are commonly regarded, like all other living things, as physical through and through. If, then, the reality of beliefs and the rest is the reality of states and events in the brain, the mental has what it takes to interact with the physical.

This combination—a causal conception of reasons for actions coupled with a physicalism of the mental—appears to promise a degree of explanatory power well able to justify its general adoption by philosophers and psychologists currently seeking to investigate the workings of the mind in relation to the body. Now at last we are liberated from the unfathomable mind–body relations which a Cartesian dualism imposes, and can look forward to the day when our everyday explanations of actions and those provided by the neurosciences, with their open appeal to causally relevant physical properties, may be seen to converge.

However, if the two forms of explanation can converge, they can also diverge, opening up the possibility that the physical reality which provides the springs of our actions is not what we identify via our thoughts and desires. A major dilemma threatens this approach. If psychological states and episodes fall outside the causal scheme, their status reduces to that of mere epiphenomena, ineffectual by-products of neural processes playing no significant part in the history of an action. On the other hand, if they are to be identified with physiological states and episodes, then, while this secures their character as potential causes, it could be that they turn out to be identical with the *wrong* states and episodes, in which case the mental is once more no better than an epiphenomenon, and a totally misleading one at that. Moreover, there is even a difficulty in seeing how, on the causal conception, any physical conditions could be the *right* ones. The causal powers of events in our brains are defined in terms of their physical properties, yet the aspect of a psychological state that an explanation of behaviour exploits is surely not to be numbered among such properties. Thinking one thing—that it is safe to cross the road—you act in one way; thinking something else—that it is unsafe to cross—you do something different. It is because of the *content* of your belief, because it is this belief rather than that, that you do what you do. This is central to the kind of explanation which we should give of your action, yet there appears to be no way of showing how such content can be instrumental in originating or modifying behaviour.

At all events, the causal conception of the mental makes for the possibility of error, and the possibility of error throws into doubt our very conception of ourselves as rational agents acting freely for this or that reason. It may be, then, that, if what we say as to our reasons for acting is acceptable, it is at best so on provisional or pragmatic grounds, while we await the great dawn of more scientifically informed neural explanations, and when these come it may be that our homely psychological explanations are revealed as without foundation, a legacy of a primitive 'folk' psychology.

However, as will be argued here at length, neither the causal conception of the mental, nor the appeal to physicalism, is above attack. Our main concern will be with the former, with the 'functionalist' conception that is so commonly, and so uncritically, accepted. In treating beliefs and desires as causes, we distort the pattern of explanation in which these commonly figure. More generally, the causal approach encourages a mistaken way of looking at the subject—as if progress in the philosophy of mind and action were unthinkable so long as we were not prepared to engage in a quasi-scientific investigation aimed at determining what causes what. We shall develop an alternative analysis of action and practical reasoning, supplemented by accounts of decision, intention, and belief which are in keeping with our ordinary use of these concepts and which make plain that our familiar explanations have nothing to fear from discoveries about what goes on at the level of neural activity.

This is not to say that we must distance ourselves from empirical findings. On the contrary, much discussion of the relevant topics is excessively abstract and general, with insufficient attention to the diverse psychological phenomena which give life to the issues. In seeking to avoid this failing, and in trying to press the analysis of the central concepts further than is usual, we shall find it useful to give attention to questions of animal mentality. The treatment of such concepts as desire, belief, sensation, and communication can profit from this extension, both in throwing light on their broader application and in providing a check on what is said with respect to human psychology. In particular, the central topic of *action* gains from a consideration of purposive animal behaviour. In following up this broader investigation it has been necessary to simplify to a greater degree than would be appropriate if animal psychology were our main concern. Likewise, topics from the philosophy of language, centred around meaning and reference, have not been developed here at length, though in both cases references to more extended coverages are given.

The present approach to philosophical questions owes much to Wittgenstein, but on a number of issues some departure from his position will be noticed. I am most grateful to Peter Hacker for his exposition and defence of Wittgenstein's thought, particularly on points where I have been inclined to diverge, and where he has often, with success, urged me to think again. My predilection for more systematic analysis is in the tradition of Ryle and Austin, a tradition which has largely given way to a scientistic approach in which conceptual analysis takes second place to a misguided quest for *theories*. Science is continuous with philosophy, in the sense that a philosophical analysis of its concepts may contribute to scientific understanding. But that is different from modelling philosophy on science, as if there were philosophical theories much as there are scientific theories, the difference residing in the particular entities—beliefs and desires, say, rather than quarks and black holes—which the philosopher is obliged to postulate. Such a comparison seems to me totally inappropriate, a misplaced pragmatism begotten of a surrender to scepticism. Whatever their limitations, earlier analytical philosophers had

at least a nose for nonsense. Sadly, so many philosophers today have
only a taste for it. I should like to think that the arguments in the following pages might do something to sharpen the former sense.

Bede Rundle

Trinity College, Oxford
October 1996

CONTENTS

ABBREVIATIONS

The following abbreviations are used to refer to the works of Wittgenstein.

BB *The Blue and Brown Books* (Oxford: Blackwell, 1958)

GB 'Remarks on Frazer's "Golden Bough"', in *Ludwig Wittgenstein: Philosophical Occasions 1912–1951*, ed. J. Klagge and A. Nordmann (Indianapolis: Hackett, 1993)

LC *Lectures and Conversations on Aesthetics, Psychology and Religious Belief*, ed. C. Barrett (Oxford: Blackwell, 1966)

LPP *Wittgenstein's Lectures on Philosophical Psychology, 1946–47*, notes by P. T. Geach, K. J. Shah, and A. C. Jackson, ed. P. T. Geach (New York: Harvester-Wheatsheaf, 1988)

LWII *Last Writings on the Philosophy of Psychology*, vol. II, ed. G. H. von Wright and H. Nyman, trans. C. G. Luckhardt and M. A. E. Aue (Oxford: Blackwell, 1992)

NB *Notebooks 1914–1916*, ed. G. E. M. Anscombe and G. H. von Wright, trans. G. E. M. Anscombe (2nd edn., Oxford: Blackwell, 1979)

PI *Philosophical Investigations*, ed. G. E. M. Anscombe and R. Rhees, trans. G. E. M. Anscombe (3rd edn., Oxford: Blackwell, 1958)

RPPI *Remarks on the Philosophy of Psychology*, vol. I, ed. G. E. M. Anscombe and G. H. von Wright, trans. G. E. M. Anscombe (Oxford: Blackwell, 1980)

RPPII *Remarks on the Philosophy of Psychology*, vol. II, ed. G. H. von Wright and H. Nyman, trans. C. G. Luckhardt and M. A. E. Aue (Oxford: Blackwell, 1980)

Z *Zettel*, ed. G. E. M. Anscombe and G. H. von Wright, trans. G. E. M. Anscombe (Oxford: Blackwell, 1967)

I

Mental Antecedents of Action

Much of what we say about the mental appears to be shot through with causal idioms. Bad news is said to disappoint or depress, a person's face to remind us of another, an unusual happening to intrigue or excite us; a chance remark may make us think of something we were meant to do, and a thought may set someone off smiling or chuckling; a sudden realization that a person means ill may send a chill of fear up the spine, and fear may in turn cause us to tremble or stammer.

Such familiar ways of speaking lead on naturally to more theoretical accounts of the mind in which use of causal notions is freely made. Analyses of perception and memory frequently turn to causation to find what makes the difference between genuine knowledge and mere chance correctness of a belief, and the explanation of action by reference to beliefs and desires is commonly taken to be a species of causal explanation. Indeed, for the functionalist, the very concept of a mental state is nothing other than the concept of a state which is apt for the production of certain sorts of behaviour. These theoretical and non-theoretical conceptions come together to form a picture of the mental and the behavioural which defines the prevailing view of their relationship, and it is this picture that I wish to scrutinize.

The examples just enumerated can be divided into two, those in which the supposed cause is mental, and those in which the mental figures as effect. In general, the second term of the relation, 'x causes y', is the less problematic, and for the most part we need have no serious reservations about the occurrence of psychological descriptions at this point. But, while the ubiquity of causation makes for an overwhelming presumption that there will be something to which a thought or feeling owes its occurrence, there is not a like presumption that a given happening will have a specifically mental event as its cause, or indeed that an event of this latter kind will issue in any effect at all. Might it not be, for instance, that movement in response

to a sensation is in reality a matter of movement and sensation stem-
ming from a common cause? Again, perhaps the thoughts which
guide behaviour can be made intelligible in this capacity without
enjoying any instrumental role whatever in its generation, both being
manifestations or expressions of a single, if complex, state. The case
for excluding the mental from the realm of causes, or at least for
querying its membership, is far stronger than is generally appreciated,
and I shall now set forth some of the considerations which favour
this underrated possibility. The emphasis in this opening chapter will
be on indicating problems and raising questions. In so far as a stand
is taken on points of substance, the necessary attempt at a defence
will, for the most part, be given only with later arguments.

1.1 DESIRE, THOUGHT, AND ACTION

It may appear indisputable that there are occasions when how we
think determines how we act, where the determination represents
causal necessity. Likewise for desire. Without thought and desire,
surely, we neither would nor indeed could accomplish what we do.
And it is true that thoughts, desires, decisions, and intentions have an
assured place in the explanations we give of our actions, as when, in
explaining our haste, we cite a belief that our train is on the point of
leaving. Indeed, when people offer such a reason there is no way of
faulting their account so long as they are sincere and understand
what they are saying.

The source of this incorrigibility is better appreciated by focusing
on the verb 'reason' rather than on the noun. To give one's reason is
to say how one reasoned, the authoritativeness of the avowal accordingly being just a particular case of the authoritativeness enjoyed with
respect to one's present thoughts generally. When someone informs
us that he is wondering whether he may be allergic to strawberries,
then, provided he is not lying, that is an end of the matter: his attention to this possibility has been put beyond doubt. This, at least, mirrors the more straightforward case. Sometimes, when the agent has
not articulated his thoughts to himself, it is more a matter of R's
being his reason so long as he is prepared to accept or acknowledge
R as a suitable expression of the thought that had been taking shape,
the consideration that had weighed with him. Contrast causal explanations. Whether or not A caused B is not a matter for an incorrigi-

ble judgement. *A* may well have preceded *B* at an appropriate time and place, and indeed have done so on numerous occasions, but then so too may a variety of other factors. It could be that, far from being a cause of *B*, *A* is simply a further effect of whatever it is that is the true cause. To settle definitively just which of the factors is operative requires us to engage in eliminative experiments, experiments whose results are not knowable a priori.

It is often complained that the vagueness of the term 'cause', or its several readings, means that we are not presented with a decidable issue if asked whether desires, say, are causes of actions. The preceding argument clearly requires a use of 'cause' according to which the identification of something as a cause must be corrigible, must be subject to the possibility of error, and I propose to tie the term to this condition—for the sake of definiteness, not because no other uses can be admitted. 'Cause' and 'reason' can interchange in certain contexts—e.g. in 'gives cause' and 'gives reason'—and 'because' can be used in connection with either. My concern is not to establish rights over either term; I claim merely that there is a use of 'cause' in which it contrasts with 'reason' in the way indicated. The range of possible causes thereby admitted is considerable, extending to causes as remote from the paradigms of agents and their acts as those given with such propositions as 'The height of the tower caused it to topple' and 'Lack of vitamin C causes rickets'. This is important. There is no question of our withholding the title of 'cause' on the basis of an excessively narrow usage.

The significance of the contrast between the two forms of explanation is a matter for further consideration, but the argument has one limitation which can be acknowledged without further ado. Granted that honest avowals of a reason for action are not open to challenge, so not to be understood in causal terms, the argument does not show that reasons are *not* causes, only that our understanding of 'reason' does not *require* that they should be. The difference revealed is one in the *concepts* of assigning a cause to one's movements and giving one's reason for acting. Compare the causal theory of perception. That the object of perception is at the same time its cause does not appear to be a conclusion which mere consideration of the concept of perception can bring to light. Seeing, certainly, is taken, if unthinkingly, to be a matter of a direct confrontation with the object seen, rather than an experience of something to be found among the object's effects. Not knowing that something comes from the object seen to the eye, and has an effect at that point, it made sense for the ancients to suppose that something emanated from the eye to the object, with any causal transactions taking place externally to the perceiver. On the other hand, this does not show that, having settled the empirical question, we shall not find a central role for causation once we set about putting flesh on the minimal account of sight which our concept embodies. Similarly, supposing that a causal role is not required of reasons to provide what we ask of them in explanations of actions, we may still ask whether it at least makes sense to view them in this light. If there is no obstacle on the side of grammar, then the truth of the causal proposition is an empirical matter—and not one that a philosopher has any particular authority to decide.

This is, of course, a large 'if'. With some mental terms we may perhaps advance as far as an empirical possibility, but, when the candidate causes are reasons, the grammar is not congenial towards even this much: witness the difficulty of transferring to 'cause' such epithets of 'reason' as 'cogent', 'unacceptable', 'misguided', 'good', 'convincing', and others appropriate to linguistically related items. A customary move at this point is to adjust the terms of the putative relation, shifting to *reasoning*, or *having R as one's reason*, as furnishing the appropriate specification of a cause. Or again, the statement of a reason is not precluded from being at the same time the specification of a cause. We shall not now pursue these alternatives, however, since our immediate concern is not so much to exclude the possibility of causation as to see whether we can render acceptable the consequences of denying that reasons, or indeed reasonings, are *required* to be causes. Since I wish to group under, or along with, these *any* of the broadly mental or psychological antecedents of behaviour—deliberation, decision, desire, belief, intention, and so forth—it would appear that any attempt to sideline causal considerations will bring us up against an overwhelming objection. As already indicated, it is surely integral to our conception of the relation between thought and action that in a vast number of cases we simply should not have done what we in fact did if our thoughts had not taken the course they did; that, indeed, without thought none of the distinctively human accomplishments *could* have materialized.

The mental antecedents of action can usefully be divided into those relating to desire and those relating to thought or belief, the former being to the fore when it is a question of what, supposedly, one *would* not have done but for the mental act or state, the latter when it is a matter of what one *could* not have done. Each in turn raises two questions. First, when is the truth of 'I shouldn't have Ved if I hadn't thought that *p* (wanted *x*)' demanded if the thought or desire genuinely is a reason for the act of Ving? Second, in so far as it is demanded, does that show the 'because' in 'I Ved because I thought that *p* (wanted *x*)' to be causal?

The clearest cases of a requirement come with the involvement of desire, cases where, with the emphasis on the reading of 'done', it can be agreed that the agent would not have done what he did if his state of mind had not been as it was, since in the absence of the desire there would have been no question of crediting him with an act of the kind envisaged. Goethe's Werther might have shot himself accidentally, but it would not have been suicide—would not have counted as such—if he had not wanted to kill himself. Or again, if Kate insists that she would not have met Harvey if it had not been her wish to do so, she must be thinking of meeting as an intentional act, in so far as she is unable to exclude the possibility that she should have run across Harvey by chance. It is a matter of 'would not have gone to meet' rather than 'would not have come across'. The intention is seen as conferring a certain character on the meeting, rather than as a necessary causal condition for its very occurrence. Likewise with the more negative acts of desisting or refraining. I should not have given up smoking if I had not wanted to. But, on one use of 'want' or 'desire', what this comes to is: it would not have been a matter of *giving up* smoking in the absence of that desire. For all I know, even without the desire I might have ceased to smoke; I might, after all, have been smitten by paralysis; but that is all it would have been—ceasing to smoke, not a resolute forbearance from smoking, an act of self-denial which I might think to my credit.

When the justification of the counterfactual proposition follows these lines its inescapability is, of course, logical, giving no support to a causal relation. Moreover, while the relevant reading of such a proposition may not be the only possible, nor indeed the most natural, it would seem that it is only along these lines that the counterfactual is sustainable. You open the drawer in search of a knife and fork. You may not wish to insist that you would not have opened the drawer had you not had that aim, since you might in that event have wanted something else. But suppose that the desire for cutlery is the only relevant desire that has to be acknowledged, actually or as a possibility. Then, of course, while we are ruling out like action on your part for any other reason, that does not commit us to denying that something which was *not* intentional action might have taken place. You did indeed open the drawer in search of a knife and fork, but for this to give your reason it is not required that you be in a position to say: had I not wanted some cutlery I should on no account have opened the drawer, not even absent-mindedly.

Likewise with thought and belief. You say you agreed to the proposal only for the sake of the peace you thought that would bring. If you had voiced your agreement without this reason, there would have been no other, you maintain, in which event your behaviour, while outwardly perhaps the same, would none the less have had a different character, being impulsive rather than calculated. In such a case it is not so much that how or what you think can be counted on to make a difference to what you *do*, taking this verb in a suitably broad sense; rather, it makes a difference to how what you do is to be *described*. Similarly, you could not have forgiven a person if you had not known what you were about; that is, it would not have counted as forgiving if you were oblivious to the character of what you were doing.

Or again, why did I go up to the bureau? To take a closer look at the photographs placed there. So I should not have made this move had I not been interested in taking a closer look? Probably not. I am not given to doing such things for no reason. However, for my explanation to hold, for my reason to be as stated, I do not have to take a stand on what would have happened had I not had this interest. It is enough that I acted in the belief that I could satisfy my curiosity by doing what I did. Clearly, the claim that I should not have gone up to the bureau had I not wanted to take a closer look at the photographs needs no defence unless it is a matter of my acting thus *only* because I had the desire cited. If it is not allowed that there should have been action for no reason, if we are not to suppose that, in the absence of the given desire, there might have been another, then the counterfactual follows immediately. There is no requirement that a causal relation be established before this inference can be drawn.

Causal overdetermination, along with the possibility of alternative ways of bringing something about, make the involvement of counterfactual considerations in matters of causation problematic. Suppose it is successfully argued that defence of the relevant counterfactual proposition is not required for the truth of one's statement of a reason; such an argument may none the less fall short of showing that the pattern of explanation given with the latter is non-causal. However, the indifference of that proposition to the statement of a reason remains of central importance, in that the counterfactual is thereby shown not to constitute a threat to the subject's authority.

There is abundant scope for causal considerations in explaining many aspects of human behaviour: the reasons given by the agent will not cover, or not cover in every respect, the manner or the timing of his activities; why he is shy, defensive, petulant, quick to react. However, while these and myriad other aspects of personality take us to causal questions, so long as thought and action are our concern it remains true that the patterns to be discerned in our ways of speaking do not impose a causal interpretation. Contrast those occasions when, rightly or wrongly, we are disposed to ascribe involuntary behaviour to a mental cause, as when we declare that the thought of a rival's success brought tears to our eyes. Here we might readily allow that, but for the thought, no tears would have been shed. We may be wrong about this; perhaps something else, some irritant in the atmosphere, explains the tears. But, while we might make the parallel claim with respect to a voluntary act and the desire which explains it, we are not *required* to be right if that explanatory role is to be preserved.

Suppose it is allowed that, as far as our customary explanations in terms of reasons are concerned, the latter are indispensable only to our conception of the character of what is done, and not, as with causal relations, to the very occurrence of the behaviour. This still leaves propositions linking thought or desire and behaviour, such as 'I shouldn't have done it for any other reason', which, as not enjoying the protection of incorrigibility, are in need of some other form of support. What, other than causal considerations, could come to their aid? So, I state—incontrovertibly, so long as my memory serves me well—that I gave up smoking only because I wanted to save money, adding, now questionably, that nothing else would have induced me to do so. I may have only shaky grounds for the latter claim. On the other hand, I may be able to say with some plausibility: that is the sort of person I am; my history shows that action of a comparable nature can be counted on not to occur in the absence of a desire of that kind, but only then. I can be right or wrong about this, just as I can when making the same pronouncement about another; there is nothing unchallengeable here, even if I am better placed than others to make the claim.

In relating behaviour to an established pattern, we are, it may seem, offering an explanation which, at least in the first instance, is non-causal. Compare explanatory observations which appeal to habit, as with 'That's what he always does'. Seeing a particular action in this light does not amount to acknowledging, let alone offering, a causal explanation. Likewise when '(Because) he is an ill-tempered (impatient, difficult, thoughtless) fellow' is advanced in answer to 'Why did he snap at me?'. Replying in these terms is like saying 'That's the sort of person he is'; not particularly informative, but it may serve to reassure us that there is nothing unusual about the behaviour, nothing out of character.

It will be agreed that the explanation of behaviour with reference to a general disposition is not particularly informative, but we may wonder whether such an appeal even purports to explain anything. At this common-sense level, explanations are thought called for when there is a departure from the norm, and, since citing a generalization gives reassurance that there is not, it would appear that what we are then doing is more by way of *declining* to give an explanation. That this is so is further indicated by the awkwardness which results from prefacing the 'explanation' with 'because'. The conjunction is quite out of place in, for example, 'Because he always does', given in answer to the question 'Why did he V?', and it is only marginally acceptable with respect to the answer suggested to 'Why did he snap at me?'. For our purposes, however, whether or not we are dealing with an explanation is of no great consequence. Either way, it is not a causal explanation, but, in appealing to a generalization, we leave it open what form, causal or otherwise, any eventual explanation may take.

It is not difficult to think of occasions when one's thoughts appear to be an inconsequential accompaniment to one's actions, with no claim to be necessary to their production. Consider movements which we engage in to make ourselves more comfortable. In such a case one might well proceed in exactly the same way whether awake or asleep, any thoughts as to the desirability of moving being very much by way of a dispensable concomitant of the activity. If they do arise, they may be simply part of the complex of thought and behaviour, not enjoying any temporal priority over the latter, let alone causal necessity. Equally, however, there are cases which seemingly point us in an opposite direction. With such a remark as 'She wouldn't have intervened if she hadn't thought you'd approve', the alternative to a causal role looks too close to a mere accident. We do have the simple pattern, as in 'She intervened, thinking you would approve', with nothing explicit by way of a connection indicated, but it surely needs more than a temporal association to bring the two into a comprehensible relation, and what else is there other than causation to fill the bill? If there is no causal interaction between thought—decision, belief, choice—and bodily movement, how can we rule out mere coincidence of the mental and behavioural episodes which seem so closely intertwined? In the absence of anything more than co-occurrence to appeal to, our position looks as arbitrary as occasionalism, with its prearranged harmony between the mental and the behavioural.

Consider patterns of illumination on a computer screen. We may have a visual representation of one cogwheel turning another, but, of course, neither wheel is causing the other to turn, even if is true to say that one of the wheels would not have rotated had the other not done so. Not causation, but then, given the computer programme, not coincidence either. There is nothing outrageous with occasionalism, thought of merely as instancing this pattern. It is only if thought and behaviour are held to be effects of a common supernatural cause that we leave sober sense behind. Again, there may be a common object, a common situation, to which both thought and action are *addressed*. Your skirting of an obstacle and your appreciation of its presence can make sense even if their starting-points coincide temporally, and we can make sense of each in terms of its character as an act bearing upon the common object.

Think, too, of animals. The fox is as capable as the hunter of engaging in pursuit, even though the hunter's manœuvres are accompanied by thought of a character to which the fox cannot aspire. I suggest that we regard the transition from the animal to the human case, not as one which introduces a new causal factor, but as one in which thought joins with action to yield a more complex manifestation of a state of mind: the hunter thinks that the fox is something to pursue and sets off after it. He has an awareness of what he is doing and what he is going to do which only the possession of language can make possible, but the thought is not causally necessary for the very occurrence of the action. In many cases it is not difficult to see how the same circumstances could make both the thought and the behaviour appropriate, and not plausible to look to the former to find the causes of the more primitive behavioural component, given that this occurs without the benefit of accompanying thought as far as all but human beings are concerned.

Or so we might argue. There are still innumerable familiar situations in which it seems initially even more implausible to refuse a causal role to the mental. When an action is a response to one's immediate circumstances—adjusting one's clothing, seeking out the shade, wiping sweat from one's brow—it is often easy to see the thought as dispensable: with nothing having to be worked out, with behaviour which may indeed be automatic, thought is simply not *needed*. When, however, there is some detachment from present surroundings, we cannot, as it were, look past the thought to these to find something to which the behaviour is a response. Kate is observed to stop in her tracks: the thought has just struck her that she has left her keys unattended in her car, and she promptly retraces her steps to recover them. Surely this must be an instance of behaviour initiated by thought, by the person's realization of what she has just done?

Once more, it is no concern of mine to deny an empirical possibility, but once more it does not appear that we have an empirical necessity. Perhaps the realization has the role suggested, but perhaps it does not always even precede the stopping, the actual moment at which we cease to move being one at which we are aware only of a vague feeling of unease, and have already stopped by the time the source of our unease has finally crystallized.

But what of intentions and decisions? To claim that these are without any causal role in the generation of action surely makes nonsense of our beliefs about the importance of reaching the *right* decision: 'I would not trouble to struggle over a difficult decision were it not for the conviction that the decision, once formed, would *matter*: i.e., would causally determine other parts of my behaviour, including its more obviously overt aspects like its effects, often physical, upon other people' (McCracken 1952: 169; cf. also Burge 1993: 118–19). We should certainly be loath to give up the idea that how we decide may matter, and at first sight there seems much to be said for the suggestion that it is as a cause that a decision has what importance it has in this connection. You agonize over a difficult choice; you reach a decision; you act. What other than your decision might reasonably be supposed to have instigated your action? It is far from clear that we can dismiss a causal role for deciding while at the same time trusting to the perception we have of its significance.

There are two kinds of decision that might be at issue here, decisions to act and decisions that something is so. The former is our
main concern, and the suggestion of a causal role, while inviting in
the abstract, becomes much less so when set against instances of this
kind. If asked why you are cutting back the hedge, you will hardly
reply: because I decided to. Since the decision does not itself constitute your reason for acting, even those who believe that reasons are
causes are as yet without grounds for thinking that the lot of decisions. Similarly, a reference to intention may explain something,
make something clear—'It wasn't an accident, I really meant to do
it'—but 'Because I intended to' would not be offered in explaining
why one acted.

More accurately, decisions and intentions are not normally to be
numbered among reasons for acting. It is not impossible to imagine
circumstances in which either could furnish a reason, but these would
be quite exceptional—as with someone who always made a point of
carrying out an intention, even when he considered that the reasons
which led to forming the intention no longer held. You decide to
pack the children's toys away. That's pointless, someone tells you;
they're going to want them again in a few minutes. You agree, but
somehow feel that you should not go back on your decision. Not a
paradigm of rational action, but it could be a case where you felt that
the fact that you'd made up your mind to do something itself provided a reason for going through with it, even though, in terms of the
original aim, the action would have to be acknowledged as futile.
Usually, however, when there is both decision and action, the reason
for the one will be at the same time the reason for the other. We ask
why you are cutting back the hedge, but the question might equally
have been: why did you decide to cut back the hedge?

The usual explanation of an action in terms of intention is not of
the form 'because I formed the intention to do so'. Is it possible none
the less that the intention should have a part in causing the action?
Not if the 'logical connection argument' is sound. According to this,
putative causal relations having mental items as one or more of their
terms are inadmissible when the specifications of these items fail to
be logically independent. For instance, it is held that, because the act
of willing is intelligible only as the act of willing what is willed, it
does not have the logical independence of the alleged effect which status as a cause requires (Melden 1961: 53). However, logical dependence is of no account so long as it does not exclude the causal

relation from holding between *distinct* worldly items, and it does not do this so long as it fails to imply that cause and effect cannot be kept apart. And this, in general, it does not threaten; even with 'The cause of *E* caused *E*', there is no risk of the two being conflated. Conversely, a logical disconnection does not ensure the possibility of a causal relation. Xanthippe's being widowed and Socrates' dying may not be in every sense the same event, but there is sameness of a kind relevant to excluding the one as cause of the other—again in the sense of 'cause' which concerns us here.

Of course, in so far as it embodies the legitimate demand for independence just acknowledged, the logical connection argument will have some application in areas which concern us. There is, for instance, no lack of occasions when we might ascribe a desire to a creature simply on the basis of its behaviour, as when the way a bird keeps coming back on course for its nest, whenever it has been obliged to deviate, may warrant the description: it wants to get to its nest. That is what it is aiming for. In so far as such descriptions are justified solely on the strength of the observed pattern of behaviour, it is clear that the want does not figure as a hypothesized cause; we are speaking only of the character of the behaviour itself, not of a 'distinct existence'. We shall enlarge upon this conception at a later point. When an intention is invoked in explaining one's action, causal considerations are, to all appearances, equally remote. In explaining why you are consulting a train timetable, you cite your intention to go to Paris, but this simply contributes to filling out an instance of practical reasoning: you intend to journey to Paris by train, and to make this possible you must establish when the train leaves. Nothing more than an appropriate place in such a pattern of reasoning is required to secure the explanatory role which the intention furnishes. Compare reasons for belief rather than action. Asked why you think that the home side will win, you reply, 'Because the opposition has been plagued by injuries.' What you offer is a ground for the correctness of your belief, its contribution on this count being all that matters. Whether it can also be a term in a causal relation is not something that has to be settled for this evidential role to be assured.

The more plausible examples of mental causation tend to involve involuntary reactions, as with feelings of fear, panic, or alarm which may follow on a realization that disaster threatens. In so far as intention is inviting as a cause, it is not with straightforward instances of voluntary behaviour, but we have to look to something like the following possibility. Suppose you decide to go upstairs, but subsequently change your mind: the book which you thought you might have to go in search of turns out to be at hand after all. However, while your intention may lapse, it is possible that, to your surprise, you find yourself going upstairs at a later time. Here there is at least a prima facie case for looking to the intention for the cause of the action. Certainly, it is a matter of *conjecture*, for you as well as for others, that the earlier intention provides the explanation of your present behaviour, so it is quite unlike the case where, having not changed your mind, you unhesitatingly give your reason: I'm going upstairs to fetch a book. Because, in the less common situation, we do not have a reason, we naturally look for another form of answer to the question why we are doing what we are doing. We could look for a cause of movement in the normal case as well; it is just that, having then a reason for the action, we normally let the matter of explanation rest at that. Whether in fact an abandoned intention might figure in a causal explanation is far from clear, but what is clear is that circumstances which favour this possibility are quite exceptional.

Very well, a causal role for decisions and intentions is questionable, but what is to take its place? Is the alternative we have touched upon so clearly superior? According to this, it is not that decisions, intentions, or indeed any other psychological phenomena are causally necessary antecedents of behaviour; rather, they are necessary only for more specific descriptions of the behaviour to apply. You may go upstairs whether or not you give any thought to doing so. It is simply that, if there is neither decision nor intention, what you do will count as automatic, unthinking, impulsive, perhaps even irrational. All the thought component does is confer a certain character on the action—as intentional, as considered, as premeditated; it does not bring any of your movements into being.

But, if this account is correct, decisions and intentions appear to be nothing more than epiphenomena, superfluous adjuncts to the accompanying behaviour. Is there not room for an alternative analysis which, while not crediting decisions with a causal role, none the less does greater justice to our conception of their practical importance? The question is one we shall have to take further.

1.2 ABILITY AND THE MENTAL

A claim that you Ved because you wanted x, or thought that p, does not require any view on your part as to what you would have done in the event that you had not wanted x, had not thought that p. Perhaps, while not wanting to V, you might none the less have done so, absent-mindedly. To this—one of the main points to arise so far—it is no objection to protest that you would not have Ved had you actually wanted not to, since this is a different possibility—more of which later. The same point holds with respect to not thinking that p as against thinking that not p, but here in particular it needs more than this distinction to silence further protest against the general position. It must surely be allowed that thought is causally necessary to the kind of creative activity of which human beings alone are capable; not simply that a person *would* not have done such and such had he not had certain thoughts, but that he *could* not then have acted thus. What are we to say to this claim? If *would not* fails, then so too, it may be said, must *could not*, but then it is unlikely that we have now to do with the same use of 'think'. It is not 'She could not have done that if she had not thought, been of the opinion, that p', so much as 'She could not have done that had she been unable to think, in the sense of *reason*'. And this latter is harder to dismiss: are we seriously prepared to allow that, without any such thought, a person might none the less engage in a series of movements which resulted in the construction of something as complex as a computer?

In one major respect, it is not outrageous to refuse to concede that someone could not have done something of this degree of complexity without the benefit of thought; it is not outrageous in so far as the ability to accomplish this project is just the ability to screw this to that, insert the result here, and so forth; not activities that a cat or a dog could master, but conceivably not too much to ask of a chimpanzee. At this practical level, the threat to 'could have' comes from a lack of the necessary strength, dexterity, and skills, in this instance of a fairly rudimentary kind. The difficulty arises more in respect of the *knowledge* required as to which component goes where. We can surely say: a chimpanzee could never build a computer, since it hasn't the remotest idea how to go about such a complex project.

However, that is to suppose just one possible case: the construction of a computer which would be explicable in terms of the constructor's knowledge of what was to be done. What we have, indisputably, is: chimpanzees *don't* make computers. We do not know that, given the right training, and other aids, they might not rise to such achievements; indeed, it is just such sequences of operations that industrial robots are programmed to perform. We do not know that evolution might not turn up a creature which, while not capable of thought, none the less produced devices which, in relevant respects, actually surpassed the computers with which we are familiar. And, if this can be described as a matter of a creature 'programmed' to perform such feats, it is not programming which requires a programmer. It might even be claimed that we do not reach the point where an attribution of thought is obligatory until it enters by way of a *redescription* of the observed behaviour, and that is not a point at which the thought is introduced as part of a causal hypothesis.

Before clarifying this suggestion, it is useful to consider remembering, a mental antecedent of behaviour which may often strike us as necessary to the latter. So, remembering that one must put salt in porridge if it is to be at all edible, I put salt in the porridge. The idea of the remembering as part of the causation of the action may lead to the claim that I shouldn't have put salt in the porridge if I hadn't remembered how vital this was, but the claim could also be made without resting anything on a causal relation—merely relying on a well-established generalization to the effect that one never acts in this way unless one has the relevant memory. Or, if that would be to go further than was warranted, one could still say: if I had put salt in, but had given no thought to the need for it, then the behaviour would have been differently classifiable—as unreflecting, habitual, perhaps even as inexplicable. And there is a further possibility. It will not have escaped notice that 'remember' bears a sense in which it would still have applied, despite the person's thoughtlessness. In that sense, I *do* remember to put salt in the porridge in the situation envisaged; that would be guaranteed by my actually putting it in, however absent-mindedly, together with certain other facts about my past.

This commonplace happening will provide an analogy to our example with thought if the activity in question is one that involves thought constitutively, rather than as an accompaniment—so with *design* rather than *construction*. If the human being, animal, or robot succeeds in producing a computer, let us say, where this is not merely a matter of assembling components, but where we could say design and/or reasoning entered into the enterprise, then perhaps we could rightly take the activity to constitute a manifestation of thought. I mean, with certain provisos, the achievement could be such that it was no mere hypothesis that the agent could think, not a matter of conjecture that he, she, or it was endowed with considerable intellectual powers. Almost anything we were prepared to describe as 'designing and producing a computer' we should also regard as giving proof of thought, but proof so conclusive, there would be no call to look *beyond* its manifestation. As Ryle put it, 'Overt intelligent performances are not clues to the workings of minds; they are those workings' (1949: 58). That the constructor could think would have been placed beyond doubt; not a matter awaiting final confirmation by a discovery that something by way of unspoken thoughts had also been taking place; no more than, with the relevant sense of 'remember', there might be doubt that the person who put salt in the porridge had remembered to do so.

This is a tempting move to make, and something like it will find support from time to time in arguments to come, but it is implausible to suggest that one might say of behaviour of the kind in question: this is, quite literally, thinking. This would be akin to the crude form of behaviourism which Wittgenstein advanced at the time of the *Blue Book*, when, in opposition to the view that there is some one mental state or process that answers to a psychological verb, he claimed that such verbs encompass a family of activities, so that, for instance, thinking could in some circumstances be an activity of the writing hand, and expecting someone to come to tea could actually be a matter of looking in one's diary (*BB* 16–20).

Very well, but without going so far as to identify thinking and acting, can we still not regard the behaviour as a *manifestation* of thought? It was suggested above that lack of knowledge, rather than of strength or skill, stands in the way of any construction of a computer by a chimpanzee. If, however, the chimpanzee were trained to assemble the components correctly, there would be a sense in which its success in this respect would show that it knew where the various parts belonged, and with this use of 'know' comes a corresponding use of 'think', justified in the same circumstances. This might be queried: here 'belonged' means 'were correctly positioned', and it is not to be taken for granted that the chimpanzee has the requisite grasp of correctness. But, in any event, we are at present concerned with the kind of thinking which designing draws upon, thinking as reasoning, and this seemingly goes beyond anything that might be realized in exclusively non-verbal activities. We shall indeed wish to speak of thought if we are willing to speak of design, of a creative application of intelligence, and not just of a mere assembling of parts, but the behaviour observed will provide good evidence for thought rather than its direct manifestation, final confirmation that thought has taken place requiring that the agent be able to put the thought into words. On the other hand, while the relation of behaviour to thought may not be logical, the relation of thought to design is, as indicated, quite different. The claim that the device could not have been put together by an unthinking being remains false, but, if it is true that it could not have been designed without thought, that is because we should refuse to speak of designing unless we were assured that there had been thought. The formal connection may be misplaced in the Rylean suggestion, but it is a formal connection—between thought and design—not a causal one, that makes thought indispensable. True, if the being is one to which thoughts cannot be ascribed, then what it is doing may well strike us as quite unintelligible, but it is not for their causality that thoughts might be wanted. A person who gives us a running commentary on his current actions may thereby throw light on what he is engaged in, but what makes his muscles contract may be as obscure, and of as little moment to us, as ever.

Again, suppose you are aimlessly doodling, barely aware of the pattern that is taking shape with the movements of your pencil. Emulating your artistry is unlikely to be beyond the scope of some simple mechanism, but your activity takes on a greater significance if it occurs as part of a more complex series of actions; not now a mindless doodle, but a representation of the circuitry of some electronic device, even if the same pattern of marks is involved. However, while this more sophisticated pursuit undoubtedly introduces the mental, what this is needed for is not the accomplishment of the physical act, but the applicability of just such a notion as that of *design*.

But it remains true, surely, that behaviour issuing in complex artefacts simply is not to be expected from beings which lack the power of thought. Such things just do not happen, except as freak occurrences, in the absence of ratiocination, and other exclusively human activities. Even with the industrial robot there is ultimately a dependence on human knowledge. It is certainly true that nothing other than human beings or their robotic surrogates is in fact found producing items of electronic hardware, but, once more, we cannot say

that it is inconceivable that an unthinking thing should do so without our assistance; it is just that, if this were to take place, the explanation would have to be of a different kind from what is available
for human accomplishments—as indeed a different form of explanation is required to explain how spiders construct their webs. Animal
life is replete with examples of behaviour which, were it attributable
to human beings, would be explained in terms of various modes of
thought, as estimating times, distances, and probabilities, but which,
for the animal, can at best be explained figuratively in such terms.

Think, too, of the 'mindless' performances of which some human
beings are capable. We are puzzled on learning that calculating prodi-
gies may report that their extraordinary arithmetical feats do not
involve a step-by-step series of mental calculations which mirror anything we might do on paper, despite the accuracy of their solutions
to highly complex problems. But if, in the last analysis, it is up to the
brain to do what issues in these solutions, it would not appear that
thought is indispensable. It is more as if, in the usual case, by having
the calculation take place within consciousness, the brain obligingly
lets its owner in on what it is up to. It is in many ways of value that
this should happen, that the calculating should take place at the personal, as well as at the sub-personal, level, but, while there can be no
result if there is no neural activity, what the subject regards as his
own contribution may not be the sine qua non of success we fondly
imagine it to be. What we can hold out for is only the lesser claim—
though still one of importance—that our concept of calculating could
not be as it is if *all* 'calculation' were of this kind.

But, if the value of thought does not lie in its instrumentality, how,
in evolutionary terms, might we even begin to account for its presence? What looks as though it has conferred an enormous benefit on
the species is not specifically *unspoken* thought, but the essential
advantage could have lain with thought whose realizations were confined to speech, or even—if this way of speaking is allowed—to
action. Tool-making is a candidate for the latter manifestation, and
the use of language to communicate is obvious for the former, both
of which are plainly suited to conferring a benefit on their possessors.
The internalization of speech may have been a further, more incidental, development—one, that is, with rather less compelling reasons, in evolutionary terms, than favoured the overt behaviour. For
instance, there may often have been an advantage in keeping one's
thoughts to oneself, though less, overall, than went with an ability to

communicate them. With such an ordering there would be no question of seeing in unspoken thoughts the foundation of these other manifestations.

We may well resist the idea of what seems to qualify as 'mindless' speech, as this development would require. How would this differ from the utterances of a device as unselfconscious as a talking weighing machine? It may be granted that the speech of our primitive man can be reckoned the expression of thought, but the epithet 'mindless' seems none the less in place when, by hypothesis, there can be no other thinking in which the person is engaged *as* he speaks. But then, while it may be very much the rule that we think while we speak, that our words may prompt further thoughts, it is also true that nothing need figure in the rich variety of preceding or accompanying thought that might be reckoned an unspoken version of the thought which receives public expression. No such antecedent is necessary to the spoken word, any more than the unspoken thought demands to be prefaced by an analogous item.

1.3 SENSATION AND CAUSATION

Our main concern relates to reasons for actions, but similar questions of causation arise with sensations, the concept of sensation being an important example of a concept which might have been thought ideally suited to playing a leading part in causal explanations, but which proves instead to link up with action rather than mere reaction. We shall now try to make clear this involvement.

The case for a causal role for sensations would appear, if anything, stronger than with thought. But consider. I touch something very hot and withdraw my hand. We shall suppose that it is not a matter of the sensation of heat or pain giving me a *reason* for taking my hand away—it happens too quickly for me even to think. Does that leave the sensation as unmistakably cause of the movement? Once the possibility of acting for a reason is set aside, a person's explanation why a movement of his took place is certainly not in general incorrigible. Is there any reason to regard instances of reflex movements as exceptions? However improbable it may seem, it is surely possible that the sensation does not lie on a causal line having the hot object at one extreme and the reaction at the other. I am not querying this on the grounds that it would present us with a mysterious detour through the mental. Let us grant that to have a sensation is to have some physiological happening occur in one's body. Then it is perfectly possible that such a happening, together with the associated reflex movement, is set in train by the same stimulus, but that both lie on distinct causal lines leading from that stimulus. Indeed, in my own case I have noticed that the recoil movement may be under way fractionally before I am aware of any sensation. And this is not just a personal eccentricity. In this and similar cases, physiologists have confirmed that experience gives grounds for supposing an ordering other than that required for the sensation to be cause (cf. Harth 1982: 100–1).

So are we simply wrong when we say such things as 'The pain made me wince'? There are claims about the causation of both winces and pains which we should not expect to see challenged—for instance, a claim that the dentist's drill may, and frequently does, cause both. However, while it may be said that 'The pain made me wince' has every appearance of ascribing causal powers to the pain, it would seem reasonable to settle for 'I winced with pain' as doing as much justice to the situations in which the former is used. Compare an explanation which puts the shaking of a man's hand down to nervousness. 'Because he is nervous' does not here amount to a causal claim, but locates the behaviour within a larger set of circumstances, within a cluster of reactions whose causal structure has yet to be disentangled.

Closely analogous to pain is the example of sound: the hearing of a loud bang can actually succeed a startled reaction associated with it, minute though the time lag is. Note that, while this rules out the auditory experience as cause of the reaction, it does not necessarily contradict the claim of the sound to be cause, since, despite the different grammars of 'sound' and 'sound wave', their points of contact may allow the sound to be credited with causing whatever is attributable to the agency of the waves. That there is, however unexpectedly, a very real possibility of going wrong when offering causal explanations of one's own reactions has been shown in a number of psychological studies (cf. Nisbett and Wilson 1977).

To pursue further the question of the relation of sensation to behaviour, it is useful to examine one well-known approach to the language of sensations. At *Philosophical Investigations* §244 Wittgenstein asks how human beings learn the names of sensations—of the word 'pain', for instance. Here, he answers, is one possibility: 'words are connected with the primitive, the natural, expressions of the sensation and used in their place. A child has hurt himself and he cries; and then adults talk to him and teach him exclamations and, later, sentences. They teach the child new pain-behaviour.' We are to relate the concept of pain to that of pain-behaviour. Which behaviour—the voluntary or the involuntary—is primarily in question? At first sight the involuntary appears the more promising. This is where primitive pain reactions, as recoiling and crying, reside. Moreover, what a person engages in by way of voluntary acts depends very much on what he believes. If he thinks he can alleviate his pain in a certain way, as by taking an analgesic, then he is likely to do so; if not, he may well do nothing. On the other hand, involuntary behaviour appears to be only accidentally associated with particular sensations; it does not of itself reflect their character as, for example, painful. May not pleasure be conveyed by cries which might in other circumstances indicate pain? Even a flood of tears does not unambiguously signify pain or the like, but can accompany grief, prolonged laughter, or peeling onions. Recoil movements look less ambivalent, but these could be a measure of the strength or intensity of a stimulus, rather than a reflection of its disagreeable character. Think, too, how contact with an electrified object may be highly unpleasant, but may also result in the inhibition of withdrawal movements.

If neither the voluntary nor the involuntary will do, we shall have to rethink this whole approach. However, I suggest that we must go back on our rejection of the voluntary. The wriggling and squirming—thought of as involving purposive effort, not a mere reflex—which we may engage in somehow to lessen a pain, the actions whereby we seek to detach ourselves from a cause of pain and to avoid things found to inflict pain, are surely central, even if other voluntary acts, as seeking a palliative, are secondary. After all, if a creature let out loud shrieks whenever a certain stimulus was applied, yet did nothing to avoid a repetition of this treatment—even sought it out, let us suppose—then we should no longer regard those shrieks as indicative of pain. Think of the blood-curdling cries emitted by vixens in the mating season. Or again, if a creature's reactions to stimuli of a kind which produce pain were confined to spasmodic contractions, if it never engaged in any purposive behaviour directed to the source of such stimuli, then, however violent the spasm, there would be no foothold for talk of dislike, and hence no grounds for speaking of pain. A monkey may bare its teeth, but the key to interpreting this gesture—as a sign of aggression rather than as a welcoming smile—is to be found in the purposive behaviour which goes with it. If we are inclined, none the less, to opt for the involuntary rather than the voluntary, this is because, I surmise, it is *spontaneous* behaviour that strikes us as central, and this is indeed behaviour that comes close to the involuntary.

If the verbal expression of pain is to be a replacement for primitive pain behaviour, we can again ask what behaviour, the voluntary or the involuntary, is at issue. The present account would favour the former, and the voluntary character of linguistic behaviour generally supports this choice. So, if we are thinking of 'That hurts!' as taking over the role of a cry, then—contrary, I suspect, to Wittgenstein's conception—it will be a matter of a cry uttered to attract attention, say, rather than a cry of the kind which comes willy-nilly, whether or not the sufferer has anyone with whom to communicate. But now, such a use of language is very much an informative, assertoric, use. In embodying a communicative intention, the words will go beyond a purely expressive function. If someone pinches another who then protests 'That hurts!', the point of the communication will be plain: he is being asked to stop it, not to do it again. Likewise when, for example, 'I've got a headache' is offered in explanation of one's crotchetiness. The cases when we have to do with utterances detached from any communicative intent will surely be negligible.

However, granted that voluntary or purposive behaviour is what we should be looking to, this is not by itself enough. For Wittgenstein, the concept of pain would appear to be interchangeable with that of an unpleasant sensation; certainly, this is all that is yielded if we confine attention to concomitant behaviour. And that is wrong. Vertigo, certain tactile sensations, itches, and nausea count as unpleasant, but not as pains. So what distinguishes the peculiar kind of unpleasantness that constitutes pain as opposed to, say, disagreeable sensations of cold, dizziness, or pins and needles? On many occasions we find associated damage to bodily tissue, as with a cut, a burn, or a bruising blow, and we should naturally look for such factors when seeking to give examples of likely pain. Of course, we have pains whose causation is quite unknown to us, but it would seem that the connection with typical causes remains the basis of our comparison. That is, pains are adjudged pains through their likeness to what is experienced in those cases where the causation is plain. At all events, it is surely in this direction, not in the direction of behaviour, that we are to seek our missing differentia.

Our concept of pain has, then, two components, one relating to associated behaviour, the other to typical causes. There is a noteworthy difference between the two. Important as it is, the connection between typical cause, or bodily damage, and what is distinctively painful as opposed to merely unpleasant, is more opaque than the relation between behaviour and sensation. Pain behaviour is geared to the character of pain in a way that reflects that character, being, as aversive, logically tied to the notion of finding unpleasant. It is a matter of behaviour for which such an experience gives a reason, behaviour which can be classified among responses rather than reactions, which makes sense in the light of the disagreeable character of the sensation. A mere reaction, by contrast, need show nothing at all beyond what is readily explicable in terms of cause and effect, need tell you nothing about the character of its cause. Compare feeling very hot. Associated voluntary behaviour, as loosening one's clothing, making for the shade, and seeking a cool drink, may testify in a similar way to the unwelcome character of the feeling, being more informative in this respect than involuntary perspiration, though again the causation of the feeling is of relevance to its identification. Or again, take laughter. There is no *logical* reason why, when something is found funny, the curious sounds and heavings which this comprises should be prompted.

A functionalist account of pain errs in making a causal role for the sensation definitionally true. It fails to address the grammatical preliminary—whether the role is even one which makes sense for pain—and, less excusably, it prejudges an empirical matter: whether, supposing the hypothesis to make sense, pains do in fact act as causes. Construing functionalism as a theory rather than as a clarification of meaning would go some way to meeting this objection, but we should then be left with just an apparently erroneous theory, and be no wiser on the question of meaning.

It is also worth noting that the behaviour for which a causal explanation is most appropriate is in the less relevant category of the involuntary. If all we ever had to go on were reactions to stimuli, then we should have no cause to think in terms of sensations, whether of pain or of anything else, but we should be dealing with phenomena offering no more of a grip to the psychological than does the twitching of a lifeless frog's leg when an electric current is applied to it. Indeed, any ascription of pain which depends on postulating it as a link in a causal chain runs a very real risk of finding itself agnostic about the very existence of pains. It should be noted, however, that to accept that pains are causally inert is not to deprive oneself of all means for explaining why they should ever occur. This might have been mistakenly inferred from our account of recoil movements, where the occurrence of the pain appeared quite superfluous, but, while, as far as the causation goes, that may be so, pain can still come into its own in the context of action, as when the memory of a pain received from a certain source gives·us a reason for avoiding that source. Action and reaction combine to give us a strengthened defence against the damage of which pain may give warning.

Causal accounts of other psychological conditions likewise threaten us with agnosticism in their regard. Indeed, the insistence on a causal role has made for a *reductio ad absurdum* of current attacks on so-called 'folk' psychology: beliefs, say, being defined as certain causes of behaviour, it is then claimed that none of the causes we can realistically hope to identify will fill the role of beliefs, which are accordingly to be dispensed with altogether. And it is not just beliefs and pains that are consigned to oblivion, but the upholders of this eminently resistible position systematically denude themselves of everything which goes to make up their character as human beings— a position which is about as plausible as the Christian Scientist's comparable claim that suffering is unreal.

Not surprisingly, the appropriate treatment of perception shows continuity with that of sensation, the concepts to be exploited here being those of knowledge and associated action, not mere reaction. This is not to deny that there will be important reactions among the behavioural indices of perception—an expression of terror may show that a snake has been spotted; salivation may show that food has been smelled. It is just that these mean nothing by themselves; nothing, that is, without the support of appropriate responses, responses indicative of knowledge acquired, not mere testimonies to the generative power of the stimulus.

2

Mind and Brain

If there is reason to query mental causation, there may also be a problem to know what to put in its place. In particular, we should like to know what is to succeed the usual accounts of action in which a causal role for thought and desire is both explicit and central. One of the preliminaries to this task concerns the scope of the mental. A loose use of this term has so far been in play, and it is worth considering what, more strictly, it embraces. We accordingly begin with some observations on this topic, before moving on to consider how the problem of defining psychological predicates should be tackled. The approach adopted is broadly Wittgensteinian, in so far as a first-person perspective is rejected in favour of a reliance upon behavioural and public criteria generally, but with less of Wittgenstein's emphasis on the expressive use of language. The behavioural slant is critical. If the position adopted here is acceptable, then our subsequent handling of psychological predicates, especially with regard to animals, is less likely to appear questionable. We then turn to a discussion of physicalism. Our reservations concerning this doctrine relate largely to the cruder versions which credit the brain with properties which can be meaningfully ascribed only to persons or their mental states, obliging that organ to become a locus of meaning and intentionality, a repository of rules, a home for grammatically characterized internal states, and so forth. We smile at the thought of medieval philosophers debating how many angels might fit on the head of a pin, but current ways of thinking about mind and brain would sanction equally meaningless conjectures about the number of thoughts which might subtend a synapse.

2.1 MIND AND MENTAL

There is a somewhat grandiose conception of the mind that may go with an ascription to it of a causally executive role. In philosophical discussions the term 'mind' tends to stray away from its natural habi-tat, which is in such specific expressions as 'have a sharp mind', 'make up one's mind', 'bear in mind', 'keep one's mind on what one is doing', 'be in two minds how to act', 'have half a mind to do some-thing', 'change one's mind', 'speak one's mind', and so forth. That a coherent use goes with its occurrences in isolation, as when the nature of mind is the issue, is not assured by these diverse idioms, which do not require us to think in terms of a recurrent allusion to a single entity—as if, when a person is said to have a good mind, to have changed his mind, and to be bearing something in mind, the same thing is being held to be good, to have changed, and to be where something is borne. Compare the term 'self'. This poses no problems as it occurs in 'herself', 'selfless', 'self-employed', and so forth, but the intelligibility of these forms does not guarantee a clear sense to such a question as 'What is the self?' when it comes to stand alone. The idea of a single item discernible in the various uses of 'mind', and such that we can ask about its relation to matter, appears to rest on a sim-plistic construal of the grammar—as though 'mind' were primarily a mass term, so inviting the question as to the kind of stuff it desig-nated—mind stuff, of course, but might that not also be material stuff? This is not to deny the naturalness of such a construal: when language goes on holiday, it often does not have far to travel.

Very differently, but equally questionably, 'mind' may be taken to signify a kind of space or place. Certain things do indeed happen *in* the mind, but the significance of this way of speaking may not be quite as it seems. With many activities it makes sense to ask where they were performed, the likely answer giving a specification of some area of public space. Sometimes, however, no answer conforming to this pattern is to hand: you performed the calculation, but not on the blackboard or on paper; rather, you performed it in your mind or in your head. This seems to offer an alternative location, one to be invoked when the public arena is ruled out, but is it in any sense an alternative *space*? In any normal space things can be variously dis-posed, some to the left, some to the right, some above others, some below. We do speak of thoughts as being at the forefront, or the back, of our mind, but these spatial expressions clearly serve to give a metaphorical characterization of our degree of attentiveness to our concerns. The orderings possible for things and happenings in space have no application to mental calculations, deliberations, and so forth, but the 'in' of 'in the mind' is in this respect misleading. A more accurate perspective is the following. We may seek to provide an answer to such a query as 'Where was the calculation performed?', if the calculation in question was as much as performed at all, and, if no recognized place can be assigned, we can at least call upon a phrase, 'in my mind' or 'in my head', which is formally of the desired kind. That is, while this looks like an alternative specification of a space or place, in reality its import is more negative; it serves to reject anything that might literally qualify as a location, but to do so in a way that keeps it in line with the more positive forms. The transition from public to private space is a transition from the literal to the metaphorical.

Consider, too, the contention, not uncommon, that sensations occur in the mind. It is understandable why some should be drawn to this way of speaking. Since sensations are not to be found by opening up a limb and inspecting the bodily tissue, it might be held that they are not literally *in* the body, so can fittingly be assigned to the mind; since, too, they are, roughly speaking, present only to an individual consciousness, they are not on a par with just any item which lacks coordinates in public space, but are deserving of the specific character which *mind* bestows. However, while it is true that a sensation is not in the body in the way a bone or a vein is, there is a perfectly good, literal, sense in which, for instance, a pain may be said to be in one's chest; and, accordingly, an awkwardness in saying that sensations are in the mind, an awkwardness which there is no need whatsoever to embrace. Incidentally, I say 'roughly speaking' sensations require consciousness. We can become distracted from a sensation, yet not regard this as showing that the sensation ceased therewith. The notion of a sensation's ceasing is the notion of its ceasing within consciousness, not the notion of one's consciousness of it ceasing. What is not possible is that we should be having a sensation when, giving our full attention to the way we feel, we fail to become aware of it.

Berkeley argued that an intense heat is at the same time a great pain, and, since the latter is in the mind, so too is the former (*First Dialogue between Hylas and Philonous*). We may query the identity: an intense heat may be given off by the fire, driving out the damp and scorching the carpet. Not so a pain. True, a sensation of heat may also be a sensation of pain, but the former is a sensation *caused* by heat, or at least one as of heat; 'of pain' does not signify an analogous relation. But in any event, if the heat has to be where the pain is, then it is some part of the body, not the mind, that gives its location.

What goes for 'mind' goes also for 'mental', which is likewise commonly taken to embrace not only thoughts, images, and the like, but also sensations. And this would likewise be wrong: it is in order to speak of an itch, say, as a *bodily* disturbance, and correspondingly unclear what it would mean to speak of it as *mental*. The assimilation in the direction of the genuinely mental is of consequence for more than one reason; most notably, the tendency to treat sensations as paradigms of the mental leads to a distorted conception of the general category, a category for which the inapplicability of locational predicates is one of the more distinctive features.

The terms 'mind' and 'mental' are sometimes used with respect to *any* object of consciousness; at the other extreme, they may be associated with happenings of which we have no awareness, as when it is said that rules of grammar of which most of us have no inkling are none the less in the mind, or as with the subconscious thoughts and desires of psychoanalytic theory. The first extension threatens to leave the terms without a useful contrast; the second is likewise a misuse, though it perhaps does not matter too much so long as it does not bring with it a form of creative definition. Thus, items covered by this extended use may turn out to divide between the behavioural and the cerebral, in which case we have a coherent, if misleading, categorization, but, so long as the relevant possibilities are left unspecified, there is the risk of embracing a pure fiction: mere ill-defined usage comes to be interpreted as the introduction of a third possibility, as delineating a novel and mysterious domain—another instance where it is assumed that we can extract 'mind' from its all-important accompanying context with impunity.

The complementary term 'physical' must also be handled with care, as is soon revealed by consideration of other terms which, like 'colour' and 'sound', have affinities with words for sensations. The public, external, reference of colour terms precludes a construal of colours as mental, yet, it might be said, they are not to be described as 'physical', their lack of depth leaving them a dimension short of what is needed for such character. However, this is one use only of 'physical'. We speak of 'physical fitness' without saddling fitness with incongruous attributes, the *subject* of the fitness being what dictates this choice of adjective. Similarly, we might speak of physical pain or suffering in so far as it is the body that is affected, rather than by way of indicating the constitution of the pain; analogously, 'mental pain' could be used in the absence of this condition—with reference to the suffering experienced by a person bereaved or humiliated, for instance. Colour might accordingly be deemed physical in the sense that it is an attribute of something physical. Colour as an attribute of something non-physical is rare, though, since it can be said that we may dream in colour, there is some scope for this way of speaking.

Compare such notions as those of a tendency, a disposition, or an ability. With none of these key concepts are we, in one sense, in any of the favoured domains—neither in that of the physical, the physiological, the behavioural, or the mental. We are in none of these domains in so far as such epithets are thought to tell us how what they apply to is *constituted*—as if a tendency of something solid had to be solid, a tendency of something ethereal ethereal. Rather, if we are to find a basis for favouring one description over another, we should look to the terms which complete these phrases, as a tendency to put on weight or a disposition to quarrel or an ability to recall. If the second is a disposition to behave, then it is, plainly, a behavioural disposition, but the logic of 'disposition' taken generally is broader than is given by this, or any other, of the categories cited. The term 'fact' is another that comes to mind. A physical fact is not more substantial than a psychological fact, a fact about volcanoes not more substantial than one to do with memory, even if what each is a fact about differs in this respect.

Compare, too, the notion of consciousness. As thoroughness is, in a variety of ways, a matter of being thorough, kindness a matter of being kind, so consciousness is a matter of being conscious. To return to consciousness is to return to being conscious, to lose consciousness is to cease to be conscious, and so on. As is typical of such abstract nouns, the model for understanding them is provided by a verbal phrase, not by names of stuffs for which questions of constitution and location might be raised. Clearly, what is conscious is one with what sees, hears, pursues, takes flight, and so forth—a man or animal, not a brain; a fortiori, not a brain of which consciousness is a baffling emergent feature or in which it is undiscoverably located. Revealing the nature of consciousness is sometimes proclaimed to be one of the remaining great scientific challenges. Whether it is a matter for science is questionable; certainly, it is a challenge which will not be met so long as the familiar grammatical misconceptions are

carried over into interpretations of scientific findings. Sadly, philosophers as well as scientists are not above disregarding the critical
grammatical distinctions, categorizations of consciousness as a kind
of stuff (McGinn 1991: 60) or as a feature of the brain, a spatial property located therein (Searle 1992: 105), being not uncommon.

2.2 EXPRESSION

A number of pitfalls await attempts at elucidating psychological concepts. We shall now draw attention to one most likely to trap the
unwary, and discuss a certain response to it. The pitfall in question,
which claimed Locke as one of its more illustrious victims, may be
indicated, somewhat obliquely, in the following way.

It is not difficult to persuade oneself that perception invariably
involves a conceptual or aspectual element—that all seeing is seeing
as, for instance, or that we cannot see without the object seen looking some way to us, or without our taking, believing, things to be
thus and so—'it being impossible for anyone to perceive without perceiving that he does perceive' (Locke, *An Essay Concerning Human
Understanding*, II. xxvii. 9). What this may mean, however, is simply
that, in the absence of some such element, the perception will go
unnoted by the perceiver. The condition advanced is one for the fact
of perception to have registered with the subject, not a condition for
its very occurrence. Compare how it may strike us, and strike us as
quite remarkable, that our minds are constantly active whilst we are
awake. Perhaps this is so, but it is also to be borne in mind that there
is no such thing as catching oneself without a thought; true, it makes
sense to suppose that one might think back to a time when one was
aware of something yet not thinking, but, this apart, any evidence
that our minds have been a blank could only be indirect, as when different times on the clock are noted without any awareness of anything falling within the period which the altered position of the hands
shows to have elapsed. If it is doubted that there can be perception
when nothing is conceptualized, we need only consider how behavioural responses of sighted creatures, men and animals, can provide
the necessary information; we do not always have to wait upon the
subject's disclosures to be sure.

Our interest is in the wider misconception that is likely to lie
behind the approach just challenged. That is, the conception of per-

ception as inextricably linked with thought is likely to rest on a more generally mistaken view as to how we are to advance our understanding of a mental state or act—namely, by giving our full attention to what is going on when we are seeing, believing, hoping, wondering, feeling, and so forth: '*the mind* furnishes the understanding with ideas of its own operations' (Locke, ibid. II. i. 5); and, as a more recent example: 'Purpose is one of various mentalistic notions drawn from introspection of one's mental life' (Quine 1992: 75). The approach is undeniably natural. After all, it is not as if we were attempting to find out about something which, as with a material substance, might reveal its nature only after further probing and examining with the help of scientific instruments, but the phenomenon appears to be given in its entirety to the enquiring mind. As, indeed, do our very selves, the referents of 'I' supposedly encountered in introspection. However, natural though it is, this approach is a cul-de-sac: directing our attention to our state of mind tells us nothing about the *concepts* of seeing, believing, and the rest (cf. Wittgenstein, *PI* §§314–16, p. 188). It gives no inkling of the network of relations in which the concepts are located and which fixes their place in the language, no inkling of what it makes sense to say by their means. More immediately, such an exercise will not reveal that, for instance, we can be said to have a belief even when fast asleep. Nor will it bring home to us the possibility of speaking of a creature as seeing without having to attribute to it an undisclosed mental state. Indeed, if the preoccupation with one's own case makes for a distorted account of human psychological phenomena, it risks making any animal variants utterly incomprehensible.

It is with respect to the language of sensation that this mistaken picture is especially familiar. How do we come by an understanding of this language? We supposedly concentrate on our sensations and read off their character as painful, as sensations of warmth, pressure, and so on. More generally, our mental life is presented as something which, in the first instance, we might report on, an array of thoughts and feelings there to be taken in much as we take in the scene before us, and commented upon, divulged, or not, as we see fit. It is, of course, as a corrective to this conception that the *expressive* use of the relevant language may be advanced—the response which we shall shortly examine—but the most important consideration is to see how readily a suitable explanation of that language can take shape without any essential reliance upon one's own case. Thus, if the question should arise whether you and another agree in your understanding of the word 'pain', you might start to make plain your own understanding by remarking that you would expect a person to speak of experiencing pain on being given a severe blow, or on coming into contact with something very hot or sharp. The other person could be expected to agree, and might go on to specify further circumstances in which talk of pain would be natural. And we could, conversely, list circumstances in which 'pain' was not quite the right word; sea-sickness may be accompanied by nausea, but sufferers of seasickness do not complain of pains on that account, disagreeable though the experience may be. Clearly, such an investigation can be carried out without the participants having to allude to their own sensations, the meaning of 'pain' being determined with reference to a familiar range of public circumstances—involving, of course, behaviour as well as causation—rather than by anything that might be taken in on attending to the sensation. True, it requires no more than attention to one's sensation to appreciate that use of 'pain' is in order, or not, but this is possible only for someone who already has a grasp of the relevant vocabulary, not for one who has yet to acquire it.

Although it seems plain enough that the meaning of 'pain' is determined in such fashion, this obvious consideration is at war with a preconception which for many holds a strong attraction. This is the idea that the definitive way of learning what pain is for someone else would require one actually to be, for a time, that other; though, since, on Locke's way of putting it, 'one man's mind could not pass into another man's body', just what this embodiment would deliver could never be known (*Essay*, II. xxxii. 15). And, in truth, what is being envisaged here is not an unattainable ideal but an incoherent fantasy. In so far as one might be said to take on the identity of another, there would then be no 'other'; no genuine possibility has been specified which would yield the knowledge sought, so no possibility by comparison with which other tests might be found wanting. The illusion that there is something to be found in this way, and only in this way, is to be replaced by an appeal to criteria which define a real possibility, the criteria given with circumstances by reference to which the relevant language may be taught. So, I stub my toe, and I wonder whether you have ever had the kind of sensation I suffer. The form of an answer is plain enough from that of the query: if you and I have experienced a sensation which we both identify as 'the sensation one receives on stubbing one's toe', then you and I have experienced the same sensation. Other questions of comparison can arise within this area of agreement, but we have learned the use of 'pain one experiences on stubbing one's toe' independently of these further differences—to which, of course, the pattern in turn extends. Locke was envisaging the problem in connection with 'ideas of colour'. It is interesting to detect the same incoherent supposition in the background of contemporary discussions of the inverted spectrum problem. And, clearly, the misconception is compounded when an improper appeal to observation is added, as when it is said that we could tell whether animals could think only if we could *observe* what was going on in their minds.

In seeking to correct this mistaken approach I have not made use of what is generally considered one of Wittgenstein's major contributions to our understanding of psychological phenomena—namely, his emphasis on the *expressive* function which first-person utterances may enjoy, as when, in certain circumstances, the avowal 'I am afraid' may be reckoned part of the state of fear rather than a report of that state. The power of the utterance to convey how it is with the speaker is then much as with other indices of fear: it is of significance for what it *shows* us about him, rather than what it tells us *qua* truth.

The notion of an expressive use appears important as a corrective to a construal of the relevant utterances which assimilates these to reports or descriptions as the latter occur with the physical world as their subject matter. A description of the scene about one will rely on the use of one's senses; it will be in place to have one's findings checked by others, to speak of verification and confirmation; it will be possible to observe the scene from a different perspective and in different viewing conditions; there will be scope for certainty and uncertainty, for knowledge and ignorance; and so forth.

This perceptual model is not an aid to clear thinking about first-person psychological utterances, but it is less obvious that its abandonment calls for a general rejection of 'report' and 'description' in favour of 'expression' or 'avowal' (*Äusserung*). True, 'description' is often not the right term: describing one's thoughts is saying what they are like—for example, confused or obsessional. It is not simply reporting them. But reporting need be no more than stating how things stand with one's thoughts, fears, and so forth. Consider 'I'm bored'. The inaptness of 'I think I'm bored' reflects the absence of grounds or evidence interposed between the state of mind and the avowal. The latter enjoys a more direct association with that state, the non-inductive status of the avowal putting it on a par with other indices of boredom, but the point can be made whether it is appropriate to speak of a report of boredom or of its expression. In pointing to the inapplicability of finding out or learning, of misidentification or mischaracterization, of doubt, certainty, or ignorance, we are pointing to features which may set *both* psychological reports and avowals apart from descriptions of a public setting.

Wittgenstein does not, of course, claim that such forms as 'I am in pain' or 'I am afraid' are never used as reports (cf. *RPP* II, §156). Moreover, it is not that, when they have such a use, the subject's relation to himself must be as to another, that what he says will be based on observation of his own behaviour (ibid., §177). Nor does granting character as a report commit us to allowing that we have to do with a statement of knowledge or belief. Information will ostensibly be imparted with the report, but that falls short of what is required for descriptions in these terms to be apposite as coming from the subject of the feeling. However, it is the expressive use that is given pride of place in Wittgenstein's scheme, and we may wonder whether it is deserving of this elevation. Such utterances as 'I've got toothache' or 'It hurts' are favoured as likely instances of such a use, but it is not until we get to something as close to a groan or a cry as is 'ouch!' that we have a really persuasive example. As an exclamation elicited by contact with a sharp object, say, 'ouch!' could readily come from someone who found himself alone, but, while 'I've got toothache' or 'My feet are killing me!' may be spontaneous utterances, they, in contrast to involuntary cries, are unlikely to be detached from all communicative or informative intent, as the rarity of their occurrence when the speaker has no company testifies. Nor is a reportive role in the least remarkable when they are offered in response to a query about how one is feeling, a query to which 'ouch!' would assuredly not give a suitable answer—and not just because it is associated with a sudden rather than a lingering pain.

Expressive uses tend to come up when there is something to register on the like-dislike scale, or at least when feeling of some sort is involved. Here we often stay close to a cry, as with 'yippee!' and 'yuk!', or we employ an expletive, as with expressions of annoyance: 'damn and blast!'. But if you have a ringing in your ears, and say as much, this will not give concrete proof of the condition in the way that 'aha!' may *be* a surprised reaction, or 'brrr!' a reaction to the cold.

Given the connections which 'statement' has with 'testing', 'justification', 'confirmation', and 'refutation', Wittgenstein considers it misleading to speak of an expression of sensation as a *statement* (Z §549). However, there are many sensations, as of temperature or pressure, which, if ever we have cause to speak of, we shall do so more often than not using language which qualifies as reportive, and even with pain we should not wish to set too great a distance between the supposedly expressive 'I am in pain' and the clearly reportive 'I am often in pain', both of which can be queried—'Surely not?'—or qualified by the speaker—'but I don't expect it to last'—in much the same way. Again, an expressive use appears to have nothing to contribute to an elucidation of such larger phrases as 'a sudden twinge of pain' or 'a throbbing pain'. Similarly, any role as a replacement of more primitive behavioural reactions is unrealistic when diagnostic, temporal, and locational qualifications contribute to the point of what is said about one's sensations, as with 'Yesterday's exertions have left me feeling stiff all over', 'This bee sting is still hurting badly', and 'I've got pins and needles in my left foot'. In playing down the reportive use, as Wittgenstein appears to do, we run the risk of neglecting a large area of use relevant to the problems of understanding psychological verbs; indeed, we risk severing the undoubted links between first-person and other-person uses, and first-person uses in other tenses. Within the overall pattern of usage, it is in general the expressive use that appears as a singularity. True, in *Zettel* Wittgenstein represents the first-person use only as being *akin* to an expression (Z §472), but with sensations generally the kinship tends to be distant.

If, with respect to a given mental state, the available words should figure only in reports, how, it may be wondered, could there be any check on what is said with them? It could not be that our knowledge of the mental lives of others was always at second hand. If all we ever had to go on were people's reports of their thoughts and feelings— as 'I'm excited' and 'I'm fed up', say, may be—we should not know what to make of such declarations: a language game which cannot be traced back to primitive reactions appears to be without a foundation. With an expressive use, the difficulty vanishes, production of the words being just one among the cluster of reactions characteristic of the state, reactions from which its very existence may be read off. Accordingly, to reject altogether any such role for a given psychological verb appears to leave us bereft of any means for answering the questions of meaning and truth which press in on us here.

This is a consideration of some force, but it is clear that an expressive use cannot carry the whole evidential burden. What would distinguish 'ugh!' from 'wow!' if we had only the expressions? And when we fill in what is needed by way of supplementation, we find that an expressive use is not essential. It may be that a report is secondary by comparison with an expression giving direct evidence of a psychological happening, but this does not mean that it has to be a verbal form that fulfils this function, let alone that there must be a historical transition through behaviour to a verbal replacement for it. It is by behaving excitedly or glumly that those who announce 'I'm excited' or 'I'm fed up' show us how they feel, and even with pain the direct ground is more plausibly sought in behaviour, given the questionable status of 'ouch' as a *word*. It might even be argued that what is of the first importance is not so much the availability of a direct manifestation of the mental as something which is criterial for its occurrence, and even a report can enjoy that status. For instance, there is no typical behaviour associated with having a tune running through one's head, but we commonly know of such a happening only if told of it by the person whose head it is. The subject's honest word becomes criterial when, as here, there is no scope for another to offer a judgement about what the subject is experiencing—as there will be with respect to sounds which are *actually* heard—so no question of the latter's losing out in any adjudication of competing claims. Whence, of course, the subject's authority. So long as he as much as understands what he is saying, what he says is to be accepted, there now being no other way for him to go wrong. True, the condition of understanding defines a real enough route to error. There is no guarantee that a person who complains of 'tinnitus' knows what he is talking about, but the gap can be closed by further explanation on his part.

With respect to pain, our departure from Wittgenstein's approach is fundamental, and it will do no harm further to highlight the divergence. Consider the question 'How do words *refer* to sensations?' (*PI* §244). On the present account, an answer to this requires us to bring in reference to certain public conditions, notably those to do with causation and behaviour, via which reference to pain is mediated, the picture rejected being one according to which the meaning of 'pain' is determined by conditions which can be taken in merely on attending to one's feeling. The question has, I should say, more to do with meaning than with reference, and would be better rendered as 'How do words for sensations relate to them?'. It is a matter of words such as 'pain' rather than 'referring expressions' such as 'my pain'. At all events, while Wittgenstein would also reject this picture, the alternative he presents is more radical. Our account is consistent with a conception of sensations which construes these on the model of 'object and designation' (cf. *PI* §293), and leaves room for the notion of identifying a pain or other sensation, but both these moves are excluded when 'I am in pain' is construed as expressive. In so far as such an avowal compares with 'ouch!', or with a cry of pain, no identification or description of a sensation is involved. Despite the superficial similarity to descriptive language, the situation is quite remote from one in which we might observe the scene about us and, perhaps after some scrutiny, identify and describe what comes to our attention. There is no question of our applying a criterion of identity for the sensation, so no question of the error which misapplying such a criterion might involve (ibid., §288).

It is no doubt true that, in so far as there is a close comparison with a cry, this is so, but I have suggested that avoidance of an improper observational model does not oblige us to draw such a comparison; that, indeed, it would in general be a mistake to do so. The scheme of object and designation is not tied to that model, but it is so undemanding, the considerations concerning the language used which warrant it so simple, that it cannot be abandoned without totally discounting the surface grammar; to such a point that we are obliged to reduce an avowal of pain to something as unstructured as a cry, thereby losing sight of the possibility that, in uttering the avowal, we should, whether through misunderstanding or lying, be misrepresenting how we feel. However, without embracing this extreme, we can insist that a report of pain, boredom, amusement, and so forth is not—exceptional cases aside—based on *evidence*; this ground for the distinction between first-person and third-person psychological ascriptions remains intact.

Although sensation is frequently to the fore when expressive uses of language are invoked, such uses seemingly have more to offer with respect to thought and belief, concepts which will loom large in the discussion to follow. However, while the notion of expression has a ready application in this connection, just *what* is then expressed may not be quite as we are inclined to suppose. We shall pick up this point shortly. First, our relevant reflections on belief might naturally develop along the following lines. While 'I believe that *p*', like 'I hope (fear, expect) that *p*', is suited to a reportive use, the simple *p* is geared to the *expression* of a belief. True, assigning the various forms to their respective classes—the reportive or the expressive—is not always straightforward, but in so far as 'I believe that *p*', or 'It is my belief that *p*', is reportive, it testifies to belief in a different fashion from the simple *p*. If we learn of your belief from your report, it is because we have taken your word for something, rather than taken what you have said as evidence on a par with your behaviour. In saying 'The key is in the lock', you make no mention of your belief, no more than you do with a bit of behaviour, but there may be no real doubt that you are giving voice to a belief, as your actions and other circumstances may confirm. As reportive, 'I believe that *p*' often comes in on the scene when the belief is already a reality, whereas the expressive form is more fundamental in furnishing the substance of the latter. The existence of the belief owes nothing to the report, whereas we may have the belief taking shape with its expression.

However, in drawing a contrast in this way we risk misconstruing the role of 'I believe . . .', which, in general, is surely to be seen as *incorporating* the expressive use. This is so whether it is a matter of a belief which takes shape with the words, or a belief which the speaker has held for some time, when the reporting will also involve reaffirmation. And there is no reason why 'I believe that *p*' should not merit both descriptions. We may express our belief with these words, and, to make them, at the same time, into a report, it is enough that we should have held the belief for a period up to and including the time of their utterance.

Does this condition yield all there is to the idea of belief as a persisting state of mind? To justify talk of persistence perhaps requires us to be more emphatic as to the settled character of the belief. The believer is not to be repeatedly reopening the question of the truth of *p*, but is simply to accept it as true, speaking and acting, more or less unquestioningly, in accordance with the belief (cf. *RPP* I §832). We might give our attention to a *question* about how things stand before saying what we believe, but we do not give attention to a state within us to check that a belief has persisted. The notion of a state of mind remains problematic in this connection (cf. Hacker 1992), but if associated with a sufficiently undemanding formal characterization, it would none the less appear to have some application. Wittgenstein recognizes two uses of 'state of mind', one associating the term with states of consciousness, the other taking in dispositions (cf. *RPP* II

§§43–5, *RPP* I §832). The latter is the one invoked in the following passage: 'This is how I think of it: Believing is a state of mind. It has duration; and that independently of the duration of its expression in a sentence, for example. So it is a kind of disposition of the believing person. This is shown me in the case of someone else by his behaviour; and by his words.' (*PI* 191; *LW* II 12). Note that in this instance there is no difficulty in taking the expression to be a statement, no difficulty in construing it as true or false. But, to take up the point which began this discussion, it is also important to note just what is being expressed. Believing that *p* may be a state of mind which one can express with 'I believe that *p*', but 'the belief that *p*', like 'the conjecture that *p*', does not signify a state of mind, but takes us to something that can be described as 'far-fetched' or 'disproved'.

To elaborate further, as something had or held, a belief can be unexpected, or typical of the believer, in which case it is the believing, the holding of the belief, that is unexpected, and the belief will be typical of *A* if it is typical of *A to* believe what he believes. Similarly, it is the belief as the believing that can be fortunate or tentative, firm or fervent. The belief as what is believed, on the other hand, may be likely, impossible, or a travesty of the truth. The belief as what is had or held is accordingly not the same as the belief as what is believed (cf. White 1972: 81–2). Note that belief as believing subdivides. If *A*'s belief is firm or fervent, this is a matter of *A*'s believing something firmly or fervently, but if *A*'s belief that *p* is unexpected, '*A*'s belief' introduces a putative *fact*: the fact that *A* believes that *p* is unexpected. Note, too, that to speak of a belief as possible may be to appraise *what* is believed, but the claim may also be that it is possible that someone holds the belief, in which case it is belief as believing that is being spoken of.

Compare other psychological terms, such as 'fear'. Someone who forgets his fear may forget, become oblivious to, his fearful state, or he may forget that he fears that such and such may happen. Someone's eyes or voice may express fear—a state of mind—but if I express the fear that our guests may overstay their welcome, the fear thus formulated is in the same category as an opinion or conjecture, the subject of such predicates as 'unfounded' and 'oft-repeated'. With an opinion we have a grammatically possible truth for which the available evidence is inconclusive, or which reflects an individual judgement only. A fear is given with words which predict the threatened occurrence of something considered unwelcome, a doubt with words which affirm the unlikelihood of certain happenings. Where we might expect to find a psychological element we find a semantic one: a belief is part of a semantic system, interlocking with beliefs which lead to and beliefs which lead from it, beliefs which it presupposes and beliefs which it makes likely. Contrast Donald Davidson: 'Much of the point of the concept of belief is that it is the concept of a state of an organism which can be true or false, correct or incorrect' (1985: 479). What can be true or false, correct or incorrect, is what can be *advanced* or *asserted*, and that is not a state, mental or physical, of any organism. It is with respect to belief as believing, as holding a belief, that the notion of a state of mind has what application it has, but belief as what is believed, as a subject of such terms as 'mistaken' or 'idiosyncratic', is not to be found in the realm of the mental. The next two sections will have more to say about belief in this latter use.

Finally, and still in connection with belief, it is worth noting that expression is not necessarily the same as manifestation. A person may *show* by his behaviour that he believes he can cross the road safely, or that he believes he can get to where he is going without hurrying, but such behaviour is not so readily regarded as an *expression* of the belief. Moreover, while a belief may indeed be manifested both in what is said and in what is done, the two conditions are not on a par: behaviour manifesting a belief is behaviour as could be expected of one whose words show him to have that belief. It is not implausible to extend talk of thinking or believing to animals on the strength of their behaviour—or so we shall argue—but the reason this way of speaking remains figurative is, I suggest, because it is not a matter of behaviour that is consonant with a belief which the creature might *also* express in words. Again, as we shall also argue, while a person's will or decision may take shape in behaviour, it is only if the agent has beliefs expressible in words that what he does can be viewed in this light.

2.3 FORMULATING PHYSICALISM

The common categorization of sensations as mental might be held to make for an unnecessary dimension of difficulty for physicalism in their regard. Sensations are rightly thought of as *bodily* happenings, this description being warranted on the strength of considerations to do with location, not with constitution. However, as we move towards the mental, properly speaking, the connection with the physical becomes insufficiently direct to be of much service in throwing light on the nature of thinking in its diverse forms. We shall now offer a few words indicating where and how physicalism might be defended, and its bearing on the questions of causation which concern us.

In trying to make out a case for physicalism, the first task is to select grammatically eligible terms in which to formulate a statement of mind–body identity, the difficulty in making sense of a mapping of the vocabulary of the former onto that of the latter being at its most severe with nouns, such as 'dream' and 'pain', and their associated epithets, such as 'lifelike' and 'sharp'. To formulate a prospective identity it helps to shift to verbal phrases, such as 'To be in pain is just to have certain events taking place in one's nervous system', or a more precise variant in which the events are specified—ideally, and irrespective of our views on functionalism, at a level of generality that would accommodate pains experienced by any conceivable subject, not just by human beings as presently constituted. This shift to the verbal form may look to be a minor emendation; in fact it marks a crucial divide between sense and nonsense, and, while it is generally regarded to be necessary to a defensible physicalism, it is all too often forgotten by defender and opponent alike. Even to claim that states of consciousness may prove to be states of the brain is to seek to match up incommensurable items. If Fness is a state of x, then x is F, but, to repeat, it is a person that can be conscious, not a person's brain.

With this shift a simple transference of epithets from 'dream' or 'pain', 'thought' or 'itch', to 'neural process' is forestalled, leaving us able to incorporate the predicate in a more manageable way. To have a thought which can be termed obsessional is not to have something that can be paired with a similarly describable neural happening, but that is not to say that the obsessional character of one's thoughts is not matched by some specific feature of their neural counterparts. For the same reason, and without any threat to physicalism, a judgement about one's state of mind may be incorrigible without the same being true of a judgement about the state of one's brain. Again, perhaps nothing which might be observed on opening up your arm could be described as an itch, but that is of no account if to say that you have an itch there is to say no more than that your arm itches, since it would not seem that grammatical propriety is transgressed by proposing that one's arm's itching can be explicated in terms of the arm's being in a physicalistically describable state. The level at which the mental may map onto the physical is such that, paradoxically, finding differences between the two need offer no threat to physicalism.

Failure to enlist the right terms for a putative identity is likely to go hand in hand with a misconception concerning the relevant psychological vocabulary. Dreaming dreams, having doubts, experiencing pangs of hunger, feeling twinges of jealousy—these are not to be modelled on verbally similar instances of *Ving x* where the grammatical object, *x*, denominates something having an existence independent of the *Ving*, as with feeling the warm air on your face or spotting a friend. The occurrence of the dream and the dreaming of it are one. If dreaming is constituted by neural events which take place in our heads while we sleep, no further problem is posed by dreaming a dream. The noun does not present us with an additional item, something which may or may not enter into this relation.

Yet another example is found with the cognitive scientist's problem of explaining how the content of a mental state can impinge upon behaviour. It is argued that a belief, say, will have effects on behaviour through being just the belief it is—that is, for having just the content it has; content, or meaning, however, does not appear to reside among the electrical and chemical properties which characterize the neural states and events in which, if physicalism is correct, the belief is realized and which can be expected to figure in any causal transactions. If the problem is to see how neural happenings can have the effects they have through meaning what they mean, it is not a problem that should delay us for long. It is not that meaning does not reside among the recognizably *effective* physiological properties; there is no question of *anything* in one's brain having meaning. Once more, the physicalist will want the neural state which realizes believing that *p* to differ from neural states corresponding to beliefs with different contents, but the differences will not themselves count as differences in content. I should add that in making this point I am not for a moment granting that belief is as those for whom there is this problem take it to be.

It may seem to be a quibble, but even the appeal to *natural* meaning is questionable if extended to what takes place inside the head. Though related to word meaning, the notion of natural meaning is

appropriately less demanding. It has yet to be explained how anything in one's brain could mean, for example, 'Neither guest wore
formal attire', but something in one's brain could mean, indicate, or
be a sign of something. However, a closer look at these seemingly
straightforward ways of speaking suggests that the impression that
we have to do with a semantic relation trades on connotations of
these locutions which are not appropriate to the relevant contexts.

Talk of a sign, or indication, is in place when there is a certain evidential or inferential ordering: we pass from the sign, S, to a supposition about something with which S is associated—that is the
movement we envisage even if there is so far no question of S's being
an indication to or for anyone. Of course, to the extent that there is
this inconvenient suggestion, it can easily be cancelled, but that is just
to say that you might as well simply speak of S occurring *because* of
what happened; perhaps not as a direct result of the latter, but there
has at least to be some form of lawlike connection between the two.
It is only in so far as S is envisaged as made use of in the way suggested that any kind of intentional notion, however primitive, is in
order. Such a use is indeed met with at the level of animal behaviour,
as when certain happenings in a creature's environment serve as signs
of danger to the creature: it forms expectations on their basis, acts in
a way appropriate to their having the origins they have. But it is noteworthy that it is things *external* to the creature that may indicate
something to it; nothing occurring in its nervous system enjoys this
role—nor, of course, the role of indicating anything to the brain—
though events in this domain might conceivably indicate something
to a physiologist. If such undemanding concepts as those of *indicating* have to be purged of the connotations which align them with
intentional concepts, it would appear that the pursuit of any richer
intentional properties within the domain of the physiological is the
pursuit of a mere will o' the wisp. But nor, I am arguing, does this
contradict any reasonable expectation.

Back to our main theme. On one common conception, the challenge presented by the mind–body problem is to show how the occu-
pants of two totally disparate domains can interact across their
boundaries; to characterize, perhaps, the physics or chemistry of the
as yet mysterious interactions between the mental and the physical.
The two domains are thus represented as having enough in common
for the problem to arise in these terms, while being sufficiently
different for it to be insoluble. A further refinement is to impose a

physicalist conception upon this scheme, thereby removing the troublesome boundaries and securing homogeneity for the items which they had segregated. But the difficulties which beset the idea of thoughts, say, as physical are in no wise diminished; they simply linger on, now to discredit the physicalism which deals in these grammatically irreconcilable fictions. Fortunately, there is no need to press this hopeless conception. It may be that no designation of a physiological process is a designation of a sensation or a dream, and yet having that process occur may be all that is involved in having the sensation or dreaming the dream. Given such an equivalence, there is now no pressure to insist on an identity at the level of the individual noun. Why, after all, should there be any expectation that the principles underlying the use of the two types of term should result in matching divisions in what they depict or report? Compare the analogous equation of persons with their bodies. A physicalism which operates at the level of the injunction 'For "I" read "this body"' would not appear tenable, yet perhaps it is possible to rewrite statements containing 'I' in such a way that the pronoun no longer figures, but reference is made to no more than one's body and its states. Such a project does not oblige us to defend the host of incongruities—'This body has forgotten the date', 'That body has an attractive body', etc.—which the cruder form delivers.

Analogies of use to the physicalist are hard to find, since they tend to be variations on the same problem—as with the supposed identity of sound and sound waves—but a parallel of sorts is provided by matter and energy. As it stands, the supposition of an identity here looks nonsensical: you can cut up bits of matter and scatter them around the room, but you cannot subject energy to anything like the same operations. Here we are dealing with a term from a quite different category, that of a *capacity*—as for work—rather than of a *stuff*. But this is of minor importance so long as it is possible to recast statements about matter in such a way that they come to make no mention of matter, but only of energy. Once more, what is now said of energy will only exceptionally be what was previously said of matter. The requisite identity may hold only at the level of the paragraph, not even at that of the sentence.

Further help can be given to the physicalist by rejecting that picture which would have the person who thinks or feels thereby observe from a unique perspective what is also open to public inspection—mental items as brain states viewed 'from the inside', and raising the baffling question: how can one and the same phenomenon present such differing facets to us?—as if the dull grey matter of the brain belied the richness of the sensory experiences which its states constituted. However much we attend to the one presentation, we gain not the slightest help in anticipating the character of the other, but the identity is more puzzling than non-identity, not less. Once more, however, this distortion is in no way an inevitable corollary of physicalism. Adherents of this doctrine should insist that, for the person engaged in the thinking or feeling, the neural firings are not the object of awareness, they *are* his thinking or feeling. There is no relation which would be easier to grasp if, when you observed something of a given colour, the nerve fibres involved in your having of the experience were themselves of that colour. Quite generally, the inappropriateness of any such demand is part of the solution, not part of the problem of defining an intelligible relation between the mental and the physical.

A similar misconception is revealed when it is supposed that a comprehensive knowledge of the neural events involved in experiencing a sensation should, if physicalism is correct, afford knowledge of what it is like to have that sensation. As this statement of the supposition makes plain, the demands made by the two forms of knowledge are quite different, the former requiring some scientific expertise, the latter requiring that one be, or have been, subject of the relevant physical disturbances. The difference is not happily expressed as one in properties perceived or detected, since the unfortunate sufferer performs no such act; nor is it a matter of the physical happenings presenting different faces to sufferer and observer. Once more it is a matter of differing subjects. The description 'nauseated', which the sufferer is in a position to offer, applies to *him*, not to the physical happenings, which attract a different range of predicates, even though it is by dint of having these happenings take place within him that this description is applicable.

2.4 THE SCOPE OF PHYSICALISM

Supposing we have at least a coherent formulation of a particular psycho-physical identity, is the question of its truth then to be regarded as an empirical issue? That might appear to be its status: we may be able to defend the position against the kinds of objection considered, but we have not shown that being in pain, say, is not an *effect* of physical happenings. This would not be a happy resting point. As though we had two hypotheses: being in pain as an effect of, and being in pain as identical with, neural processes, further empirical investigation being required to decide which is correct; or, perhaps, no such investigation being capable of yielding a definitive answer, one or other alternative is to be preferred on grounds of simplicity, or of some comparable desideratum.

If the mental has a physical realization, it surely cannot be a mere accident that this is so. But how might one rule out any alternative as incoherent? One possible approach derives from a form of argument due to Saul Kripke: it makes no sense to suppose that something composed of a given substance, as a suitcase made of leather, might have been composed of a different substance—of plastic, let us say. It would simply not have been the same thing, the suitcase we are now contemplating, had it been differently constituted to that degree—or indeed, if it had been leather, but not this leather. Likewise, if your current feelings or imaginings are in reality neural phenomena, then it cannot be admitted that they might have had a totally different, non-neural, character.

However, it is not clear that the considerations which in general hold good for this line of argument extend to the psychological, since here the relevant criteria of identity are not concerned with matters of constitution. I see no ground whatever for saying: it simply could not have felt the same if nerve fibres had been involved other than those whose stimulation resulted in your feeling pain. Equivalently, it does not follow that you could not have had exactly the same experience if your physiology had been different, where sameness is as normally understood—namely, sameness in how it feels. This point is perhaps overlooked because it is the crude form of the doctrine that is considered: pain is identical with C-fibre stimulation. It should also be mentioned that Kripke's appeal to the modal standing of the relevant identities is actually presented as an objection to physicalism: the doctrine is held to fail if, as is commonly insisted, it is specified that its identities be contingent (1980: 146–55).

Kripke is wrong, incidentally, in thinking that the necessity in question is not linguistically founded, but 'metaphysical'. Let us agree that this suitcase could not have been made of plastic. Had such a suitcase been before us, it would simply not have been *this* one. It is the constraints on what counts as *this*, as the *same* suitcase, that are

being brought into play here, rather than the emphasis being—as in
the more usual case—on the associated general term. Kripke is misled, I suspect, by the occurrence here of a referential term. Could anything be this very object and not be composed of molecules? he asks
(ibid. 47). There is indeed an extra-linguistic reference here, but, for
all that, 'could anything be . . .?' might also be put 'would anything
count as this very object . . .?'. It is not, after all, a physical possibility that is at issue. At all events, leaving aside the seeming irrelevance of the argument when constitution has no part to play, nothing
in any case follows concerning pain generally, given that the necessity in question relates to the conditions pertaining to the use of 'this'
in 'this pain' rather than to the general term 'pain'. Kripke thinks
otherwise. He holds that 'the identity of pain with the stimulation of
C-fibers, if true, must be *necessary*', that 'the identity theorist is committed to the view that there could not be a C-fiber stimulation which
was not a pain nor a pain which was not a C-fiber stimulation' (ibid.
149). However, suppose we allow that those instances of being in
pain which are in fact C-fibre stimulations could not but have been
C-fibre stimulations. This tells you nothing about how other
instances of being in pain are or may be realized. It simply reaffirms
the identity conditions of the given instances.

But it will no doubt still be felt that, if the psychological is
reducible to the physical, this is no accident, and it is up to us to
show why other alternatives are to be ruled out. The only way I see
to meeting this challenge is by putting pressure on the relation which
any alternative would appear to involve—namely, that of causation.

Asked to produce ways of speaking which reveal our everyday
notion of cause at work we should not be at a loss for specimens,
such verbs as *cut*, *scratch*, *bend*, *roast*, *soak*, *scrape*, *chew*, *twist*, and
melt being representative of the large array (cf. Anscombe 1971: 137).
Causation is not a mysterious relation, in the sense of one which may
not be apparent to observation. It would be ridiculous to deny that
one could see shoes being polished, wood being chopped, or toast
being burned. What appears to be common to these notions is the
idea of one thing's acting upon another. However, while it is surely
in some such terms that our primitive idea of cause is to be understood, there are also terms which are thought to introduce causal
conditions of a less dynamic character, as with the constitution,
arrangement of parts, and properties generally of an object. Suppose
you pluck a string on a stringed instrument. Your plucking would be

held to be the cause of the sound, but there are other factors which can be said to contribute to its production and character, as with the tension, length, and constitution of the string, and the nature of the body to which it is attached. In identifying a cause, we tend to opt for the activating, initiating, or triggering cause, rather than the conditions against which this operates. The latter might even be refused the standing of causes, as the notion is commonly understood, but they enjoy a similar role in the way they may be indispensable to the character of the effect.

A defence of physicalism requires us to justify a certain interpretation of sequences of the following kind: a burn causes a volley of neural impulses, whence your arm hurts; decay brings about neural activity, and your tooth aches. At some point the neural activity just is to *be* your arm hurting, your tooth aching, whereas for the anti-physicalist these experiences will never be more than *effects* of such activity. To the anti-physicalist we may now put the question: *how* do such happenings cause your arm to hurt, have your toothache as an effect? What model do we have for such causation?

The dynamic character of these happenings suggests that their role is, if anything, that of a causal agent rather than a causal condition: they are to cause your arm to hurt by doing something to it. But that is the role reserved for the burning or cutting, happenings which assuredly do cause pain by acting upon your flesh. The neural firings do not cause your arm to hurt by mimicking these familiar causes; there are not these firings *plus* a change in what they are supposedly acting upon—to wit, your arm—an altered state which they induce and which might linger on when they have ceased. What grounds are there for saying that these, taken as a whole, *act upon* anything at all? Any changes to which a noxious stimulus might give rise are to be found among just these happenings themselves; or, if not here, then in the gross movements of the body which then ensue. We remain locked within the physical system, the barriers to breaking out being erected by grammar—nothing would count as a causal relation which did not keep us within that system.

But this, it might be said, is to take an excessively narrow view of how we can learn of the effects of physical causes. We also know of the effects of burning, say, by experience, not simply by observation and investigation. Very well, we know by experience what effect contact with a hot object can have, but this does not mean that the experience of the burning sensation is not constituted by the physiological happenings. Moreover, to find out what the effects of such contact involve it is surely relevant to follow up the sequence of events which it sets in train, and this means relying now on techniques which another can enlist as readily as can the subject. In so far as following up that sequence confines us to the physical, and in so far as we can make no sense of a transition from this space to another, we can claim to be characterizing whatever it is that that stimulus brings about. As already observed, the neural happenings do not act upon our bodies to produce the pain we feel—they do not *hurt* us—but the most it would seem we are entitled to say is that they *result* in our feeling pain, where this is explained in the following way.

We can distinguish two kinds of process. With those that involve action of one thing upon another, we can speak of generation, construction, transformation, alteration, destruction; on the other hand, we may have a movement or other change having a certain terminal state as its result or outcome, but where this is an end phase or upshot of the preceding happenings, rather than an effect of those happenings upon something. That is, there is greater continuity, comparable with successive phases in a uniform development, than we have with cause and effect. In speaking of pain as resulting from neural happenings we need be committed to no more than is involved in a process of the second type: being in pain is simply a final phase of those happenings rather than an independent effect, something of a different character to which they give rise. We have no reason, I suggest, to favour the action-upon model over this physicalistically consistent alternative.

If, at some point, the neural happenings just *are* the subject's feeling pain, and not a causal prelude to such feeling, it may seem that we have confined pain to a domain where its causal potentialities are assured. This need not be so. We still have no licence to extract the term 'pain' from the more general condition 'to be in pain is . . .' and attach it to something which is an object of observation to the physiologist. If I experience a sharp pain, it does not follow that some neural events within me can be described as sharp; merely that having such an experience equates as a whole to some physiologically describable state of affairs. Conversely, if the relevant events can be traced from arm to brain, it does not follow that this defines the location of my pain. And the same consideration applies in the matter of causation: the neural happenings may issue in further physiological events, but that does not make the pain subject of this relation, does not make it any more acceptable to say that a pain can act upon something, that it might initiate the movement of a limb, for instance. The correspondence is such that we can move from causation of the physical to causation of the 'mental', but not sufficiently close for the converse relation. It was suggested that finding differences between the mental and the physical need offer no threat to physicalism; by the same token, in so far as we have identity, this is not guaranteed to advance our understanding of the mental.

With 'belief' and 'desire' we are even further away from anything which might denote the physical: 'the belief that p' is a phrase which may attract such descriptions as 'dogmatic', 'nihilistic', 'controversial', or 'cherished', 'the desire to V' one which may be joined by 'unrealistic', 'altruistic', 'heartfelt', or 'overweening'. There is no guarantee that such predicates will characterize a mental state, and no chance that they will characterize a state of the brain. Likewise with a forlorn hope, a groundless fear, a painful realization, or a vain wish. It is sometimes suggested that such attributions stand in the way of a physicalistic reduction of beliefs, but, if the reduction has the mental as its target, it will not have to cope with beliefs any more than it will with conclusions or conjectures, diagnoses or diatribes.

The same observations are relevant to the dismissal of physicalist reductions on the basis of 'twin-earth' considerations aimed at showing that different thoughts can supervene upon identical physical states. According to Hilary Putnam, the meaning of a term like 'water' is dependent on the character of water in such a way that, if what corresponds to the word on earth is H_2O, but what corresponds to it on another planet is a substance with the same readily observable properties, but a different chemical constitution, say XYZ, then the meaning of the word on that planet is different from its meaning here. In consequence, the content of mental states is dependent on extra-mental, and indeed extra-physiological, facts (Putnam 1975).

The account of meaning which this argument relies upon is misconceived. If, when speaking of 'that liquid', you mean wine and I mean water, then what we respectively mean is different just in virtue of the difference between wine and water, but this does not require 'that liquid' to vary in meaning correspondingly. For that it would be necessary that the criteria for the application of the phrase should be different for each of us. This, in Putnam's example, will indeed be so if for us the meaning of 'water' is given by 'H_2O', whereas for those on the other planet it is given by 'XYZ', but this will be a matter of how each party *understands* the word. That is, whereas a difference in what is meant in the first use is founded in a possibly unknown difference in the world, a difference in meaning of the second kind requires a difference in the acknowledged criteria for the word's application. Indeed, if we are speaking of the ordinary understanding of 'water', 'H₂O' does not provide an equivalent, the understanding in question being explicable without presuming a grasp of 'hydrogen', 'oxygen', or chemical valency. It could not be correct to say that, for all we know, 'water' might have a dozen different meanings, but this would be a real possibility if unknown features of what is referred to with the noun could enter into its meaning. This is not to say that meanings are 'in the head', but it is to acknowledge a central place to the notion of how a word is understood. It is unfortunate that English uses the same word for these very different uses of 'mean', but it is clear enough that they are different. While any number of distinguishable substances may be meant by one who says 'that liquid', we are unlikely to speak of correspondingly different *meanings*, the use here of 'mean' not being one in which the verb readily nominalizes. The distinction, which is elaborated in Rundle (1990: ch. 6), will be touched upon again in §4.2.

Putnam's argument is deserving of further critical discussion, but in any event, and as has already been observed, when *A* believes—hopes, fears, etc.—that *p*, there is not in general anything *mental* that collects such predicates as 'controversial', 'vain', or 'unreasonable'. If the belief, hope, or fear that *p* is not mental, it is not, a fortiori, a mental *cause*. At best, believing and the rest can be causal conditions, yet it is thoughts as the bearers of crucial semantic properties which, it is frequently claimed, must somehow be shown to be causally relevant, and relevant in virtue of these properties, if the mental is to play a genuine role in explanations of behaviour. Moreover, it is implausible to suppose that there is much here that can be handled within the confines of physicalism. In hoping and fearing, disliking and distrusting, we have conditions which infuse the subject's verbal responses, involuntary reactions, demeanour, gestures, and behaviour generally. Even with respect to sensation, such a complexity remains to be addressed. In general, certainly, physicalism mirrors the narrowness of a Cartesian conception which would affirm a clear and distinct division between inner and outer, with fear and the rest placed firmly on the former side of the divide. Give the wider

conception its due—one that finds a place for the multifarious manifestations of these conditions—and we are left with little more than
the uncontentious truth that you cannot hope, fear, and so forth,
without a brain. We might also add that what A's thought is *about*
is often, ultimately, a matter of what A would identify or pick out
non-verbally as his concern. It is not just that something external to
the thought, to the thinker's mind, has to be invoked; it is something
pertaining to what he might *do* that is crucial.

Physicalists have a tendency to deal in impossible generalities:
everything real is physical; experience is real, so experience is physical. It is a worthwhile project to see if there is a level at which the
radically different vocabularies of the physical and the psychological
can be found to converge on a common reality, but no success in any
aspect of this enterprise could have us conclude that thoughts or
experiences were physical. That makes no more sense than it would
with such notions as those of *inconvenience, chance,* or *discretion.*
However, the considerations which show that physicalism need not
embrace such impossible identifications also suggest that the doctrine
will have little to offer by way of clarification of the terms which
occur within the psychological descriptions which, as a whole—and
if such there are—have physicalistic counterparts. The conviction
that the mental has properties other than those of the physical is in
no need of a defence against physicalism. To repeat the general point,
it is coherent to maintain that there can be properties shared by both
the mental and the physical—as those relating to duration—but also
properties pertaining to the mental only, even though there is a
level—that of events—at which the mental is identical with the physical. However, to the extent that the kind of autonomy which the
mental enjoys is to be defended in this way—in terms of a form of
'non-reductive physicalism' (cf. Kim 1993)—there is no firm expectation that our understanding of specific psychological concepts stands
to gain from advances in neurophysiology.

Suppose, for instance, it can truly be said that to have a mental
image is just to have certain physiological events taking place within
one. An appreciation that this is so would not mean that our puzzlement about the psychological happening would thereby be at an
end, since our uncertainties here are uncertainties encountered in
relating our psychological concepts to one another, or at least to
other equally familiar, non-physiological, concepts. Just how like seeing is having an image? How like a photographic image is a mental

image? It is the place of the concept of *image* in our everyday language that we wish to see clarified, its relation to the concepts to which we naturally turn when offering an explanation that we wish to see more perspicuously displayed. So long as confusion reigns at this level, we shall be confused about what it is that knowledge of the underlying physiology might somehow illuminate. And this is not the only way in which a physicalist approach may prove unavailing. A consideration of thought and belief has revealed a further misconception as to what can be reckoned to the domain of the mental, a further limitation on the possible relevance of physicalism. Finally, even where physicalism may be correct, it loses much of its significance so long as, in speaking of the mental, we are not speaking in a veiled way of the causal determinants of behaviour. And this remains very much a live possibility.

2.5 OBJECTS OF BELIEF

The problems presented by psychological verbs, such as 'think', 'dream', and 'imagine', are often problems which centre on the associated noun-clause construction, as when we speak of thinking that we are late, or dreaming that we are on a desert island. We have already remarked on the misleading mislabelling of pains as 'mental', and it is noteworthy that the clausal construction does not have the same place with respect to the vocabulary of sensation as with the strictly mental. On the other hand, and as already indicated, when thought or hope is a matter of what is thought or hoped, something specifiable by a noun clause, talk of a mental object is yet again, and even more strikingly, out of place. Just what the clausal construction involves will now be considered.

Thoughts and beliefs, hopes and fears, are commonly taken to be objects of a 'propositional attitude'. However, it would be wrong to regard thinking that p as relational, whether it is to have a proposition, conceived of as an abstract entity, as one term of the relation, or whether, as the nominalistically inclined would have it, it is to take a sentence as its object. It could be true that Kate thought that p even though the proposition which would give expression to her thought had not been formulated, let alone addressed, at the time in question, in which case one term of the supposed relation is simply missing. A thought is the upshot of one's thinking, not its pre-existent object.

The person may acknowledge that the words are right for the situation as it presented itself to her, but that is not a question of comparing the spoken word to an unspoken version to see if they tally. To construe thinking as relational is much the same error as noted with other instances of 'internal' accusatives, as dreaming a dream or feeling a twinge of jealousy.

True, when belief rather than thought is in question, there is greater scope for the notion of a propositional object to enter, believing often being a matter of accepting something that another has said, something already in circulation, as it were. There is then something which can be entertained, then endorsed or dismissed. However, this is one possibility only. When taken as the general pattern, it is as if we introduced 'proposition' to apply to any of the things that are believed when there is something towards which we can clearly be said to adopt an attitude, as with a report, a rumour, or a confession, and retained the term even when the only 'object' which might be in the offing is one which we can at best say *will* be produced with the expression of the belief—with perhaps the added paradox of deeming this the central case in which we have to do with a proposition.

My quarrel, I might add, is not with the notion of a proposition, which, even if it is wrongly invoked in this connection, allows of an innocent enough interpretation. A proposition is for me something you can write down or hear, find illegible or inaudible. This makes it something 'concrete', but it is something abstract in so far as two people can write down the same proposition or repeat it slowly. A usage which allows for the latter is not mandatory, but it is both intelligible and useful. One aspect of its usefulness is seen in the way it makes it possible to say that 'It is raining' and *Il pleut* are the same proposition. Not that they in some way 'stand for', but that they simply *are*, the same proposition. And that is intelligible. If it is thought not, that is no doubt because it is supposed that sameness must be taken as strict identity, when there is also sameness as given with an equivalence relation—sameness in some respects, so a relation which may reckon as the same linguistic forms which, while differing in sound and spelling, agree in the all-important matter of meaning.

However, while the notion of a proposition may be blameless, the conception of thought, belief, hope, fear, expectation, and the rest, as mental states with meaning or content appears, if not an irretrievable muddle, to be sorely in need of clarification. It is the former, I suggest, if meaning and content are treated as equivalent.

Clearly, the notion of linguistic meaning does not have direct application to hopes, fears, and so forth. You can enquire after the meaning of words which express a hope, but not after the meaning, in the same sense, of the hope itself; if you express your thought out loud, what you say may bear more than one meaning, but the thought cannot be said to be ambiguous. Prior to such expression there need be nothing of which one might say that it had meaningful parts—'concepts'—the same structure, or others of the features exhibited by the arcane entities thought to shadow our words. It was suggested above that mental items to which such predicates as 'muddled' and 'mistaken' apply cannot be counted on to exist when it is true to say, for example, that Kate thought mistakenly that p. It does not require Kate to have articulated the thought to herself for this to be so, but Kate's preparedness to voice her thought in these terms, or to accept such a formulation, is all that is needed. Whether as predicates or as part of a coordinate construction, it is primarily *what is said* that descriptions such as 'mistaken' or 'implausible' latch on to.

On the other hand, the logic of 'content' is not interchangeable with that of 'meaning'. You can speak of the content of a belief, just in so far as there is something that is believed, so, if we should be able to answer the question 'What is it that is believed when it is believed that p?', we can take our answer to contribute to an elucidation of the notion of content. Linking the notion to the clausal form, *what is believed*, imposes grammatical subtleties on the former which differentiate it sharply from any propositional term, as we shall soon see.

The above remarks hint at a conception of belief in which its verbal expression has a primary role, a conception which has obvious attractions: there is far less of a mystery if belief and thought are to be identified through their expression, rather than being inner items against which the speaker must check what he says to be sure that he is saying what he thinks. Certainly, if the appeal to thought is an appeal to something modelled on overt speech, the explanatory value of the former *vis-à-vis* the latter will be fatally compromised.

How might a reference to the spoken word be incorporated into a characterization of belief? The usual strategy is to explain thinking or believing that p in terms of a disposition to say that p. There has to be something to this approach, given the readiness with which we may alternate between saying, for example, 'I thought there was no one about' and 'I'd have said there was no one about'. However, it takes a number of assumptions to keep the account in the running. First, while thinking that *p*, we may have no inclination whatsoever to give voice to this thought; there need be no general disposition to say that *p*, but, at best, we need to introduce an appropriate restrictive condition, as 'if asked to give my opinion . . .'. And even then there is a supposition that we are speaking truthfully—a matter of saying what we really think. This condition has a habit of intruding itself into otherwise promising analyses, reflecting the awkward consideration that truthful speech has, in some sense, to answer to thought.

In concerning ourselves with such qualifications, do we not perhaps betray an overly literal-minded reading of 'I'd have said that *p*' or 'I'd say that *p*'? The superficial grammar invites completion of these forms by an if-clause, but, on the relevant reading, they would surely state something false if the speaker did not think that *p*, rather than be representable as truncated forms which would be revealed as true once the missing clause, as 'if it were my intention to deceive', is supplied. That is perhaps so, but it is still plausible to maintain that the relevant use is made possible only by taking for granted some unspoken condition. Most obviously, it is assumed that the speaker has the aim of saying something true. Making this assumption explicit, we might suggest the following characterization: (*c*) *A* believes that *p* if and only if, having the aim to speak the truth, *A* is prepared to affirm or to agree that *p*. The relevant aim is not, we may note, to speak truthfully, which would again reintroduce thinking, but to say something that is in fact true.

I speak here of an *aim* rather than an *intention*, since one can still be said to have truth as one's aim even when being right in what one says is not within one's control, so not something one can so readily be said to intend—a distinction we shall touch on again in §5.4. But, even with this refinement, there still appears to be something secondary about (*c*), with respect both to its appeal to an aim and its appeal to truth. Considerations of truth arise only once we have, or envisage ourselves as having, something assessable as true or false. As you look about the room, you will doubtless come to have various beliefs; and, once these have formed, a question of their truth may be entertained, but any such concern is subsequent to their formation. The matter of an aim arises once we give voice to our thoughts or beliefs, speaking, as a voluntary act, being one which can involve a variety of aims or intentions. The latter, however, are not introduced with thinking that *p*, but this is something we *find* ourselves doing; our thoughts take shape willy-nilly, a matter of a *reaction*. When I think that the seat will support my weight, I judge, infer or conclude that that is so, but I need not at this stage—nor, indeed, later—entertain any aim or intention.

Again, while 'I'd say that *p*' may be a fair approximation to 'I think that *p*', with the shift to the past tense a further complication arises. So, you ask me how many people were in the room. I may be happy to reply, 'I'd have said there were around twenty-five', even if at the time I did not give the consideration to the matter which 'I thought there were around twenty-five' would require. My present attention to your question is the occasion for my *coming* to think that *p*. In the past situation I may have had the relevant information at my disposal, but I did not then make anything of it, did not reason, infer, form an estimate. Thinking, in the sense we are concerned with, is not just having a thought, but is linked to these other notions. 'Believe' as we shall later see, has somewhat different affiliations.

The notion of a preparedness to say that *p*, given the aim of saying something true, appears, then, to be secondary, to leave out of the picture the notion of a mental happening, as when it occurs to us that *p*, or when we seemingly realize that *p*. Again, does not (*c*) merely specify a condition for what *A* says to *report* what *A* thinks? That this is so is suggested if we press the notion of agreeing which features in (*c*). Reference to agreement seems called for, since this is just as good an indication of belief as is advancing *p* itself. Moreover, agreement is something one could signify without being able to speak. Such an inability does not exclude thought, but *A* surely must at least be able to indicate concurrence with *p*. However, suppose that even this is beyond *A*. In that case, we are left with nothing more, on *A*'s part, than recognition of a form of words as adequate to formulating the thought or belief. Some such recognition must be possible if we are to make sense of *A*'s holding the belief that *p*, yet the apparent sufficiency of this condition just seems to emphasize the secondary character of any affirmation or agreement. These are further matters, quite dispensable to having the thought which they presuppose.

However, these objections have now taken us to a one-sided picture: (*c*) could be a condition for what *A* says to *be*—not to report—what *A* thinks, with no implication that in uttering *p A* will simply be repeating a thought out loud. Or again, in signifying agreement,

A may simply be endorsing what has been put to him, rather than acknowledging that it expresses a belief he already has. The terms seemingly indicative of a mental episode, as 'It occurred to me that *p*' or 'I realized that *p*', can be accepted in this capacity, but they relate to the dawning of a belief or realization, a notion to be explored in §7.2. The more long-lasting state which begins in these ways is belief in a sense which (*c*) better captures, though with some such happenings presupposed, as was granted in our handling of the objection to the possible equivalence of 'I thought that *p*' with 'I'd have said that *p*'.

'Think' may relate to an episode, but it may also signify a state, as in such a context as 'Kate thinks her daughter will be a successful lawyer'. A move to the past tense brings with it a blurring of the two uses: 'Kate thought her daughter would be a successful lawyer' may report an enduring belief or a thought which the person had, something which struck her, on a particular occasion. It is not that we are dealing with two radically different concepts of thought—what may begin when the thought strikes you that *p* may endure in the belief that *p*—but, in so far as the notions of a state of mind or a disposition have application, it will be with respect to the latter.

Is there not a further possible divergence between the forms with 'think' and those with 'say'? Asked how old an article of furniture is, you reply: I'd say it's early eighteenth century. This may be nearer to a guess than to an opinion, to a view you are prepared to stand by. Very well, there may be such a divergence, but it is not that with 'I think . . .' the speaker must be reporting a mental episode, whereas with 'I'd say . . .' he need not be; the difference is in the same plane, a difference in the degree to which the speaker is prepared to stand by what he says. What follows 'I think' is presented as having the standing of a view or an opinion, not a query or a conjecture, but the phrase can convey that character without there being an antecedent unspoken judgement to which the words give expression. *p* is what I think if that is how I find myself judging, whether out loud or to myself.

To highlight the main point of this discussion, the kind of case which keeps our thinking about belief on course is one where the belief arises in the context of describing events unfolding before us: we respond verbally to what we see, our words, our attention, having an exclusively external orientation. Our aim will be to give an accurate description, but that is a matter of our natural response—to describe things as we see them. We are not now giving an account of what it is to think to oneself that such and such, or what it is to have the thought that such and such cross one's mind. The idea of mental events or other items central to having the belief, let alone items to which our belief is directed and which we perforce report in expressing our belief, need play no part in the instances of belief being envisaged. That anything mental can be bypassed in this way will be argued further in §3.2.

Back to the grammar, and to the question of the objects of the propositional attitudes. Making sense of hoping, fearing, suspecting, or expecting that *p* as hoping, fearing, suspecting, or expecting a proposition is a challenge to which I am unequal. Moreover, if you expect that *p* and I believe that *p*, then what you expect is what I believe, but, since 'proposition' cannot be introduced in the former case, it cannot serve to characterize what is both expected and believed (cf. White 1972: 75; Hacker 1992: 258). So, while it makes sense to speak of believing a proposition, it is not a way of speaking that is suited to the construction with a noun clause. How, then, is believing that *p* to be understood? Just *what* do we believe when we believe that *p*?

As a preliminary, consider the analogous query in terms of suspecting: what is it that one suspects when one suspects that *p*, or when one suspects, simply, *p*? With respect to the latter we are not tempted into casting *anything* in the role of object, and would indeed be in error were we to do so. With 'Kate suspected that the milk had been adulterated', there is the possibility of a passive transformation: 'That the milk had been adulterated was suspected by Kate.' This possibility warrants the parsing of 'suspect' as transitive in this context, with the noun clause as object, but, when 'that' is omitted, this mark of transitivity is lost. The intransitivity of the verb is further shown by the way in which 'Kate suspected' can now be moved about the sentence: 'The milk had, Kate suspected, been adulterated', 'The milk had been adulterated, Kate suspected'. Here two coordinate verbal forms are being variously combined, rather than one being subordinated to the other as direct object to transitive verb. Moreover, while we can speak of an 'object' with respect to the form with 'that', this is so in only a formal, grammatical sense. To take the further step of construing the clause as *naming* something, for instance, would force the inappropriate reading of 'suspect' on the verb. You do not suspect a proposition, nor even a suspicion, but in the absence of any such term it seems we can do no more than repeat the clause, or some more general version of it, in answer to the question 'What does Kate suspect?'. So, Kate states—sincerely, we shall suppose—that she suspects that the milk has been adulterated. Since, in saying this, she has already said precisely what it is that she suspects, a persistent questioner can be answered only by ringing possible changes on the clause. Kate suspects, she elaborates, that some impurities have been introduced into the milk.

Again, if the general question is posed, 'What does one suspect?', we are obliged to settle, somewhat lamely, for an answer as woolly as 'all manner of things'. There is little limit to what it makes sense to speak of suspecting. You suspect that a fuse has blown, that the figures have been altered, that the cat will never return, and so on indefinitely. To accommodate this generality, something like the 'general propositional form' might be enlisted: one suspects that things will be thus and so. If we do not wish to leave room for any and every instance of such a form, we may introduce a restriction—in accordance with, for example, the consideration that one often suspects that something discreditable is so—but what is significant is that such a form, whether qualified or not, clearly respects the clausal character of any completions of 'A suspects . . .'. Moreover, we have reason to insist that any alternative completions should be rephrasable in line with this grammar. If I suspect a conspiracy, the conspiracy—if such there is—is not the object of my suspicion—as if *it* might have done something untoward—but it is simply that I suspect that there is, or has been, a conspiracy.

It appears, then, that the question 'What does Kate suspect when she suspects that the milk has been adulterated?' is in no need of an answer if one as much as understands the words; it is not as if the item sought after were something awaiting *discovery*. Moreover, while a more general query makes sense, it is to be answered simply by elaborating the trivial answer in an appropriately general way. That any coherent elaboration should make use of a noun clause, or its equivalent, is in no way unsettling. We do not feel that there is something which has eluded us, some specification of an object of a different type, since putting any such specification after the verb results in patent nonsense. Asking what can be suspected amounts to asking what noun clauses 'A suspects' can join with, and the answer may be: pretty well any.

Belief is more problematic precisely because it does make sense to speak of believing a proposition. Our claim is, however, that, while this is so, it is not correct to construe '*A* believes that *p*' as, in effect, elliptical for '*A* believes the proposition that *p*', that the situation is in fact just as with 'suspect'. To repeat: what prevents us from appreciating this basic sameness is simply the availability of a term like 'proposition', which gives an apt specification of an object of belief in certain other contexts. As with 'suspect', so too with 'believe', there is a question, though one of detail, as to what range of clauses may complement '*A* believes', but, if we are obliged to introduce restrictions, these will be within the domain of clauses, not within that of (what we might call) objects proper. Dissatisfaction with an answer which simply gives a clause in all probability reflects a lingering attachment to the idea that, while it may need improving upon, the answer given with 'proposition' is essentially of the right type. The break with this style of object must be far more radical if we are not to impose a distorting pattern on the construction with 'believe'. If you ask me what I believe when I believe that I have been very fortunate, the answers are required to be elaborations, not designations, of what I believe, as when I reply that I believe that what I had lost has been found.

But do we not say such things as that what *A* believes is a foregone conclusion, or is a travesty of the truth? Yes, we do, but by way of passing a *comment* on what *A* believes, not by way of specifying a *kind* of thing believed, as one might say: on that occasion a foregone conclusion was believed, or a foregone conclusion was what was then believed, as if 'foregone conclusion' had its place in an inventory of believable items, along with 'rumour', 'allegation', 'confession', and 'tittle-tattle', from which we were obliged to draw in seeking an answer to 'What does *A* believe?'. It is simply that what *A* believes—that the candidate will lose his deposit, say—is, moreover, a foregone conclusion. Compare 'What *A* believes is a fact'. To say this is not to specify a sort of thing believed; not: a fact is what is believed, but what is believed—namely, that the candidate will lose his deposit—is a fact. Once more we come back to the clause as what dictates our understanding of these forms. In '*A* believes that the candidate will lose his deposit', the clause simply gives an oblique rendering of terms in which the belief might be expressed. To think or believe that the candidate will lose his deposit is simply to have a thought or belief expressible *thus*: the candidate will lose his deposit.

A particularly perspicuous variant is given with a form which can be reckoned intermediate between *oratio recta* and *oratio obliqua*—

namely, that exemplified by 'The candidate will lose his deposit, *A* believes'. Here '*A* believes' purports to indicate the standing of the accompanying words, envisaged as uttered by *A*, but we are in no way tempted to elucidate what this involves by invoking the pattern of a relation directed to an object. This variant is perspicuous in the way it draws together reports in which a speech act is explicitly characterized, as with 'He had been deceived, *A* protested (lamented, explained)', and those in which a psychological verb occurs, as 'He had been deceived, *A* suspected (believed, feared)'. Despite the difference in the two types of verb, there is overall agreement in the way the shared affirmation, 'He had been deceived', purports to report words which the person used, or might have used, in expressing a protest (lament, explanation) or suspicion (belief, fear). It is, in either case, a matter of words *with* which an attitude is conveyed, rather than words which are the object of an attitude. Here we may note that, if a verb *V requires* that there be something propositional towards which an attitude is taken, then the construction with the that-clause is in general *not* allowed. So, you can ridicule, endorse, dismiss, contradict, or misunderstand my claim that the earth is flat, but you cannot ridicule, etc., *that* the earth is flat.

However, what emerges from this discussion is not so much that the notion of a proposition cannot legitimately be invoked in this context, but that it is not to be introduced to provide a term in an inappropriate relation. To explain, in the form 'The candidate will lose his deposit, *A* believes', it could be said that the words appended to '*A* believes' present us with a proposition, where 'proposition', like 'assertion' or 'statement', is used, not with respect to a clause within an utterance, but with respect to the complete utterance. This might be taken to define a sense in which '*A* believes that *p*' may be said to involve a proposition—that is, there is this involvement just in so far as the clausal form is replaceable by a variant in which the noun clause has given way to an affirmation, complete in itself—but accepting this proposal still would not warrant us in saying that '*A* believes that *p*' involves a relation to a proposition. On the contrary, the construction in which a proposition is acknowledged to figure is patently one in which we have two coordinate forms, rather than one which conforms to the model given with '*A* believes the story (allegation, rumour, etc.)'.

The clausal construction brings us, I have suggested, not to something *towards* which we take an attitude, but to something *with* which an attitude is expressed. To this it may be objected: since it can be only to *words*, or their equivalent, that we are brought with the latter, we have lost the greater generality which the notion of an object of a propositional attitude enjoys; this might, after all, be something purely mental, an internal sentence couched in the language of thought. But if, as has been argued, belief is to be understood in terms of the expression of belief, there is no real loss. If there is belief only in so far as there is a form of words which the believer may affirm or endorse, if the expression of belief does not have to be reckoned such through its standing as a report of something mental, then nothing but an illusion is lost. If, on the other hand, there is a question of words said silently to oneself, these are to be compared with the expression of belief, rather than with something towards which one's belief might be directed.

A final, not uninteresting, point. It is natural to suppose that the most straightforward, as well as the most basic, instance of *Ving that p* comes with *saying that p*. The most straightforward, in that here 'words' can be given in answer to the question, what is said? This is, of course, a pattern which those with reductionist aspirations for 'believe' have cherished: show that what is believed is a sentence, and our problems are over. However, in the use of 'said' that is relevant to '*A* said that *p*', or to ' "*p*", *A* said', what is thought straightforward is just false. ' "I am going to sing", he said' belongs with such forms as ' "I am going to sing", he warned'. Here 'he warned' purports to characterize the act with which the quoted words were uttered; it is not a question of warning the words, or anything to which they might refer, and this remains true with 'He warned that he was going to sing'. Likewise with 'protest', 'boast', 'complain', 'lament, 'conclude', 'insist', 'conjecture'; and, indeed, 'said'. It is just that the characterization which this last gives is much less specific than these other verbs provide. Of course, we do have the form 'He said the words, "I am going to sing" ', where 'said' may be replaced by 'uttered', but adding 'the words' after 'said' in ' "I am going to sing", he said', distorts the latter, and even replacing 'said' here by 'uttered' is inappropriate. It is not that an analysis of '*A* says that *p*' can make do with something as concrete as words as object, whereas '*A* believes that *p*' introduces something mental, but to make a contrast in these terms is to reveal just the misconception we have been exposing. Once more, the final say rests with the unifying observation: if you believe that *p* and I say that *p*, then what I say is nothing other than what you believe. The identity does not fail because I am dealing in something as gross as words, whereas your belief is directed to something ethereal. On the contrary, what I say is *just* what you believe. The agreement could not be bettered.

There is, evidently, much more to be said by way of demystifying the 'propositional attitudes' (for further discussion, see White 1972, Rundle 1979: ch. 7; 1990: §9.4; Hacker 1992). Our aim has been merely to sketch a way of analysing the *oratio obliqua* construction which steers clear of the common assumption that thought, belief, hope, fear, and the rest present us with mental items which have the content, the representational role, of linguistic forms, and which might enjoy a causal role in explanations of behaviour.

3

Mind, Animals, and Behaviour

We turn now to consider the possible application to animals of psychological predicates relevant to an analysis of action. This topic has the potential both to mislead and to bring our thoughts back on course. It has the potential to mislead by adding an imagined dimension of difficulty to any problems posed by these predicates, as happens when the lack of a language is taken to set an obstacle to knowing what is going on in an animal's mind rather than as making for the senselessness of any hypotheses about a mental life in anything but an extended sense. On the other hand, animals provide a useful reminder of more primitive manifestations of various psychological states which we are apt to lose sight of when concentrating on sophisticated human capacities. In particular, while familiarity with our own agency may encourage a common conception as to how action is to be clarified—namely, by following a path which begins with a mental event and terminates in behaviour—consideration of animals points us towards a less provincial, and less mentalistic, perspective.

3.1 ANIMAL ACTION AND DESIRE

It may seem puzzling that animals should ever come to do much of what they do—as feeding, grooming, and protecting their young—without knowing why. My claim is that to act in a certain way a creature, whether animal or human, does not have to know why it does so; it is just that, if it does not know, then a certain kind of explanation of its behaviour is not possible. But it is true that the way an animal responds to certain perceptual cues—stopping, starting, modifying its movements in the light of what is happening about it—brings its behaviour close to human action which rests upon knowledge and belief, closer than with a reflex act, for instance. So close, indeed, as to give a foothold to these notions, though not to the extent of enabling us to say that the animal knows the rationale for what it does. Clearly, the continuity between us and higher forms of non-human life is considerable, and there is surely a presumption that the intellectual capacities, centred around language and thought, with which we are endowed are to be thought of as grafted onto what we and they have in common; certainly, there is danger of distortion if we insist on tying knowledge, desire, and so forth, inextricably to the mental. Or, rather, there is such danger if mind and the mental are to be considered a human prerogative. And that is how I see it. There is, I wish to say, something for us to know about a creature which lies outside what can be learned from observation of behaviour and physiology only if there is something which that creature might divulge, or alternatively, keep from us. You may remain quite impassive as I speak to you, but my conception of you as a person allows that all manner of thoughts should be racing through your head, thoughts of which I shall be apprised only if you inform me of them. A mental life in this sense is denied to the rest of the animal kingdom. We can credit the dog with watchfulness, timidity, fear, a state of expectancy, and its nervous system, like ours, is abuzz with neural goings-on, but the former we read off its behaviour, and the neural happenings are likewise in the domain of the detectable. We never have cause to suppose that there are facts which pertain to an inner life and to which we are denied access.

It is often observed that we are carelessly anthropomorphic in our ways of speaking about animals. That, undoubtedly, is so, but the present emphasis is different. There are numerous predicates which qualify as broadly psychological and which are fittingly ascribed to animals, but we can acknowledge this, I suggest, without having to accept that any mentalistic notion is here mandatory in any substantive way. What I mean by that should be clear from the preceding demarcation of the mental: notwithstanding the range and variety of such predicates, there is nothing to be learned about the animal that it is beyond the combined resources of a physiological and a behavioural investigation to reveal.

How might this position be defended? In so far as it involves my conception of the mental, there is doubtless a degree of stipulation which leaves it vulnerable, but the point of substance is that the assumption of anything further than what may be disclosed to observation is quite gratuitous, and hence that there is no call to invoke *mind* in any significant sense. At this point the thesis concerning mental causation, or the lack thereof, becomes important. Suppose it is claimed that a creature's behaviour shows that it *must* be able to think. If I accept this, it is because I am persuaded that its performance warrants a *redescription* in these terms; not because thoughts are required to account for the causation of the behaviour. For the moment, however, I wish to look at some sample psychological terms to see to what extent a non-mentalistic construal of them is independently plausible.

A concept pre-eminent in explanations of human behaviour is that of *action*, where the term is accorded a more circumscribed reading than it has in many non-philosophical contexts, being restricted to things which an agent does rather than things which merely befall it, to the activities involved in designing and building, say, rather than to such episodes, possibly quite unwelcome, as slipping, shivering, blushing, and retching. Action and agency are commonly treated as mysterious categories, a sense of agency being as ineffable as it is inescapable, yet it is noteworthy that much the same division into action and non-action is available with animals other than men. When a cow's head twitches as a result of a fly alighting upon it, we have a type of reaction which may be distinguished from other movements which the cow might engage in to dislodge the fly, as rubbing its head against a tree. The reflex movement is one that is over and done with very rapidly, leaving little or no time to modify it in such a way that it is more effective in the given circumstances, whereas with other movements—rubbing against something, shaking the head—a more flexible pattern may be observed. Again, we might contrast the non-actions of slipping and falling with the actions of swimming and flying.

There are, of course, complexities in identifying the two forms of behaviour, action proper and mere reflex. It can be far from obvious how animal grunts and cries are to be categorized, and the confusingly rapid movements displayed by birds, say, may make it difficult for us to discern the plasticity, the adaptability, which would mark them as actions. Contrast the movements of a monkey in peeling a banana, where the ability to adjust and adapt is evident. A behavioural episode may encompass both varieties. Perhaps, for instance, the cessation of an action, when the creature is brought up short by something in its environment, is often to be thought of in reflex terms—as it may be with us. Or again, a hovering hawk maintains a steady position despite variable air currents. If we speak of deviations or departures from this position resulting in a correction, we have a schema into which, conceivably, either style of explanation can usefully be lodged.

The problem of making sense of purposive behaviour is essentially a problem of finding a way in which the notion of a *goal* may play a part, given that we may not, when invoking the notion, be introducing anything which has any reality at the time of the action, so not anything which could then furnish a real term in an explanatory relation. With animals, we have, in the general case, to make do with the idea of a pattern of behaviour which, through adjustments to circumstances, typically culminates in a certain state, albeit a pattern detached from any conception of a state aimed at. If we have to consider some species of psychological ascription as fundamental to our understanding of animals, it will not be a matter of *thinking* that such and such will lead to a desired goal, but priority goes to a less problematic condition—namely, that of being able to recognize when things are as they are at the various stages en route to the goal. The bird building its nest does not have to have any conception of an overall plan into which its successive acts fit, but it has to be able to take in the successive states of affairs which result from its efforts and which dictate the next step in its operations. If we may be allowed a degree of harmless metaphor, we may say that at each stage of the construction, what the bird has brought about can be seen by it as right or wrong at and for that stage. Certainly, some idea of recognizing, of being able to tell—figurative though these ways of speaking may be—is difficult to avoid, as a glance at any text on animal behaviour soon reveals, with accounts of female ostriches identifying their own eggs, stags gauging each other's strength, rats recognizing which of their fellows are healthy, which not, and so forth (cf. Dawkins 1993: ch. 2, for these and other examples). True, the ability to recognize a condition is not the same as an ability to recognize it for what it is—in a way, that is, that involves understanding. The stickleback's defence of its territory when another male intrudes is prompted by the sight of the red coloration which develops on the underside of the male—in general, a good indication of the presence of a threat, but the same response can be elicited by other objects, including even a passing mail van, provided the colour is right (cf. Dawkins 1993: 21). Red things are differentiated from things of other colours, but with no understanding of a rationale for the particular behaviour which gives proof of the discriminatory ability.

Our ascriptions to animals of actions, desire, knowledge, and perception are clearly interdependent. The behaviour which leads us to say that the monkey wants to get the banana which it is heading towards, that it is engaged in purposive action to this end, is behaviour of a kind which might also be invoked to justify a claim that the monkey can perceive the banana. A demonstration that a creature can see is not furnished simply by noting its possession of a light-sensitive organ which mediates reactions to the environment. Sunflowers have something of this combination, without sight, and we could easily construct a device which gave a rich range of differential responses to visual stimuli, but which could no more be said to see than can a light meter. The sunflower is found wanting through the restricted range of its sensitivity. It is quite incapable of responding to any structure which might be found in a light array, to differentiate among the visually diverse things which might confront it, but it is bare sunlight that prompts its movement. On the other hand, a suitable electronic device might mirror a wider range of visually definable features, but be wanting on the side of concomitant behaviour, behaviour appropriate to the presence of these features. The creature or device is to show that it has learned something about its environment; its behaviour is to be such as to allow us to speak of a manifestation of knowledge on its part, to reveal an appreciation of the presence of something, if not of its character as something to be pursued or avoided.

It is sometimes said that the crucial concept missing from the behaviourist's explanatory scheme is that of intention. The behaviourist has some reason to balk at the introduction of this concept if it comes in the form of *intending*, or *having an intention*, to V; where, that is, an intention has supposedly taken shape in advance of behaviour which puts it into effect. However, as providing a characterization of action engaged upon, *intentional* can interchange with *purposive*, a concept which the behaviourist can include in his repertoire without sacrificing any of his principles. And even talk of intention is not altogether excluded. Suppose that when a lion has manœuvred itself into a favourable position, a certain attacking strategy is likely to ensue. The behaviour predictable in this situation might well be behaviour which we can say the animal has an intention to engage in. Here, while all the lion may be doing is watching and waiting, we are in effect envisaging a pattern of behaviour already under way, so it is an extension of the kind of situation which

invites application of 'intentionally'. It is when an intention is supposedly formed in circumstances remote from those of its execution
that we risk going beyond what makes sense for the creature.

Certainly, to give an account even of animal perception some
notion of intentionality is called for, since, as just intimated, the kind
of behaviour which gives proof of perception is precisely purposive
behaviour, as when a creature examines something, or chases after it.
This is not to say that it makes no sense to attribute perception in
the absence of behaviour. On the contrary, the idea that a sighted
creature should be able to see something, yet do nothing, is important to our concept of perception. The relevant 'doing' is not a matter of simply reacting, but of initiating action on the basis of what it
sees, and it might 'choose' not to do anything. The sleepy cat opens
its eyes, takes in the scene, and closes them again. It has seen what
is before it, we suppose, but what does that mean? What event has
occurred in which its perception could consist? Neither brain nor
behaviour would appear to have anything to offer. Not brain, since
our concepts antedate any appreciation of the role of this organ; not
behaviour, since by hypothesis there is nothing at all on this front.
But, of course, such inactivity is consistent with the creature's having
learned of the presence of things around it. The change is a change
in respect of what it knows, and therewith of its capacity for action.
If we speak of a changed *state*, it is not an internal state in either a
physicalistic or a mentalistic sense; indeed, it is not a state deserving
of the description 'internal' in any sense at all.

We may not find it easy to spell out exactly what we know when
we know that the cat sees the mouse, but it is inappropriate to speak
here in terms of a *theory*—as if there were invariably something less
than conclusive in our ascriptions of perception, something which we
were obliged merely to postulate. One source of a contrary view is,
I suspect, a misreading of the term 'perception'. There is no doubt
that an ascription of perception can be well founded, if this means
no more than a claim that the creature can perceive, but, if 'perception' is construed on the model of 'image', then crediting the creature
with perceptions—note the plural—may well be thought to take us
beyond anything that can rest on a secure observational basis.

The potentiality for the grammar to mislead is similar to what was
noted above with respect to consciousness. That animals can be conscious is indisputable—that is just what we have with a wide-awake,
alert, observant dog. To ask whether the creature is endowed with

consciousness should simply be to have recourse to a stylistic variant using noun rather than adjective, but for some the noun appears to introduce an issue enjoying an altogether different order of profundity and difficulty, consciousness being hailed or lamented as a mysterious phenomenon quite beyond anything which science might hope to explain. Of course, whatever part of speech is used, there is a more demanding question when consciousness is a matter of self-consciousness. The awareness involved in perception establishes the former, but for self-consciousness we should want the creature to appreciate *that* it sees, hears, and so forth, whereas for a cat, dog, or other non-language-user, it would seem that anything that might be thought to show an awareness of seeing the mouse turns out to testify to no more than an awareness of the mouse (cf. Rundle 1972: 127–31). More on this shortly.

When action is the focus of interest, desire has to be a joint concern. To take the latter further, we note that we do not, for the most part, have anything over and above the animal's actions as grounds for an attribution of desires or wants. We may be presented with distressed behaviour—the dog whining and scratching at the door when it wants to be let out, the plaintive mewing of a cat caught up a tree from which it wants to get down—but these do not of themselves ensure the purposiveness that wanting may involve. When, with the distressed behaviour before us, we conjecture that the dog wants to be let out, what we are conjecturing is precisely that the animal will act in such a way as to give direct proof of this desire if the circumstances allow—if the door is opened and the way made clear for it to go out, for instance. The distress has what significance it has essentially as an indication of the creature's preparedness to engage in the appropriate goal-directed behaviour. Once more, there is nothing 'theoretical' in saying, for instance, that the dog wants to get its bone, but what furnishes the basis for such a claim is simply the character of the creature's movements as purposive; not the inflexible, stereotyped pattern of reflex movements, but the adaptable responses shown in the animal's interactions with things, in its persistence towards a goal. In the central cases, the marks of desire simply coincide with those of action. We do not have the further task of ensuring that an appropriate 'inner' state is also in attendance, let alone that it has a place in some form of mechanics of action. Of course, the description 'theoretical' may be in place in the sense of 'conjectural', as when we have yet to ascertain whether a variation in the position of something we think is being pursued will lead to a corresponding change of course on the part of the creature. But uncertainty on this score can in principle be removed. We are not grappling with a hypothesis which is, as it were, irredeemably theoretical.

Note that to say that behaviour can give proof of desire is not to reduce wanting to behaving, since a state of readiness, or a propensity, is not a form of behaviour, though it is, of course, a matter of a readiness or propensity to do certain things. What is important with desire, as also with knowledge and belief, is that, while they may be thought of as states which mediate between informational input and behavioural output, they are secured by a redescription, being logically guaranteed by no more than what observation can yield—the conception to which functionalism approximates, but of which it falls short. A mentalistic approach is tempting precisely because in very many cases the psychological description under consideration patently does not apply directly to behaviour. That it therefore attaches to something mental may, however, be equally unwarranted. Of course, while single-minded endeavours in pursuit of a goal offer a ready purchase to 'want', there is no easy entry for other related psychological terms, such as 'wish' or 'hope'. The reason is plain enough: both involve beliefs as to the likely futility of action to attain a desired goal, and the consequent detachment from action means that any application to animals stretches the use of the terms way beyond the literal.

If wanting is simply a disposition requiring nothing more than behaviour as the medium of its expression, then behaviourism is clearly not without the means for handling animal desire. However, this might be thought a one-sided account, dealing with 'standing' but not with 'occurrent' wants, an occurrent want being conceived of as a mental event or process present to consciousness, whereas a standing want is a more enduring disposition or propensity to have an occurrent want (cf. Goldman 1970: 86).

There is more than one way in which we might distinguish among wants, but the division just indicated appears misconceived. Given that the object of a standing want is the object of some occurrent want, I wish to say we have to do with a *single* want or desire, a want or desire that is sometimes brought to mind, but which it also makes sense to attribute to a person even when his thoughts are elsewhere—just as with belief. Whether or not we think of the desire as before the person's mind, we are talking in either case of a disposition, of a preparedness to act, if and when circumstances permit, to attain the given end.

Perhaps desires are thought of as mental because we often do not know that a person wants something unless he tells us—just as we may not know what he can see until he speaks. This, however, does not show that *what* the person may or may not disclose is something mental; it may mean only that the opportunity for manifesting the want in behaviour has not yet presented itself; not that it is not something that can be fully disclosed in this way. What is true is that there are some desires, as a desire to write a novel, which can be ascribed only to a being capable of thought. Again, neither the intensity nor indeed the identification of another's desire is something of which we are obliged to remain ignorant: how much one wants something is a matter of the steps one is prepared to take to get it, and the 'identification' of a desire is not something that follows on inspection of some mental item, but it is a matter of what the desire is a desire *for*, the thing or state of affairs wanted. Hence my talk of sameness with respect to so-called occurrent and standing desires.

3.2 THOUGHT AND BELIEF

Behaviourists are often accused of making improper appeal to the notion of behaviour, using the term as a cloak for something more than mere bodily movements. That charge is sometimes justified, but it is not that a richer notion of behaviour must presuppose a mind behind what is observed. The concept required is that of behaviour which qualifies as a response, not as a mere reaction, behaviour which, in being geared to the character of whatever the response is a response to, offers a foothold to a range of crucial psychological descriptions. We shall shortly take the question of animal thought a stage further, our aim being to show in greater detail how, in so far as the notion of the mental has application to animals, it is only as part of a more adequate conception of behaviour, and not as demarcating a mysterious and inaccessible domain of mental life.

Before embarking on this topic, it is worth looking further at the concepts of thought and belief in their more straightforward uses—namely, as applied to human beings. 'Straightforward' is, admittedly, relative. Many of the difficulties presented by 'think' are traceable to its heterogeneous character, the verb being used to cover happenings as diverse as reasoning, musing, calculating, reflecting, deliberating, imagining, and believing. At all events, focusing on even just the more evident features of our usage soon makes it apparent how much is presupposed therein which can have no direct application to animals.

The general direction of the argument in the last chapter was to make the verbal expression of thought central. This is not, of course, to deny that 'A thought . . .' may relate to something that went unsaid, but what is important is that what went unsaid could have received expression in words, and that, when it does, there does not also have to have been an accompanying, silent, thought. Certainly, the role or function of language is not primarily to express thoughts, thus conceived, nor does understanding another speaker involve making some kind of inference to such a thought. However, there is no shortage of considerations which seemingly tell against the priority of speech. When a person states that *p*, we can always raise the question whether that is what he really thinks. Perhaps he is not being truthful, perhaps further reflection will lead him to retract what he has said. Either way, it would appear that priority goes to an underlying thought. Again, it is a familiar experience to find oneself unable to come up with any words that are adequate to express one's thought. Similarly, we may note how a good writer's turn of phrase will have us acknowledging a formulation of a familiar thought more apt than anything we have been able to muster—Pope's 'What oft was thought but ne'er so well expressed'.

However, to repeat a point made with respect to belief, if asked 'Is that what you really think?', there is no necessity that you should do anything which would count as reflecting on a thought which you have brought to mind; it is your (continuing) affirmation or endorsement that is being sought or questioned; you are being invited to assess or reassess the likelihood of a certain happening, let us say. Again, if what you say may be contradicted by what you think, so too may your thought. You say, *or* think: we've been invited out on Friday. You then remember: no, it's been cancelled. In many cases, too, the suggestion that we compare our words with our thoughts is to be met by observing that there is nothing which one's words *follow* and against which they are checked by the speaker, though something relevant may follow *them*. I may reply to a question without giving any thought to the answer, but having given my reply have 'second thoughts'. But that does not mean that what I first said was not at that time genuinely what I thought: I was saying what I said as my view, offering an ostensible item of information, even if I subsequently retracted it. Again, I use the wrong word, saying, 'bought' when I meant to say 'brought'. Notwithstanding the time-reference of 'I meant to say', whether I meant to say *w* depends, not on anything that went on in my mind prior to my saying *w*, but on my reaction to *w* once said.

Finally, if I agree to your way of putting things, perhaps preferring it to my own, it is not because what you say does greater justice to a thought before my mind; rather it measures up better to the *situation*, say, which it aims to portray. Thus, with reference to the quotation from Pope, it is not so much that we can lay claim to having had the thought in question; more that we can appreciate the fittingness of the superior description. There stands a person in full view. I could venture some form of description of him, but what you say far better captures the peculiarities of his appearance which I had been groping to describe.

But to appraise what is said in relation to our surroundings we have to have some awareness of these, and it may be queried whether this can be done without thought. In this connection it is worth recalling the tendency to suppose that 'think' and 'believe'—more especially the former—have application whenever something in or about our surroundings comes to our knowledge, is in some sense taken in by us, a supposition which risks overstating the pervasiveness of thought. Suppose that, from where we stand, it is apparent that a certain shrub is nearer than a certain tree. If asked subsequently whether we had thought that the shrub was nearer, we might be reluctant to say we had. Perhaps nothing of any relevance even entered our heads. Again, while it may not come as news to you to be told that you have just passed a group of four children, all facing the roadway, at the time you may not actually have had the thought that there were four children, or that they were thus positioned. And so on with countless other features of the scene. If we formulate an observation to ourselves in words, however partially, if we conclude, infer, judge or reason that something is so, then we shall, plainly, have thought. Likewise if we wonder, raise a question, then reach an answer. So, I thought he was going to say something, that someone had left the door open, that she was looking preoccupied. The connection with 'reason' and 'infer', with a need to judge, or assess, is a dominant strand in the use of the verb. You think to yourself that a friend is looking distressed. There will then be something which occurs and which deserves to be called a mental episode in a way that need not be so when certain things, as that there is much wind and rain, are simply obvious features of the setting. When this more minimal form of learning or awareness is all we have, it will be possible to invoke a verb of perception: we agree that we *saw* a group of children, even if, once more, it puts it in the wrong light to say that we *noticed* them. We might also mention *finding something F* as a psychological notion less problematic than that of thinking. We may hesitate to say that the toddler thinks that *x* is interesting—it is not of that opinion, has no such thought to report—but there need be no doubt that it finds *x* interesting.

The step between being aware of an *x* that is *F* and having the thought that an *x* is *F* is often so short as to seem to be no step at all. Indeed, if we concentrate on situations in which we are presented with familiar things having unremarkable features, situations in which we could readily put words to what we perceive, the step may seem even shorter. It is also true that, while what we perceive and recall provides an important backdrop to our thoughts, it would be a distortion to suppose that we always say what we say with at least half an eye on something which qualifies as what we are talking about. But the case remains an important one for the way it lends undeserved support to the priority of thought; it encourages us to insist that we *must* have thought if we as much as had some awareness of our surroundings, so that there can be no question of what is perceived providing something against which people's words can be judged; as if reality could not provide the relevant constraint, but that there had always to be a thought interposed.

It would appear, then, that the degree of awareness sufficient to enable us to appraise a judgement for truth does not have to be such that we must already have had the thought which the judgement expresses. Mere awareness of the scene does not require the mastery of concepts which thought as judgement demands. Two people can have a common awareness of a single thing, but the thoughts they may have about it are not thereby determined, since these will depend on the principles of classification, the concepts, which they command. To think that the creature scurrying across the patio is a lizard involves being prepared to offer a particular characterization; it is to judge the creature to fall in one of the many categories in which it might belong. This reliance upon concepts goes beyond what is required for mere awareness of the lizard, and makes for a crucial link between thought and language (cf. below, §4.2).

So far we have been treating 'think' and 'believe' as more or less interchangeable. However, while our present interest is principally in the area of usage where the two undoubtedly do overlap, it is worth enquiring whether even here there might not be a significant divergence between them. One apparent difference lies in a greater tentativeness for 'think': 'I believe that Kate is sincere' may be held to repose more faith in Kate than does 'I think that Kate is sincere'. True, if the stress is carried by 'I' rather than 'think', this suggestion will weaken considerably, but in general there can be said to be a difference in these terms. Relatedly, 'believe' may often have a solemn ring to it, expressing a commitment to a position which does not allow of proof, an acceptance of something on faith: 'I believe that God will provide'—not a happy context for 'think'. It is a word favoured by politicians as well as by the clergy, there being a suggestion that it is to one's credit that one believes, is prepared to take the plunge. Here we note that we can believe a person as well as what is said, a matter of placing trust in the speaker's veracity.

The more solemn use of 'believe' is not the only one, but we also have such observations as 'I believe this painting is by Canaletto'. There may be little to choose between this and 'I think this painting is by Canaletto', but, in so far as there is a difference, it is likely to relate to the respective grounds, 'believe' introducing a reference to what others have said, 'think' being based on one's own reasoning or opinion. Saying I believe is like saying I gather, or I've heard say and have no reason to doubt. In this use, the philosophical favourite, 'I believe it is going to rain', is likely to report information picked up from a weather forecast rather than be a remark passed on looking at the heavens. However, the latter is not impossible, the allusion to another's views not inevitable. Compare 'I believe we've met before' or 'I believe I can handle it'. It may be that evidence is being treated as akin to human testimony, but the relevant point is perhaps more that one is placing trust in one's memory or abilities. However, there is little if anything to differentiate this use from that of 'think', and even less with such a sentence as 'He believes he's being followed'.

To see the basis for a more general contrast, consider occurrences of 'think' where 'believe' is likely to be incongruous, as with 'I think you look great in that dress', 'I thought his speech was funny', and 'I think I'll spend the weekend pottering about in the garden'. One may believe that a speech was funny—that is how it has been reported—but thinking that it is funny is not, on the more probable interpretation, a matter of holding a belief; it is more a matter of *finding* the speech funny, of actually being amused. The concern which 'think' reflects may be simply to record one's own reaction or appraisal in a way that makes it quite inappropriate to add, 'but I may be wrong'. Similarly with 'I think you look great in that dress'. In venturing such a comment there is no question of accepting something which might be established by another party, something which one might have to take on trust, though, once more, it is not that the matter is one that *could* not be established independently of the speaker's own reactions, so not that 'believe' could in no circumstances be apt.

The use of 'think' in 'I think I'll spend the weekend pottering about in the garden' is interesting. One possibility is that the speaker is announcing an inclination towards an action, but with the implication that he has not quite made up his mind, has not decided irrevocably. Once more, however, such diffidence is one possibility only, one arising when 'think' is stressed. In general, there is no more a suggestion of tentativeness than is found with 'I think you look great in that dress'. 'Think' offers the opportunity to convey diffidence, but it need not be taken up. So, 'I think I'll give her a call' or 'I think I'll turn in now' may be said just as one sets about the act. In so far as it is thought to be up to the speaker to do what is proposed, addition of 'but I may be wrong' is again inappropriate, the considerations which weigh with the speaker being considerations which concern desirability rather than feasibility. Contrast 'I think I am going to faint'. Imminent fainting may be thought likely by the speaker, but it is not up to the individual whether or not it comes about, so there is no question of a judgement in its favour being what settles the matter. Here 'believe' is also possible.

'Think', then, covers a wider range of possibilities than 'believe', having a use in which the possibility of error plays no part, and, when the thinking merges into a behavioural reaction, taking us off in a different direction altogether. In the abstract, this latter possibility appears counter-intuitive, but thinking as finding something funny, sad, or shocking is a matter of being amused, saddened, or shocked, and here the behavioural component is plain. The range extends even further when we take in such acts or activities as thinking about something, thinking something over or through, thinking of a name or of something to say, thinking what, how, or why something is so. Unlike 'believe', 'think' often relates to the voluntary: you may be asked to think of a number; having made up your mind what to do, you can be invited to think again. In many of these contexts thinking often is, or is bound up with, an activity, or with an episodic happening. As such, it may not qualify as a state of mind, but as such it may also be remote from thinking as believing. Here we may note that one may think (= reason) to oneself or out loud, but not think (= believe) in either way; I may keep on thinking that I must do something about the dripping tap, but I cannot keep on believing that I have a weak heart. Thinking as an occurrent activity, something which may take the form of an interior monologue, which may be interrupted, pursued with determination and concentration, is very different from being of an opinion or holding a belief, yet views on the latter often appear to take the former as their guide, exaggerating the degree to which inner speech is involved in thought as belief— Plato's 'the inward dialogue carried on by the mind with itself without the spoken word' remains the model (*Sophist* 263e, *Theaetetus* 189e).

Finally, let us return to an earlier point about the importance of the non-psychological dimension of the psychological verbs. The frequent closeness of 'believe' to 'gather' is worth drawing to the attention of anyone who would seek to explain 'believe' by characterizing the state of mind which it reports or expresses: what is to the fore with this use has as much to do with the *history* of what is being advanced, a matter of information gleaned from a person, or other source. Similar points were made in the last chapter with respect to 'fear' and 'doubt', and could have been made for 'expect', 'suspect', and 'be sure', the degree of evidential support which these variously imply being a central feature of their use. In elucidating 'I'm sure that p', we might naturally introduce reference to a state of mind or disposition: one is sure that p to the extent that one is prepared to bet that p, to base one's actions on the eventuality that p, and so forth. However, such considerations are secondary to the evidential issue. If questioned whether you are sure that p, you will cite reasons for thinking p true, rather than dwell on your feelings of confidence. So, are you sure you locked the garage? Yes, you say, you distinctly remember replacing the key on the shelf, something which, in the circumstances, you consider a firm ground for your assertion. Again, 'You can't be sure' alleges a deficiency in this respect, a lack of grounds which would license your categorical assertion, and when, similarly, you say that you *cannot* believe that *p*, this is not an admission of weakness on your part, but your claim is that what you know rules out the possibility that *p*. Similarly, if there cannot be a dissenting view, nor greater or lesser assurance, nor support to a degree, then there is no place for 'I think'. So not 'I think I'm bored', 'I think I'm overjoyed to see you', but just the plain 'I'm bored', 'I'm overjoyed to see you'. It is the standing of these words, the nature of the possibility advanced, that rules them out as the expression of an opinion, not any limitation on one's powers of thought.

3.3 ANIMAL THOUGHT

The question whether animals can be ascribed thoughts or beliefs is more complex than the parallel question concerning desire. The affinities of 'believe' with 'accept' and 'gather', on the one hand, and, on the other, the affinities of 'think' with 'reason' and 'judge', suggest that the application to animals of either requires at the very least an extended usage. This is not to say that talk of desire is just as it is with human beings: the purposive animal behaviour which invites description in these terms is not behaviour directed to bringing about a state of affairs which the creature envisages and finds attractive. None the less, we surely stay closer to literal truth when we say what the dog wants than when we say what it thinks. However, despite difficulties which ascriptions of thought present, it may be held that they must be allowed, since there would otherwise be many occasions on which we should be quite unable to make sense of what an animal is doing. To take a familiar example, a dog is seen to run excitedly around the base of a tree after a squirrel has vanished into the upper branches; we should surely wish to explain the dog's behaviour by supposing that it believes the squirrel to be up the tree. How, without such a supposition, could we hold out any hope of a satisfactory explanation?

A natural response to this challenge is the following. It is premature to speak here of explanation, but there is a case for appealing to such behaviour to *give sense* to an ascription of belief to the animal. It does not go without saying that we can understand such attributions; on the other hand, animals behave in ways which make it plausible to extend this way of speaking to them. Cast the belief in an explanatory role and we generate an intractable problem about what the behaviour is evidence *for*. We have in effect excluded the right conception at the outset in speaking of an explanation, which makes us look for something substantial when all we have is a redescription, the adoption of a convention. It is a convention that some, of course, would not wish to adopt, but for those who accept it, it is again not the mental that is in focus, but the appropriateness of the terms in which the content of what is believed or known is specified.

Though essentially correct, this is too short a way with the issue. The excited behaviour can be regarded as no more than evidence that the dog has learned of the squirrel's presence, behaviour that is fittingly explained by supposing that it has acquired such knowledge. It is thus comparable to the distressed behaviour which may be associated with an unfulfilled desire, as with the whining of a dog which wants to be let out. However, the important point is that, just as with desire, it will not be something beyond behaviour that we look to for proof of what is thus conjectured. Not so much excited barking—which has the secondary status noted—more the purposive behaviour which reveals an appreciation of the squirrel as situated at a certain place. Given such a response, and considerations relating to the part played by the dog's senses, we can confidently say that it has seen the squirrel, and therewith come to know of its presence. If we choose to rephrase this in terms of belief, our description will, of course, inherit the non-mentalistic character of the condition on which it is based. We shall not have to think of what is postulated as something for which behaviour can give less than proof; it is just that some forms of behaviour are less central than others, and, while they thus make it appropriate to speak of an explanatory hypothesis, they may thereby mislead us into misconstruing the relation of that hypothesis to the creature's behaviour.

My starting-point is that it is not clear what is meant by speaking of a dog as thinking or believing that something is so, just as it is not clear what it means to say that an octopus may feel queasy or a hyena suffer from nightmares. For someone for whom these are propositions with a clear sense, it may be possible to say, for example, that the dog may be having the specific thought that *p*; we just cannot tell. And such a person might suggest that we advance it as a hypothesis that an animal can think, proceeding then to see to what extent that hypothesis is confirmed by subsequent happenings. With my starting-point, none of this makes any sense at all.

To take another example, suppose I pretend to throw a stick for a dog to fetch and the dog runs off in the direction the stick could have been expected to travel—just the kind of case where we might be drawn to saying that it thinks I have thrown the stick. These words have a role as a description; do they also have a role as an explanation? The occasions on which this might be so are simply those where some of the information which licenses the words as a redescription has not been made explicit. So, you see the dog racing off and you wonder why. I may enlighten you by saying: Sarah thinks I have thrown the stick. What this points to is the gesture of mine, the movement as of throwing the stick, which you presumably missed and which would complete my justification of the description. Nothing would be explained if you were already aware of this.

But if we cannot explain in such a case then we cannot predict, and if we cannot predict there is nothing that deserves to be called belief. Not at all. A cuckoo lays its egg in the nest of another bird—a bird which, it may be said, then thinks that the fledgling which hatches is one of her own. But all that means is: she treats it as one of her own. Whichever description we favour, we can predict likely behaviour on the bird's part—and, if there is something that only the psychological description licenses, that will show that this description is not having its interpretation dictated by the behaviour, as it should. True, the terms which describe that behaviour will not simply detail 'mere bodily movements', but will impute purposiveness. That, indeed, is why there is some plausibility in appropriating belief to the relevant performances, but this does not make it any the less a matter of behaviour. What is important is that such descriptions as 'runs after', 'searches', 'watches', and 'waits' may be warranted without our first having to switch to the vocabulary of belief.

But there are other difficulties with that vocabulary, the most pressing being that an animal's behaviour is often not sufficiently specific to warrant any precise attribution of belief, to make 'The mouse thinks that the cat will bite it', say, more compelling a characterization than 'The mouse thinks that the cat will harm it' or 'The mouse thinks that the cat will attack it'. This is clearly so. Even when the belief relates to present rather than future, as with 'The dog thinks there are two squirrels in the tree', or 'The dog thinks there is a dead squirrel in the tree', we may look in vain for the differential behaviour needed for the attribution—behaviour peculiar to the circumstance of there being two and only two of a kind, or of something dead's being present. However, this does not mean that every ascription of belief is incurably arbitrary. We can say indifferently that the dog thinks that the squirrel is in the tree or that it thinks that the squirrel is up there, pointing in the requisite direction, either locational phrase being acceptable as an identification of the region to which the dog is giving its excited attention. True, it is frequently claimed that ascriptions of belief will not tolerate variations in the referential terms used without altering the content of the belief, and it might be held that the same strictures apply to these identifications of a place. I have argued elsewhere that this view is wrong-headed (Rundle 1979: §§19–20), but it should in any event be clear enough that what the creature's behaviour is directed at is all that matters, the question, under what description the dog picks out the thing or place, being as irrelevant as it is incongruous. You say: 'Sarah thinks that that ghastly chap you just introduced me to is about to give her a biscuit.' As is typical, the concerns of speaker and audience are here in focus with the choice of designation, not those of the person or creature whose thought is being reported. Sarah can be a child, an adult, a cat, or a dog, as far as the acceptability of the mode of reference is concerned.

At this point it is worth noting two ways in which belief may relate to action. Accounts which invite us to turn to its manifestation in behaviour to gain an understanding of belief have to confront the difficulty that all manner of actions may be associated with the same belief. If pretty well anything goes—including even inaction—it is difficult to discern the basis for an illuminating relation. Here it is clearly belief which gives a reason for action that is being envisaged, the kind of case where we seek to *explain* an action by hypothesizing a belief. So, we are inclined to suppose that Kate thinks the object she is holding is dangerous, as she is handling it so gingerly, but it could be that she thinks it is fragile. However, the behaviourist should be making out his case only with respect to more primitive instances, those in which the action gives a direct manifestation of belief, where the case for speaking in these terms—however figuratively—is to be argued by having regard solely to the behaviour, with no hypothesis as to unspoken thoughts.

This is also the case to consider when confronted with the following familiar dilemma: we cannot ascribe a belief to a creature unless we make an assumption about what it wants; conversely, we cannot ascribe a desire without an assumption about what is believed. The conclusion? Possibly scepticism concerning these states of mind, possibly a retreat to a problematic holism where one ascription waits upon the propriety of the other, which in turn waits upon that of the former. So, if Ving has C as a consequence, we can explain A's Ving by supposing that A knows or believes that this is so, and wants C; but the same behaviour is consistent with the supposition that A does not want C, but does not have this belief. However, any explanatory role for belief and desire has to be secondary, the fundamental cases simply being those where we aim at giving no more than a redescription. Thus, the difficulty would not appear to arise in the important case—important to the identification of action—where the animal's behaviour makes equally manifest both its knowledge of the whereabouts of what it is fleeing or pursuing and its desire to do the one or the other.

Here we might mention a way in which, for human beings, doing something with thought may be understood. According to Ryle's well-known account, the motorist or tennis player who 'thinks what he is doing' is not doing two things at once, not combining such activities as steering the car or hitting the ball with the separable activity of thinking. Rather, he is doing just one thing, but doing it in a certain fashion—intelligently and attentively (Ryle 1968). If the description 'is thinking what he is doing' does not point to anything going on behind the scenes, an accompanying but unobserved activity, then it would seem we need have no scruples about describing comparable animal behaviour in the same way.

However, this account may be queried. The descriptions just offered with 'intelligently' and 'attentively' are surely preferable to any in terms of 'thinking', even with respect to human beings, never mind animals. Consider a tiger as it stalks its prey, creeping stealthily, watching closely its victim's every move, stopping when its own movements might give it away. Such descriptions are frequently in order, but it is questionable to say that the tiger is thinking, that it is giving thought to what it is doing. For that, as indeed for the tennis player, we should want not just a style of performance, but such intellectual exercises as thinking ahead, raising possibilities, and thinking them through. The tiger may be totally taken up with what it sees and hears, attentive to every movement, to every relevant alteration in circumstances. But what this more obviously describes is a creature that is *not* thinking. That is, its mind is not on matters with which only thought can put it in touch—the non-present possibilities, rather than the present scene.

This response, however, does not give the particular idiom 'thinking what one is doing' its due. We say that a person is not thinking in this sense if he does not have his mind on what he is doing, is not sufficiently alert to his activities as to be able to guard against or correct unwise moves. Such thinking may shade into the more intellectual form just alluded to in so far as the person is taking into account likely consequences of his actions, but it may be that consequences do not have to be worked out, that they are already known and appreciated. If, for the tennis player, thinking what he is doing comes to keeping the ball in play but as far out of his opponent's reach as possible, there may be nothing to work out, no competing alternatives to weigh up. It would accordingly seem possible to justify some use of 'think' on the strength of the animal's undoubted attentiveness and alertness, its responsiveness to present circumstances. On the other hand, while the kind of thought here at issue may be inseparable from behaviour, that means only that there could not have been the thought without the behaviour, not that there must be the former whenever there is the latter, and a deep difference remains in the way a person, but not an animal, *knows* what pitfalls he is guarding against. There is, for us, a form of awareness, a thought which might be expressed, where for the animal there is no more than the sensitivity to what happens that its behaviour reveals. Note, incidentally, the difficulty of matching up 'thinking what one is doing' with either a state or an activity exclusively. The notion of a state, or disposition, certainly has a place with respect to being attentive, on one's guard against untoward developments, but thinking as an activity, as might go with reasoning, is, as regards thinking what one is doing, a possibility only. The conception we find hard to shake off is, none the less, one of such thinking as essentially an activity which accompanies our behaviour (cf. Wittgenstein, Z §106).

A further observation about thought is worth making at this point. You may fail in your first attempt to open a door if the door unexpectedly opens outwards rather than inwards, and, while the question of which way the door opened may not even have occurred to you, you may still correctly say that you thought it opened the other way. Similarly when a stumble at the foot of the stairs is explained by saying, 'I thought there was another step', or when we go to lift something, preparing ourselves for a considerable weight, only to find that the object is lighter than we thought it would be. Here we need not consciously prepare ourselves for a demanding lift, but we quite unthinkingly put just so much effort into raising the object and are surprised when, our effort being in excess of what is needed, the article jerks off the floor. The use of 'thought' here may strike us as odd—it is precisely the kind of case where, in one sense, we have given no thought to the matter in question; moreover, while the thought that the door opened the other way might be a matter of something thought by the person more generally, and not something that occurred just before opening the door on that occasion, the more limited time reference seems appropriate with respect to lifting the case.

Even here, however, the phenomenon is not deeply mysterious: we have simply learned to expect certain happenings, a certain behaviour, from things which look a certain way; our reactions have become automatic, with no need repeatedly to rehearse the reasons behind them. It is to be noted that, while this use of 'I thought . . .' is most common when there is an unexpected turn of events, it applies equally when things proceed smoothly; it is just that in this case the question is seldom raised. Sometimes it is true that I think I can safely overtake a car, in that I have given some thought to the question and arrived at this conclusion. On other occasions it requires no deliberation, no estimations or calculations, but the description 'He thought he could overtake safely' is still applicable to me. Here it might be said that the belief is made manifest in the behaviour.

There is another important strand in this use of 'think'. First, when our execution of the action proceeds without a hitch, we may be able to speak in terms of *knowledge*. We know that doors open inwards in a certain building, and pull or push as appropriate; we know that the suitcase is a heavy one, and measure our efforts accordingly. Lack of attention by the subject to what he can say he knows is no embarrassment to our speaking of knowing: I knew that there were several children in the room, that it had windows, that it was daytime, and so forth, matters to which, it might again be said, I gave no thought. Likewise with respect to our actions: we have learned so much, and so much is obvious, that no weighing up, calculating, excluding of alternatives, is necessary. We just go ahead and act. If, however, things are not as we unreflectingly take them to be, then we say, notwithstanding, that we merely thought things were thus and so; 'merely thought' recommends itself through cancelling the commitment to being right, but it is in another respect not entirely satisfactory, since with its use we incur a suggestion of giving thought to the matter which is undesirably strong.

Similarly with animals. We might say of a monkey which takes refuge from a snake by going up a tree that it knows that it is safe there, or knows that the snake cannot get it. We might say this, because the monkey is no longer agitated, behaving as if in imminent danger, but observes the snake in a detached, impassive, fashion. However, while we may be prepared to use 'know' here, we may be less happy to say that the monkey *thinks* that it is safe. That threatens to demand more of the monkey's mental capacities than we are willing to concede. Likewise with 'believe', especially when this approximates to 'gather', or to some other term which suggests an acceptance of something that has been advanced. On the other hand, we need a description for the case where there would be knowledge that *p* but for the fact that *p* is false—as with an example above: we pretend to throw a stick and the dog races off to fetch it. Such terms as 'think' or 'believe' are suited to this circumstance, but have the disadvantage of suggesting a mastery of concepts, an inner mental response, which it would be fanciful to attribute to the animal. At all events, if it is the creature's behaviour that warrants talk of knowledge, the same behaviour is the basis for an ascription of belief, not any questionable hypothesis concerning the creature's mental life.

Does the example of unreflecting action provide a good model for animal thought? You walk through a doorway without pausing to gauge its height, yet it is true to say that you thought you could pass through without banging your head. Given that there would appear to be nothing in this performance which could not equally be matched by the cat's assured behaviour in making for a hole in the fence and passing through it, the extension of thought to the cat on the same basis might strike us as totally unmysterious and undemanding. Or is this to ask for too little?

With human beings, this use of 'thought' is in place when something to which we once gave our attention has become automatic. Our behaviour follows a certain course without our having to address the various possibilities; we act in the unthinking assurance that such and such is so. That, after all, is something we have learned. But, it may be insisted, the earlier stage, one where we were fully conscious of the matter in question, is necessary to the description 'I thought . . .'. Similarly, automatic behaviour will be describable as intentional only if at some point there has been a conscious aim. Suppose that, engrossed in a book, you turn the pages without even noticing you are doing so. That these acts are none the less to be considered intentional is indicated by your reaction on finding, say, that you have turned two pages instead of one, when you might well say that you had meant to turn to the next page. This is again an instance where the familiarity of a pattern of behaviour dispenses us from having to think, but there will have been other occasions when such actions were executed with greater deliberation and awareness. If, with the animal, there are no earlier occasions of this character, no occasions when it gave explicit thought to what it was doing, then it would seem that a comparably botched performance on its part should not lead to our offering the description 'It thought . . .', even in the reading which, as far as present circumstances are concerned, is so undemanding.

Or is that so clear? First, it appears wrong to insist that the appropriateness of 'thought' *must* be dependent in the way suggested on the agent's earlier history. It is more plausible to look to a comparison with the use in circumstances in which the reasoning is more explicit: on some occasions the size of the suitcase is consciously taken as a ground for judging it light; in the present case the size, or some comparable index, is taken in by the person, but not explicitly considered in this capacity. But in any event, animals too may engage in unhesitating behaviour after an initial stage of learning. Suppose the cat misjudges the width of the opening as a result of having had its whiskers trimmed. Why should it not then be right to say that it thought the hole was wider than it was?

In our own case, the straightforward execution of the action is no bar to talk of thought, but there is at least the possibility of an expectation or assumption's being disappointed, and this seems to presuppose thought in a more significant sense—a realization that what we thought has proven mistaken, not something that is in its turn just another item of behaviour. The idea of surprise is made central in Davidson's account of belief. Not without reason. Compare the following observation from D. J. O'Connor: 'The vast majority of our beliefs neither merit nor require formulation in language. Indeed, one of the commonest ways in which we are brought to recognise that we have held a particular belief is our surprise when experience fails to bear it out. The majority of our beliefs are implicit unformulated expectations' (1968: 4). The involuntary character of our expectations mirrors an important element in belief. However, it is less than obvious that, as Davidson contends (1985: 479–80), a creature can be surprised in the relevant way only if it possesses the concepts of belief and objective truth. Clearly, the most that an animal can muster will be patterns of behaviour which merit such descriptions as 'bewildered', 'confused', and 'disoriented', and these will hardly allow us to say that it can reflect on its beliefs, as Davidson requires. But is it in any event necessary that the animal should have this ability, have itself the concept of belief, for talk of belief in its regard to be in order?

As well as the form 'I believe that p', we have with the bare p a suitable form for the expression of a belief. When the former qualifies as reportive, it presents us with a more reflective use, a use which would not appear to be demanding of a place in the speaker's repertoire in order that something should count as the simple expression of a belief on his part. Possession of the concept of belief does not appear to be required even for language-users, so can hardly be insisted upon for animals.

However, to probe a little further, we may note that, if a surprised reaction is forthcoming, this will not of itself show that the creature was *aware* that it had had a belief which had now been disconfirmed. If an ascription of belief can be sustained, then there must also be a place for learning of something which contradicts that belief, but on the present scheme that just means that a switch to behaviour appropriate to what has been newly learned can be expected; it does not require that there should be two beliefs whose contradictory relationship is appreciated by the animal. Any surprise evinced could simply accompany the change from behaviour appropriate to the old belief to behaviour appropriate to its successor. On the other hand, the minimalist character of this account brings home just how large a component of typically human belief is missing; in refusing any association with self-consciousness, we surely make plain that we are dealing with belief in one of its more peripheral realizations.

To sum up our position, there are uses of 'think' and 'believe' which have no place in sober accounts of what goes on in the animal kingdom. Equally, however, there are less demanding uses which may be enlisted, even if only with some broadening, some sympathetic extension, of the usual senses. Certainly, we do no violence to language in speaking of *knowledge*, and, while it is not the most suitable term, 'think' has, as noted, an intelligible role in those cases where we are obliged to retreat from 'know'. After all, the move from

knowledge to thought or belief can hardly be a move to a state which
is more problematic *psychologically*, as it were, given that it is made
solely on the strength of the failure of a purely external condition.
Again, if the unwanted connotations of 'think' are found too dis-
tracting, there are the less misleading alternatives given with perceptual verbs, as in 'Sarah saw that her bowl was empty'. It is perhaps
not unproblematic just what pattern of behaviour would verify such
a statement, but verification can surely proceed without even the suggestion that anything as dubious as a canine thought has to be taken
into consideration. It is a matter of the animal learning by using its
eyes, so a conception which stays close to the less problematic case
of knowledge.

Whatever disagreement there is on these matters, it should not be
allowed to affect one of our main contentions—namely, that nothing
of substance is here at stake. There are circumstances when I should
be happy to say that the dog believes there to be a squirrel in the tree,
but it would be quite out of place for me to put this forward as a
matter on which I was quite certain, certain beyond reasonable
doubt; as if there were something I knew that some did not. It is simply: I am prepared to go along with that way of speaking.

3.4 ANIMAL SENSATION

With animal desire, knowledge, and belief, what is important is that
the states interpolated are states which, while they may be thought
of as intermediaries between stimuli and behaviour, are secured by a
redescription, being logically guaranteed by no more than what
observation can yield. Sensation, it would seem, is more problematic.
Could talk of an animal as in pain ever amount to no more than a
redescription of the observable?

With pain, the character of the sensation as an object of experience
appears to defeat the pattern invoked with these other states and to
defy any purely behavioural analysis. How could such an analysis
possibly succeed when it takes no account of the notion of something
which happens to the sufferer, something which often follows on
injury and which the creature's behaviour is directed at lessening or
avoiding? Moreover, we may wish to make room for the possibility
of pain which is not manifested in behaviour, even if only in circumstances where the relevant behaviour has been inhibited.

Given that what is identified in following up the causal chain that begins with a putative cause of pain will lie in the creature's physiology, it would seem that something of this character must be added. And in the light of our discussion of physicalism, this might appear a step we can take with some confidence. However, tempting though it is to bring in reference to the sufferer's physiology on the basis of such considerations, these are none the less secondary. After all, it is not as if discoverable happenings in the body are anything we might point to and declare: that is the pain, but, if we are to define the location of pain for an animal, it would seem appropriate—as it might be with us—to do so in terms of the area towards which the creature's relevant behaviour is directed, that part of its body which it favours or protects. Even when behaviour is inhibited, we are to think in terms of how the creature could be expected to behave in altered circumstances. We do not begin with a physicalistic account of animal pain, but any physiological state is found to supervene on the behavioural.

But, so long as we confine ourselves to detailing what is discovered by observation and investigation, is it really clear that there is a psychological description which deserves to mention 'pain' in reporting what turns up? Even if we are allowed to bring in physiological considerations, such a description may be thought unfounded. Certainly, it is easy to find striking differences in what goes with our use of sensation words, as ordinarily understood, and what can be said in speaking of animals.

Human beings experience a host of sensations, pains included, which do not show themselves in behaviour. Indeed, pains are somewhat exceptional in being particularly disagreeable, and so being more readily linked to behavioural criteria than the many mild feelings of warmth, pressure, and so forth, which we constantly experience. What is important is that we can attend to, reflect upon, take note of, compare, and so on, these sensations—a whole series of thought-involving acts which we can make no sense of with animals. Subtract what you cannot make sense of in these terms and, it would seem, you are left with no more than *behaviour* as the concept to invoke.

This is not to say that we can find no place for animal consciousness. It is, in general, quite unproblematic to ascribe consciousness or awareness to animals: the dog makes abundantly plain its awareness of the cat, as the cat of the mouse. This is where it stops, however;

the responses which give proof of perception give proof of awareness, and we can take other behavioural responses as giving proof of dislike and other affections, but there is nothing in the animal's capacities which provides any foundation for the idea of an undisclosed response, as occurs when unmanifested pain registers with us. Yet this—some form of response on the side of the subject—appears to be necessary if awareness is to mean anything in such a case. When we experience pain there is something to which we can give our attention and which we find unpleasant. What would either of these conditions mean for the animal when not somehow realized in observable activities? Recall the example of the cat which opens its eyes, takes in the scene around it, and closes its eyes again. It has learned of the things around it, and there is much that it could in consequence then do, even though it does not in fact stir. This account gives substance to the difference between seeing and not seeing, despite the total inactivity, but not in such a questionable way as if we had said there was something which the creature had learned but which it then kept to itself. There is an unrealized disposition or capacity for action, but not an inner registering of its surroundings.

To make sense of an inner life in which awareness of sensation or sensory qualities figures, it would seem we have to make sense of an inner life in which there are thoughts. But what thoughts? They cannot be such as to be impossible for a being which lacks the classificatory language; we can be aware of a sensation without knowing its name or being able to describe it. That is right, but *some* thought centred on the sensation is necessary none the less. Consider taste. You may chew something without being aware of its taste, without giving the slightest thought to it, but, when the taste comes to your attention, it has to impinge upon you in some way: so, it may strike you as sweet, as pleasant, as unusual, as a little like the flavour of strawberries. Again, consider the notion of seeing the colour of something. Here, too, some thought has to be prompted. Seeing the colour of the sky may involve seeing that it is reddish or noticing its intensity, seeing what colour it is or being struck by something about it; or, it may be that a question is prompted—you wonder what the colour is. Various thoughts are possible, but there has to be something of this character that makes for the difference between seeing the colour and being oblivious to it. And, if it does not take a behavioural form, as with some discriminatory act, in what, for an animal, could the difference between being conscious of a sensory quality and not being thus conscious consist?

We do not reach a point where we have even an analogy with human sentience until, as with pain, we have a non-accidental link with a behavioural manifestation, and even then it may be wondered whether there really is a psychological description of animals that makes justifiable use of 'pain'. Still, the animal's reaction to the hot object with which it comes into contact makes it plausible to say both that it felt the object and that it disliked what it felt, and this may be taken to warrant *some* use of 'pain' in its regard. But is it pain as a conscious experience? Lacking thought, the animal is quite unable to reflect upon its pain, quite unable to be aware that it is in pain.

The phrase 'conscious experience' is not the happiest—what would count as an unconscious experience?—but it is none the less worth considering whether it has any application to animals. To try to characterize the animal's position *vis-à-vis* our own, it is natural to turn to cases where we are engaged in some activity of which we should ordinarily be fully aware, but which, on the occasion in question, is performed automatically, without any thought as to its occurrence. Examples commonly cited in illustration of this possibility include the familiar circumstance of driving a vehicle while giving no thought to what is offered to one's gaze along the route, but where it is apparent from the way obstacles are avoided that these have registered at a lower level of consciousness. Or again, the example of 'blindsight' may be invoked: a person suffering from lesions in the striate cortex may deny any awareness of objects in an area of his visual field, yet his behaviour may show him to be aware to some degree of such visually given properties as those of location, motion, and orientation.

These comparisons are not entirely satisfactory, since they make the animal out to be like someone who is not fully attending to something, or who is not capable of doing so, when in fact the animal may be completely engrossed in the scene before it, totally attentive to, say, the movements of the creature it is watching. So in what sense might it be said that seeing is not, for the animal, a conscious experience? Or if, in the light of the creature's undoubted consciousness, this is not the right way of posing the question, how at least might the sighted animal differ from us in point of consciousness or awareness?

One answer is to observe that, however alert the animal may be, however sensitive to what is unfolding before it, its consciousness has an exclusively external orientation. Its awareness of the visual world may be in no way wanting, but its awareness of itself as seeing is nil.

Its awareness can be said to be lacking on two counts: its awareness of *itself* as seeing, and its awareness of itself as *seeing*. For each it would seem that what is lacking is the necessary *concept*. To take first the seeing, it might appear that if one can be aware of what is seen it needs only a shift of attention to be aware of one's seeing, but the shift here is a grammatical one, to an object of awareness in a totally different sense of this phrase. Seeing is something we can indeed be aware of, but only in the sense of being aware *that* it is occurring, *that* we are seeing; so in a thought-involving way that makes sense only for a being possessed of the relevant concept. What, in the end, it comes down to is simply that we, in contrast to an animal, can *say* that we see.

Consider now self-awareness. It does not require possession of the concept *tree* in order to be aware of a tree; the tree will do perfectly well as object of awareness. But when we are aware of ourselves as seeing, this is not because we have ourselves in view, as with the object seen, but what we do have, and what is necessary, is the concept given with the first-person pronoun. This calls for further clarification. Suppose that, after developing the ability to identify verbally things currently perceived—with 'Teddy', 'juice', 'car', and so forth—the child eventually comes around to using the fuller forms, as 'I see Teddy'. Use of the pronoun 'I' may mark an important advance, but it is not as if something the child had hitherto overlooked—a *subject* of the experience—has now at last come to its attention. Rather, as far as a knowledge of what the world contains is concerned, the conditions warranting its employment are just the conditions for being able to say, on the basis merely of its visual experience, that such and such an object is present—just the conditions satisfied at the earlier stage. But, although knowledge of an extra entity is not called for, there are, of course, other conditions which must be fulfilled if the concept is to be correctly ascribed to the child. In particular, an appropriate range of contrasts remains to be mastered. For instance, as such a question as 'Does Mummy see Teddy?' would reveal, the child might come to appreciate that ascriptions of seeing to others are in order. If it came out with 'I see Teddy', and the like, but with no appreciation of relevant contrasts, then such declarations would amount to no more than the more primitive naming uses. However, when it comes to exercise the concept *I* in, for example, perceptual reports, this does not require it to make an identification which it failed to make when a thing perceived received no more than the bare name. What warrants use of 'I' is the character of the knowledge of existence as knowledge at first hand, not the identification of a subject: awareness of 'other' suffices for introduction of a term for 'self'. Similarly, the mere fact of experiencing pain would be enough to justify 'I am in pain'. This, of course, sounds trivial, but it is important for the way it makes plain that no identification of a subject, so no identification of anything material, nor anything immaterial, is involved. To repeat the main point, the child comes to appreciate that not all seeing has to be *its* seeing, so there is the basis for a distinction on its part between itself and others as subjects of perception, but, while it identifies another when it says 'Mummy sees . . .', when it says that it sees it bases this simply on the known presence of a visual object, there being no question but that it itself is seeing the object, no place for an identification of a subject as well as an object.

However, to return to our original question, it might be countered that a subject's awareness of itself as perceiving is among the more sophisticated possibilities one might consider, that it is not clear that failure to live up to its demands means that a creature's seeing cannot be described as a 'conscious experience'. Let us agree that, for this description to fit, there must be more than the acquisition of knowledge in the form of a practical ability, that some appropriate *thought* must take place—one, for example, as to the identity of what is seen. The more demanding cases go beyond this in their requirement of a more specific thought—to wit, the thought that one is seeing, or seeing such and such. What we then have deserves the title more of 'self-conscious' seeing: the subject's attention is no longer totally taken up with what it is seeing, but it stands back, as it were, and reflects on its experience. But, while lacking the concepts *I* and *see*, might it not be, none the less, that a being should acquire knowledge which took the form of relevantly acquired thoughts? It could not be said to be conscious of seeing, but, given the way its mind entered into perception, perhaps it would be right to count this as a conscious experience. Perhaps, but this is not a matter which our present purposes require us to decide, since, even with this more minimal requirement, we clearly stay at some remove from anything of which an animal is capable.

Animal sensation, rather than animal perception, has been our main concern, and this discussion of awareness has done nothing to deflect the account of the former—as minimalist as the companion account of animal belief—that was looming. While, that is, it may be considered problematic to look to behavioural and other observable conditions to justify saying that a creature felt something when there is no capacity for thought, it would seem that either we do just that, or we abandon talk of feeling for such cases. We have seen reason for adopting the first alternative, for speaking of animals as capable of feeling pain, but, if these considerations are on target, it is left to the physical and the behavioural to provide the categories to which we can have recourse in explaining the concept in this use.

4

Reasoning and Language

We have looked at animal thought where this is a matter of something akin to belief, but what of thought as reasoning? This would appear to be a less tractable possibility. Whereas 'think' as 'believe' can profit from its relation to 'know', a verb which connects readily enough with behaviour, there is no such relation for 'think' as 'reason' to exploit. None the less, in the face of apparent examples of creatively intelligent behaviour, there is a strong temptation to attribute thought to animals as an indispensable part of an explanation of what is observed. That is, it is not considered merely that the description 'thoughtful behaviour' may be licensed by having regard to no more than the behaviour and the course which it takes, but the supposition is that the creature *must* think or reason in order to do what it does; there is genuine explanatory power in the ascription of thought, and indeed no hope of any adequate understanding without it. We have, by implication, dealt with this supposition when considering human thought and behaviour, but it will do no harm to give the specifically animal case an airing. Within the discussion, the topic of animal language comes to assume importance, and we shall also make a brief foray into this area.

4.1 ANIMAL REASONING

Good examples of apparent thought are provided by Köhler's apes, which were observed to make use of sticks to drag in food from outside their cages, and even to slot one stick into another to provide themselves with a longer stick when the food was otherwise out of reach. Köhler (1927: ch. IV) was impressed by feats of this latter kind, in that it seemed to him that the ape had thought out a solution, that a sudden insight had dawned, a realization that the problem could be solved by extending a stick in this fashion. That, after all, would describe the parallel human accomplishment, supposing it not a matter of mere habit. However, a closer look at what is going on suggests that this somewhat dramatic language is introduced to cope with something well within the capacities of a languageless creature.

We shall suppose that the ape has learned that it can sometimes bring wanted objects within reach by making use of a stick—the sort of achievement which does not in general impel us to speak of thinking or reasoning. One possibility is simply that, while playing around with two sticks, the ape finds itself with a longer stick on its hands, one which it then puts to work in a straightforward application of past learning. What grounds could we have for dissatisfaction with this account? Most obviously, the possibility of an accidental production of a suitable implement may be discounted if we suppose that the creature's past experience affords it knowledge of the properties of sticks of the kind in question which can be exploited in constructing the elongated stick. Certainly, we should naturally make appeal to the creature's likely learning history if chance is to be excluded, and, if there is no need to speak in terms of thought in the first case, the same surely holds here as well. The question now is whether any significantly different possibilities remain.

That we have covered the real possibilities is suggested by a comparison with the human case. When a man joins together two sticks with a view to making the longer one needed, his action will be dependent on earlier experience, whether it be an action that is a familiar part of his repertoire, or whether he has to reason his way to the conclusion, perhaps hitting upon that conclusion with a sudden flash of insight. Even in this latter case, that is, there is no getting away from past experience: the man does not know a priori that sticks can be lengthened in this way, but his realization that he can extend the stick rests on knowledge he has of the behaviour of rigid bodies, of what is possible when one such has an opening of a certain size and another is of a slightly lesser width.

We are unperplexed by the ape's performance if it either came about by sheer chance, or else was the result of previous learning, and my suggestion is that there is nothing further we need consider. Our human subject does not take us outside these alternatives, but the difference between him and the ape is a matter of his greater ability to apply the lessons of past experience. So, we can imagine an animal that was able to repeat this solution only when conditions were very close to those in which it had learned this way of proceeding; only when, say, identical sticks were to hand. A more intelligent creature, by contrast, will derive more extensive knowledge from the same happenings, learning that a range of sticks can be used for this purpose. That they should be the original sticks themselves will not be treated as necessary, nor that they should be of a certain colour or smoothness, and so on. The greater powers which we have in this respect may make it appear that we are not even drawing upon experience when we come up with an answer. However, remote though present circumstances may appear from anything we have encountered, any solution that is at all likely to succeed will rest on past experience.

The point is important. Mindless application of lessons learned is one thing, it may be said; when the conclusions are novel, an altogether different framework is required. Thus, it has been suggested that we can pin down two essential elements in thought, internal representation, and transformation—working out what will happen in changed circumstances—and that we can then determine by experiment whether an animal is thinking, the situations which favour this possibility being those in which there is sufficient novelty to defeat any procedure which relies solely on pre-set rules (Dawkins 1993: 126). However, it is difficult to see how experiments could differentiate between the case where the brain as 'computer' is responsible for performing the requisite tasks, and where, in addition, thinking takes place. There could be experimentation aimed at showing that something was going on in a creature's head literally, but could any investigations show that something was (also) going on in its head figuratively? Talk of experimentation is premature, in that what is needed at this point is to give *sense* to the hypothesis of thought on the part of a languageless creature. Looking to its manifestation in behaviour rather than to its verbal expression is the obvious way of meeting the difficulty, but what is then required is to see whether the behavioural patterns warrant the relevant redescription. It is not a question of drawing an inference to unobserved mental activity.

To take another example, it may be that, at least over a certain range, a cat is as good a judge of distances as are we—as when it is required to judge whether a gap between a wall and a tree is sufficiently narrow for it to be able to jump across. This is a species of thought which might be considered the most demanding of recognition as non-behaviourally realized. When the cat proceeds to jump, we may wish to say, just on the strength of this behaviour, that it thinks it can bridge the gap, but there is also, surely, something to be said about the cat's thoughts in the moments before it took this step. Does the cat not survey the gap and arrive at a conclusion about the feasibility of the leap contemplated?

If you wish to say that the cat has calculated that the leap is within its powers, then the fact that it jumps after close inspection of the gap, and has some experience of success and failure, is prominent among the sorts of consideration which lend respectability, though not inevitability, to that way of speaking. But, it may be protested, if it is just a question of sanctioning a certain description of what is observed, then the contribution made to an explanation of the animal's behaviour is surely minimal. That is right. But it is only in so far as a thought ascription approximates to a redescription that it stands any chance of being acceptable. To extract an explanation from the ascription would be to go beyond anything which the pattern of behaviour licensed.

Is there perhaps more of a problem with purposive animal behaviour which is not triggered by environmental cues, as when a bird returns to its nest or a squirrel sets off to dig up nuts it once buried? It is not uncommon for those who seek a scientific understanding of such behaviour to suppose that the creature must, in some mentalistic way, represent to itself a scene beyond its present environment; or again, that it can recognize a familiar route only because it has representations with which to compare what it sees. How, otherwise, could we make sense of its behaviour?

Some of the more interesting navigational feats performed by animals offer little scope for any appeal to a mental representation of a destination, the animal having never been near the place to which, for instance, it is migrating. Since we are going to have to cope with such feats, and since the invocation of imagery is only dubiously intelligible, a scientific account would be better served by trying to seek out environmental cues which somehow guide the animal—cues which, like magnetic lines of force, presuppose no familiarity with the regions passed through. Even when the creature is revisiting a familiar scene, it could be that it successively recognizes landmarks en route, that it does not in any way picture its final destination.

Imagine a swallow, skimming low over a pool in search of flying insects, then tracing an arc beyond the pool before coming back into line with the water for a further sortie. It has, surely, to keep the pool and its whereabouts in mind if it is to come back on course; it cannot be a matter of: out of sight, out of mind. But how would it help the swallow if it had an image of the pool when this is lost to view? If its flight takes it away from the pool to the right, it has in some sense to know that the pool is behind it to the left, but simply picturing the pool to itself will not tell it that.

Consider what happens with us. It is not enough simply to bring to mind a past scene for such recall to have a place in an explanation of our subsequent action, but it is only as it occurs in connection with relevant thoughts that it can perform this role. Without these surroundings it may be just a matter of aimless musing, or other unrelated thoughts and reflections. But then that is to take us back to the familiar pattern of explanation in terms of the course that our thoughts take, and this, once more, appears to have no application to animals. Moreover, while success in a performance analogous to the swallow's would require us to retain the relevant locational information, we need in no way annex an image to this information. Recalling what one's destination looks like is an incidental addition to the task of making one's way to it. In steering its course by observed features of the setting, the bird is like us, but it differs in its inability to put the relevant information into words.

I wish to say that, as it occurs in imagining—not as in hallucinating—having images is a possibility only for a creature which can also think. That, it might be surmised, stems from an error parallel to the one already exposed with respect to thought and perception. Reflection on an instance of perceiving is indeed calculated to have us agreeing that thought is inseparably bound up with perception, but the comment for which this calls is that it could hardly be otherwise: we could have no direct knowledge of perception which was not thus accompanied, the thought being necessary not for perception, but for its registering with the subject. But, while we have behaviour (and memory) to fall back on in giving substance to the idea of perception in the absence of thought, there is not the same scope for a behavioural realization of having an image. Certainly, the crucial intentional acts of imagining or picturing into which images might be incorporated seem not to admit of any purely behavioural variants.

What of the apparent reasoning manifested in oddity tests, tests where the animal reveals an ability to recognize sameness and difference at a highly abstract level? The chimpanzee is presented with three objects, two of which are the same, one different, and it is rewarded if it chooses the odd one out (cf. Davis *et al.* 1967). There is a degree of abstraction here not met with when a specific quality, as redness or sweetness, is to be discriminated. That is true. The creature has learned that there is something in common between a situation where it is presented with two triangles and a square, and a situation in which it sees two yellow blocks and a green one.

Puzzlement about the animal's performance might be expressed in the following way: how on earth can the creature manage to work out where the reward is if it cannot think? The answer may well be: it cannot; 'work out' has no application in that circumstance. Compare the following. Faced with someone who has succeeded in solving a complicated mathematical problem, we might well say: he would have been quite unable to work that out if he hadn't been able to think. However, we must allow that he could have produced the correct answer none the less. This shows that we consider there to be more to solving the problem than simply producing the right answer; indeed, the solving, the working-out, is likely to be regarded as itself an exercise, an instance, of thought. The impossibility has, we may note, nothing to do with causality: we are saying merely that producing the correct answer would not count as actually solving the problem if there had been no thought.

Very well, but if, with the animal, we cannot speak of working out, of thinking—at least in any literal sense—how is it that it finds the reward with such consistency? We do not know, but it would seem reasonable to suppose that an acceptable explanation will build on familiar considerations concerning the recognitional powers of animals, much as with the problem-solving feats using extended sticks. The ape begins, let us suppose, by associating the reward with a single square in the company of two triangles, then with a single green object placed alongside two yellow ones, and eventually with a single object of one kind which it can discriminate joined with two objects of another kind which it can likewise discriminate. Why should this one-against-two pattern not be something to which it can become attuned unless it commands a symbolic representation of the possibilities? It is, after all, a matter of a sophisticated response to something *present*; not, that is, the kind of case where, say, a mere possibility is to be addressed, and where some mode of representation accordingly appears indispensable.

More generally, in so far as thought is necessary, it is not for any causal powers it may have, but for features which it shares with language. In connection with problem-solving, with thought as reasoning, this may be so in two ways. First, the specification of the problem may involve language; that is, the problem may be one in, or of, language, as with a crossword puzzle or a riddle. Secondly, and less obviously, it may require language to engage with the problem. Thus, much problem-solving is in answer to a question, even if only one that the subject has put to himself. How can I get to the other side of the river? Where can I find a longer branch? How would the room look with the sofa facing the other way? No words need pass through our mind as we attempt the imaginative exercise which the last question invites, but it is difficult to see how any imagining which merited the given description, 'imagining how . . .'—note the interrogative construction—could arise for a being incapable of taking in and addressing the question.

Again, consider a puzzle which is solved by fitting variously shaped blocks into matching holes. Although we may be able to say such things as 'I saw at once that this one wouldn't fit there', this may well be an example of wordless thought. On the other hand, to have the solution of the puzzle as our *goal* in any full-blooded sense requires thought which is not simply realized in skilful manipulation, since any such sense surely requires that we have taken in a possibility, and not just have attended to what is before us. Similarly, working out where food is located requires one, if not to have wondered, asked oneself, where the food is to be found, then at least to have engaged in hypothesizing, inferring, and so forth.

Although we have found no room for animal thought or reasoning—at least as covert mental activities—the kind of explanation sketched counts as psychological rather than physiological: the creature comes to *recognize* a situation in which there is one shape of one kind, and two of another, and it *learns* that the food will be found under the odd one out. These characterizations I regard as warranted merely on the strength of the creature's behaviour, and not as requiring supplementation by appeal to reasoning. If carried out in the head, that would mean engaging in thought which presupposes mastery of some representational form, as a language, and moves made with this form, such as hypothesizing and deducing, which we simply do not know how to make sense of in this connection. The sticking point is, to repeat, not so much the psychological, broadly construed, as the linguistic dimension.

The psychological character of the explanation sought is acknowledged in the very question 'How is the creature *able* to V?'. We do not ask how someone is able to blush or faint, but, for an act to be the exercise of an ability, it has to be in place to speak of the subject as *succeeding* in Ving, and that is appropriate only if Ving is something the subject can have as its goal. We accordingly take some liberty with the notion when we extend it to a machine, as when we ask how a computer is able to do this or that. We may, it is true, give the same answer to the question how the problem was solved whether computer or person provided the solution; in each case it is, let us say, a matter of using such and such an algorithm. Differences continue, of course, to be discernible, both in the notion of *using* and in the way in which operations in accordance with the algorithm are effected in either case, but it is of interest, however obvious it may be, that it is not by increasing the range and complexity of operations at this level that we shall transform our computer into anything to which any psychological notions are strictly applicable. So long as the relevant operations are not incorporated within an overall purpose, made subservient to the attainment of an end, what we have is mindless, whereas an animal may at least display behaviour of a kind which makes it reasonable to repudiate this description on its behalf.

Consider now the intriguing possibility of behaviour which bears all the marks of an intention to deceive. To take a much discussed example, vervet monkeys have been observed to make use of alarm calls for leopards, eagles, and snakes—a different one for each. On hearing the alarm given for leopards, they take refuge in the trees—where they are difficult to catch—whereas their response to the eagle alarm is to look up in the air and make for the bushes; finally, on hearing a snake alarm they stand upright and survey the ground around them (Cheney and Seyfarth 1990: 102–3). Suppose, as was evidently observed, that two troops of monkeys are engaged in a fight, and that one on the losing side gives a leopard alarm, even though there is no sign of the relevant predator, an alarm which sends both sides scurrying off to the safety of the trees, thus ending the skirmish and avoiding a defeat for the vervet's group (ibid. 213). This, surely, is prima facie evidence of reasoning and foresight. A plan has been devised and put into action.

It would seem perfectly possible that a monkey should learn that such a call in such circumstances is advantageous and that it should put this learning to use. This would secure a precursor, if not a rudimentary form, of intentionality—it will be true to say that the monkey is acting thus because of the consequences of doing so. The problem is in putting together all that has been learned so as to yield a pattern of reasoning when it cannot be said that something takes place in the creature's head which might be reportable in such terms as these: monkeys scatter on hearing this call, and, if they should do so, the monkeys in my troop will gain a respite in the fight in which they are coming off second best. I shall accordingly give this call. Once more we have no way of giving substance to such reasoning, so no way of admitting it as a real alternative to an explanation in terms of chance and/or learning. Indeed, I do not believe the point can ever be reached when it can be said: this behaviour can be explained *only* by supposing that the creature thinks. Rather, as indicated above, it is only if the creature can think that a certain *kind* of explanation will be possible.

But, if it can be said that a person may think that *p*, even when he has not put that thought into words, might there not also be reasoning without words? However, given that in this instance the creature is required to be running over possibilities and drawing out their consequences, a problem remains of specifying how such activities might be realized in the absence of any capacity for verbalizing them. How, for instance, might we make sense of the suggestion that the creature is arguing in accordance with *modus tollens*, reasoning in a syllogistic fashion, or, indeed, reaching a *conclusion* by any means?

With thinking in some of its forms, it may be difficult to dispense with words or their proxies: silently counting or keeping score, for instance, will involve the recitation of number words to oneself, or perhaps the visualization of some notational device. With other forms, thinking will not be simply a matter of saying something to oneself, but, with thinking as reasoning of any complexity, the description fails because it is only like this to a degree, a matter more of fragmented, disjointed, inner speech. Our familiarity with principles of reasoning and calculation dispenses us from having to articulate them to ourselves with the detail we should offer when seeking to justify our procedures, but, if we were unacquainted with any formulation of a given principle, there would be no grounds for saying that we were guided by it.

The fragmentariness instanced with inner speech is worth a further comment. First, it is clear that this is also a common feature of the spoken word: utterance of someone's name, say, could abbreviate any number of larger phrases, the context making their further elaboration unnecessary. Just as someone might say 'I'll ask Angela', meaning 'I'll ask Angela to the school dance', the prior conversation making the explicit reference dispensable, so someone, having been thinking about the school dance, might silently say the shorter phrase to himself. The completeness of the model by which inner speech is judged fragmentary is more the completeness of the contextless written word. There is also a sense in which other imaginative acts might be considered fragmentary: we can think of singing or dancing without our thought taking in much of what would be involved in such performances. But, just as it would not be appropriate to speak of thinking of running rather than hopping if our thought did not take in certain aspects of the activity, so there has to be something which differentiates one instance of reasoning from another, and here the train of thought which unfolds in inner speech is likely to be crucial.

However, while words undoubtedly enjoy a constitutive role in some forms of thinking, the fundamental dependence of thought on language is not to be found in a contribution of this kind. It is not that some words at least must be recited inwardly—the key words on which the thought turns, as one might suppose—but the importance of words is as already indicated above (§2.5): it rests with actual language to specify the thought, to determine its very identity, whether or not anything passes through our heads. I suddenly say to myself, 'Oh God, the dentist!', or I think wordlessly of the dentist or his surgery, but knowing that does not put you in a position to say that I must have remembered that I had a dental appointment the next day, rather than that it had struck me that I had forgotten to ring for an appointment, or whatever. There is no question of attributing a particular thought to someone if there is not a formulation of that thought that the person can accept as expressing what he thinks. The person may not actually be able to express the thought himself—he may be dumb—but he has to have the capacity to recognize some formulation as apt.

While the animal's lack of language limits the range of thoughts which can meaningfully be ascribed to it, it is not as if the choice lies between allowing such an ascription and accepting what is observed as unintelligible. Lack of thought is no embarrassment to the spider in its highly complex web-spinning activities, and when the behaviour is learned rather than instinctive there is the familiar Skinnerian scheme into which it can be fitted while steering clear of any such ascription. Thus, in terms of this scheme we might seek to explain a blue tit's habit of pecking at the foil on a milk bottle to get at the milk, surmising that it is because of the consequences which this activity has had in the past that the bird is currently engaged in it. The tit need not have been applying a lesson of past experience when first it pecked at the foil, but the success which this possibly chance episode met with has led to its repetition. No need here to make sense of the bird as *thinking* that it can get at the milk by this means; or, in so far as it might be appropriate so to speak, this can be a description which is taken to be warranted by nothing more than the relevant behaviour, taken in the light of its past history of successes. And there is a further variation on this pattern: the creature is doing what it is doing because of what *happened* to follow on some past occasion, where there is no implication that the activity actually led to what followed. Behaviour in accordance with this scheme could correspond to mistaken belief. We could imagine quite complex patterns of activity built up from routines drawn from these two types.

4.2 LANGUAGE AND CONCEPTS

Since language is beginning to assume such importance, it is worth enquiring whether what is known about the linguistic capabilities of any animals provides the basis for a significant extension to what can otherwise be said about their mental life. According to Anthony Kenny (1975: 2), the mind is the capacity to acquire intellectual abilities. If we should be in doubt whether gifted chimpanzees have minds, this will be because there is some doubt as to whether they are using language, and thus manifesting an ability for intellectual activity. Our use of 'mind' and 'mental' has made for a different, though related, contrast, having a mind being associated with the capacity for having undisclosed thoughts—the use of 'mental' found in 'mental arithmetic'. It is the character of our unspoken reasoning, calculating, wondering, and so forth, as episodes that are fully actual while not made known at the time, that is so important to our conception of a mental life. Prima facie, some command of language is possible without any such capacity, enough perhaps to show possession of a mind in Kenny's sense, but it is of interest to consider what uses of language would show a creature to have a mental life in the sense we have favoured.

In seeking to assess the significance of what animal language there is, we might consider two questions: whether a given system of calls or other signs may be reckoned a language, and whether the use made of the elements of this system is describable as *linguistic* in anything like the sense that applies with human communication. I wish to lay emphasis on this latter question. We could call a complex representational system a language, as with the dances of worker honey bees which reflect the distance, direction, and quality of food sources. If it is protested that this is to stretch the use of the term 'language' unjustifiably, then take 'could call it a language' as 'could, for all that would show us about the mental capacities of the relevant creatures, call it a language'. At all events, it is not the co-variation with circumstances that shows a mind; only a more advanced display of intentional behaviour could do that.

The division just drawn matches an important distinction between two uses of 'mean' alluded to above in §2.4. This verb is associated indifferently with persons and words as subject, but it is surely not the case that a word can mean something in the way that a speaker can. Indeed, in many languages there would be no temptation to see the two cases as in the least comparable, different words being assigned to each. German *meinen* and *bedeuten* give one such pair, and it is noteworthy that the latter, which commonly takes linguistic items as subject, may also be used in connection with something like the bees' dance. The more difficult questions feature 'mean' in the other use; in particular, can the bees be said to mean anything by their dances?

The apparent mastery which some apes have attained of the use of lexigrams, or of American sign language for the deaf, provides the most comprehensive evidence of genuine linguistic use on the part of a species other than man. True, there has been some controversy over the interpretation of the apes' performances. According to Herbert Terrace (1987: 125), a frame-by-frame analysis of videotapes of one chimpanzee's signings showed it to be responding mainly to the urgings of its teacher to sign, much of what it produced being in imitation, full or partial, of its teacher's prior gestures. Other studies have shown that imitation need not be operative to any significant degree (cf. Greenfield and Savage-Rumbaugh 1984), but objections remain. Thus, Terrace places considerable weight on the child's use of language in sharing information, as when indicating to another that it has noticed something. The use which chimpanzees make of language, by contrast, is dominated by an acquisitive goal, a desire to attain something by its means. Terrace writes:

there is no evidence that suggests that an infant ape is interested in communicating, to another ape or to its human surrogate parent, the fact that it has noticed an object, *as an end in itself*. To be sure, chimpanzees will communicate with one another about food locations, or about objects of prey. It is, however, important to recognize that such communication is in the service of some concrete end and is not intended simply to inform a companion that something has been noticed. (1987: 129)

This difference between apes and children no doubt tells us something of importance about their respective intellectual capacities, but it is not clear that it casts doubt on the propriety of saying that the ape makes a genuinely linguistic use of signs. Such a use can still be acknowledged if it is merely a matter of the language's embodying a purpose *in addition* to one of simply conveying information. The more important question is whether the creature in fact communicates by means of the signs, and does not simply use them as instruments in its acquisitive designs, with no more communicative intent than is involved in pressing buttons in a sequence required to trigger off the delivery of food. Suppose that a chimpanzee learns that by signing 'out' it can get someone to open a door. There is then intention in its use of the sign to this end, but not necessarily any communicative intention. True, 'communicative' can be taken at more than one level, but in the present connection it might be considered reasonable to demand that the ostensible communicator should appreciate that successful communication requires that the being with whom it is attempting to communicate *understand* the mode of communication used. The animal has acquired a strategy for getting a door opened, but a strategy which does not require it to think of the person who opens the door as a being capable of understanding, rather than as, in effect, a door-opening mechanism which the sign activates. Even if it should learn that the recipient of a request must be within view and attentive to the producer of the sign, that still does not guarantee that communication is involved in a relevant way. Production of the utterance could still, in its essentials, be isomorphic to a clearly non-linguistic pursuit, such as poking or pecking at pictures on buttons.

Before looking more closely at some of the relevant findings, it is worth pointing out that our concern is not essentially with what animals can in fact do—absorbing though that topic is—but with what it would make sense to attribute to an animal possessed of certain practical abilities. In keeping with the argument to date, we shall find that the choice is not between (i) a narrow behaviourism which forgoes any use of psychological vocabulary, seeing everything in terms of environmental events which increase or decrease the probability of a given response, and (ii) a position which argues that the observed behaviour makes it likely—though still a matter of a fallible inference—that these creatures enjoy an inner mental life. There is good reason to suppose that higher animals should come to develop a concern with the beliefs and desires of their fellows, but no call to see them as capable of ascribing episodic, unspoken thoughts to them, let alone as needing to do so. They may have to learn to 'read' behaviour, but as involving anything more than this, the so-called problem of animal 'mind-reading', of the animal as having to develop a 'theory of the mind', is unreal. Or so, I hope, our investigations will suggest.

Before considering the demands of communication, of speaker's meaning rather than sign meaning, let us consider whether a grasp of the latter has any mentalistic implications. It is a real enough question whether a monkey treats an alarm call as having an external reference, as indicative of the presence of a predator, say, and does not merely react in fright to the call. For some, the former possibility is thought to require that the monkey should, on hearing the call, form a representation or idea of the predator in question (Cheney and Seyfarth 1990: 165). Certainly, there is one psychological notion that appears inescapable here—namely, that of expectation. If the call is associated with a particular threat, then we should look for behaviour appropriate to an expectation that the source of the threat is in the vicinity: the creature will adopt an alert, fearful stance, and scrutinize the area where the predator might be expected to be found— on the ground, say, if the call is a snake alarm. But, as it applies here, the notion of expectation can be spelt out in terms of a disposition to the relevant behaviour. The account is not incomplete, the behaviour unintelligible, until we have assured ourselves that the creature has called to mind an image of a snake, any more than it need be for a human subject. Here we may note that the notion of 'natural' meaning—utterance of the call is a sign of the presence of a particular threat—is the only notion of meaning we need invoke.

But the monkey does not just have a cry with the meaning, roughly, of 'snake!', it also surely has a *concept* of snake. This claim is of considerable relevance to our enquiry in general, so let us see where it leads. The ascription of concepts to animals will not get far if possession of a concept requires mastery of language. Moreover, there are innumerable concepts which, on any view, lie quite beyond the attainments of a languageless creature, as a quick inspection of any technical volume, such as a computer manual, immediately makes plain: concepts such as those given with *format*, *debug*, *DOS shell*, and *RAM drive* are light years away from a place in the brightest of monkeys' repertoires. On the other hand, the use of language which shows a person to have such and such a concept will not occur in a vacuum, but there will be underlying abilities, notably those of a broadly recognitional or discriminatory character, which give substance, as it were, to the word usage. By itself a word is nothing. To gain significance its use has to be backed by some such ability. In many cases—the example of *snake* being one in point—it will make sense to ascribe to animals abilities not too remote from our own, the quite specific behaviour which the vervet monkey evinces on being confronted by a snake testifying to a relevant capacity on its part. True, we have to proceed here with caution. If the monkey should prove to behave in much the same fashion towards ground-based predators in general, we should be advised to employ a more general specification of what it was that it recognized. Again, for E. Sue Savage-Rumbaugh's chimpanzees taught to sort foodstuffs and tools and to label them as such, the operative distinction appeared to be that between the edible and the inedible (1986: 257). None the less, we could have adequate grounds for crediting these animals with the relevant recognitional ability.

But is this enough to warrant speaking of the grasp of a *concept*? We do not have, in addition, to assure ourselves that some form of abstract, internal representation has occurred in the simian mind, but it is true that we have focused on one aspect only of concept possession, the fully developed case presenting us with a *cluster* of capacities: not merely the ability to respond differentially to things which fall under the concept, as can be realized with a non-language-user, but also the ability to apply or, indeed, to misapply a concept in a judgement, to extend it to new cases, to abandon it in favour of an alternative concept, to invoke the concept in the absence of things to which it applies, and so forth. Failing a word or other sign whereby possession of the concept might be manifested, it is difficult to make sense of these possibilities. Even our intelligent monkey does not exhibit enough of the relevant cluster for us to say that it has the concept *snake*, I should say, but at the very most it can be held to enjoy a limited grasp of that concept—and this in an extended sense only of 'having the concept'.

Many of the points to be made about concepts are of a piece with our earlier observations concerning belief. The key features of either failing to be features of linguistic items, we are tempted to turn instead to the domain of the mental to find more suitable bearers. In either case, however, it is not that mere words are inadequate where their mental counterparts can rise to our demands; rather, the identities which would assign verbal forms a central role are unacceptably crude. As a comparison, we may rightly deny that facts are true propositions, but that does not rule out the possibility that anything said using 'fact' might not be said in a more roundabout way making use of the phrase 'true proposition'. Likewise, a concept is not a word, but that does not mean that having a concept is not explicable in terms of an ability to use a word.

On this account, association of a specific call or cry with recognition of a snake is not a minor step, but a key stage in the development of other features of the full cluster. And, indeed, if concept possession makes this demand, it is a demand which, it would seem, is not beyond the bounds of what is possible for animals. To take one suggestive example, an African grey parrot is reported as learning not only to name certain objects correctly, such as corks, keys, and pegs, but even to answer the question 'How many?' when presented with a small number—up to six—of such items (see Pepperberg 1987). What can be inferred from such performances? Supposing that a creature is capable of recognizing a given object or condition, it is not a problem to conceive of it signalling as much with an utterance. Recognition will in general be manifested by responses which have proven advantageous in such circumstances, and we have only to imagine another item of behaviour, one of uttering, annexed to these. Like them, the utterance serves an end for the parrot, which is rewarded by receiving the objects—which it liked to chew—when and only when it gives the right answer.

How might the character of the utterance as one of meaningful words be brought into the picture? After all, it could be that the bird had learned that coming up with w in circumstances c brought a reward, but not have any conception of w as meaningful. And, even if such a conception on the creature's part is not necessary to w's having a meaning, it can be difficult to know what that meaning is. Consider the word 'cork'. An actual cork is only one element in the circumstances in which the parrot learns to say 'cork', and we have to be able to justify equating it with our 'cork' rather than with, for example, something more like 'I want a cork'. If, like a child, the parrot uses the term without acquisitive intent, but just to acknowledge presence of the object, we have a basis for detaching the allusion to desire, so to this extent there is point to Terrace's strictures. The structured character of the parrot's responses—'two corks', 'three sticks'—is further evidence of an appreciation of the individual contribution of the component words, but still without ensuring an overall force of 'Here are . . .' rather than 'I want . . .'. Thus, Savage-Rumbaugh notes that chimpanzees which had shown some mastery of symbols none the less tended to link together a range of signs which had been appropriate in similar situations, producing combinations such as 'Give orange me give eat orange me eat orange give me eat orange give me you', where there was no need for the specific references of the individual signs to be understood (1986: 26; cf. 179).

Again, that the chimpanzee knows what the lexigram for 'orange drink' stands for may be thought demonstrated by the evident delight which it shows when the symbol is produced (ibid. 123). However, this may be a matter simply of 'natural' meaning: production of the lexigram is a prelude to production of the substance; having learned of this association, the chimpanzee's expectations are aroused, but it could attach the same significance to other happenings, happenings of a patently non-linguistic character, which were likewise signs that an orange drink would be forthcoming.

So long as natural meaning only is at work, the messages into which the sign can enter will be restricted. The creature will not have an appreciation of the lexigram as a sign *for* rather than merely a sign *of* something. The parrot, it is said, is rewarded when it gives the right answer. But does it have any conception of 'the right answer'? If, having no such concept, it cannot appreciate *why* it was rewarded, *what* it has done *correctly*, then something vital to an understanding of the language in question is surely missing. However, making good this lack is not a step we are obliged to rule out. Situations in which a creature is given *w* as a reward for producing the lexigram for *w* do not force a properly linguistic interpretation, but we meet with a more significant development when, as happens, the chimpanzee learns to give the correct name on being shown food, where the reward is some *other* food. Here it is more plausible to hold that the reward is made for giving the *correct* answer, for saying something *true*; it is not simply knowledge of the efficacy of producing a lexi-gram which has been found associated with a single thing as a means to getting that thing (Savage-Rumbaugh 1986: ch. 6).

However, a large question remains as to the animal's ability to dis-cern any communicative intention behind the use of signs, to have any appreciation of meaning in the second of the two senses indi-cated—*Meinung* rather than *Bedeutung*. The conditions relating to intention, understanding, and belief which communication involves might well be thought to take us beyond anything of which an ani-mal is capable.

4.3 LANGUAGE AND COMMUNICATION

Let us begin by considering this notion of meaning in connection with imperatival uses of language. Imagining a chimpanzee in the role of one issuing, rather than receiving, a request or an order brings us up against one of the problems indicated: how can we know that the ani-mal is doing more than treat the recipient of its request as simply a device which production of a symbol may activate? It is not difficult to attribute to the chimpanzee a desire that its instructor should act. Chimpanzees want people to do all manner of things, as give them food and play with them. Nor is it difficult to see how production of a symbol could be learned to be effective in getting a desire satisfied. It is, it would seem, the character of the instrumentality that is want-ing for a linguistic use to be in question.

Suppose that whenever you shout 'Cower!' or 'Cringe!' at your dog, it cowers or cringes. This could simply be a reaction on the dog's part induced by the sheer vehemence of your utterance. As a mere reflex, what it did would not count as obeying, but, if we are dealing with a *response* to a request, matters are different: we have a type of behaviour which is at least a possible candidate for a mani-festation of understanding. If, in its turn, an animal thought that requests or commands 'worked' according to the former scheme, it would have a mistaken conception of their role; but not only is this misconception one of which the animal is surely incapable; it would not appear that it need have any more positive knowledge as to how its signings of 'out' and the like function—any more than does the child who has mastered the use of the cry 'Teddy!' as a request to its parent to pick up a teddy bear thrown from its cot. If, when the chimpanzee signs 'out' to you, you respond by opening the door, and if you know that the animal wants you to act thus, and is using the sign as a means to this end, then it would not be unreasonable for you to say that you have complied with its request.

There is, I suggest, enough here to warrant *some* talk of a communicative use of a sign, but a closer look at the comparison with the child's cry of 'Teddy!' reveals a divergence of some note. Such a cry can also be reckoned the expression of a desire, a role which appears to be central to, but more general than, that of an injunction, being in evidence possibly both before, and indeed after, the cry is enlisted for the further purpose of requesting. This stands in marked contrast to the action of operating a mechanism to achieve one's end, where there is no such expressive function to be exploited, and it also brings the cry into line with standard imperatives, as we shall now see.

In seeking to elucidate the imperative form we naturally invoke an association with an intention—most notably, an intention to elicit action. However, any comprehensive account has to find a place for uses, as with 'Get well soon' or 'Have a nice day', where the speaker is merely giving voice to a wish or desire, with no intention that—as in a Gricean analysis—the person should form an intention to act (Grice 1968). On the contrary, fulfilment of the wish may be thought quite out of the hands of the person addressed. True, intentionality is to be acknowledged in so far as the speaker will wish to communicate his wish or desire, but the intention is one that attaches to the act of uttering, rather than one that defines the imperatival form. It is invoked in answering the question: why did you say that? If the person is asked whether he meant what he said, he is not being asked whether he intended anyone to know of his desire so much as whether he really did want the person addressed to get well soon, or to have a nice day (cf. Rundle 1990: §5.3).

With some uses of the imperative—as in instructions and recipes— this account of the relation to desire has to be refined, but, this complication aside, it would appear possible to define the form in terms of a use to express desire, and then proceed to explain the various intentional uses in terms of this role. Clearly, this association is found when action is considered to be a real possibility, and in this case the way the imperative 'works' is evident: by making known our desire to someone, we stand some chance of getting that person to act to fulfil that desire, provided that it lies within his power to do so. Whether our authority is what gives reason for compliance, or whether we are relying on the person's goodwill, will further determine whether the injunction counts as a command or a request, an order or a plea.

An expression of desire thus provides an instrument to the end of having one's desire satisfied, but a very different instrument from a suitably connected button, or other such device, since its use in this role involves the intention of making known one's desire. The chimpanzee may intend to elicit action from its instructor by keying an appropriate lexigram, but it is not clear that we are warranted in interposing the further condition—namely, that it intends to achieve this by getting the instructor to know what it wants, and thence to act to satisfy that desire. The animal gets its instructor to act by making an appropriate sign, and that, it would appear, is all.

But suppose we have an animal cry which qualifies as an expression of desire. Finding itself unable to get down from a high tree, the cat starts to mew plaintively. This comes close to a request for help if the mewing is sensitive to the presence of potential helpers, increasing in intensity when there is someone around who might help. With such variation we do indeed have relevantly purposive behaviour, not simply a stressed reaction, but there is still no call to say anything more than that the cat is adopting a strategy to a certain end. That is, if the mewing is not simply a reflex, then it is something which the creature has found to work, but that lesson does not require that it conceive of it as working by communicating a desire.

The second possibility to consider is that of the animal in the role of recipient, the question of understanding now taking over from that of instrumentality as the central issue. If the animal is to be a participant in a linguistic transaction, it must understand the order or request addressed to it, and that looks to be less than straightforward.

But how is understanding manifested, if not by acting in a way that compliance requires? Could it not be said, for instance, that a dog understands 'Fetch!' if it knows what to do on being given the command? True, it is the *command* 'Fetch!', not the verb 'fetch', that is at issue. Having our concept of fetching is more a matter of understanding the form that is common to 'Could you fetch . . .', 'I'm going to fetch . . .', etc. None the less, there would appear to be a measure of understanding on the part of the dog.

Or is that so? Is a dog, chimpanzee, or other animal truly capable of understanding what is wanted of it? We must not be misled by the simplicity of the infinitival construction in 'knows what to do on being given the command'. The condition involved is of some complexity. A Gricean account of meaning something by what one says imposes somewhat daunting conditions for human beings to meet, let alone for animals, but even with our simpler scheme the demands made of an animal are still considerable. Thus, when a person, X, makes a request of another person, Y, it would appear that, in order to introduce the communicative dimension, we should require that X want Y to learn from his utterance that he desires Z, say, and, recognizing that this is X's desire, to act to fulfil it. Suppose, now, that Y is a chimpanzee. So, on being shown a lexigram for a tool, the chimpanzee goes off and fetches the designated article and presents it to the instructor. Certainly, it has responded to the instructor's use of the lexigram as to a request, but is there genuine communication here? Has the instructor made known his desire to the chimpanzee? Or has the animal simply learned a trick, a trick which it can perform without having any conception of the producer of the symbol as having some purpose in doing so, some desire to make known?

There are two desires in play here, the desire which the request formulates, as with a desire to be brought something, and the desire or intention that the recipient should act to fulfil the former desire. The problem for the animal is not that the desires which it is to recognize are unwitnessable inner states, since it is required only to discern the relevant pattern in the instructor's behaviour. But it is often enough of a challenge for us, let alone for an animal, to identify the end state which deserves to be described as what is aimed at when there is no question of relying on the agent's verbally given identification. Still, perhaps the animal could learn that certain forms of behaviour tend to be varied in such a way that particular outcomes are favoured, that what we should call satisfied behaviour tends to follow on certain developments. Certainly, it is possible to speak of an animal as recognizing a desire in so far as it can recognize distressed or demanding cries and the like—as with the importuning behaviour of its hungry young—and act accordingly. Such instinctive responses do not involve understanding or reasoning, but they allow some notion of recognition to get a grip. If they can also be invoked when learning plays a part, as in the present contexts, then perhaps the instructor's behaviour can show the chimpanzee that he wants it to retrieve something indicated, in which case it may be possible for the chimpanzee to learn that in such circumstances the instructor also says 'Fetch!'. This might allow the utterance itself to figure as a sign of the desire, and thus to be used as a means for its communication. It could then be said that the creature knows what is wanted of it by one who utters the command, and hence that it knows what counts as obeying 'Fetch!', the central semantic relation that has to be given its due somewhere in our account.

However, while it is possible that an animal should become sensitive to our pleasure or displeasure, the way we have characterized recognition it is not required that the creature which recognizes a certain condition should be capable of recognizing it *as such*, that it should have any appreciation of the condition beyond what it signals of concern to the animal. A display of pleasure in certain circumstance may become for the dog a sign that it will receive a reward, but that may be all the significance it has for the animal; what, in our terms, the display means may be quite beyond anything it is possible for the dog to grasp. As with issuing imperatives, so too with receiving them it would appear that patterns of behaviour of the kind described do not suffice to endow production of the relevant signs, or responses to them, with the psychological implications, the content, which they have for us.

What of uses of language to impart information? Can an animal take in what is said to it by way of statement or assertion? Once more, it is the psychological element that is problematic, the intention behind the message rather than the message itself. Thus, the animal's behaviour may make it plain that it has learned what it was intended to learn from what was said—for example, the whereabouts of food—but an actual appreciation that this is what the producer of the signs wanted it to know is not required for such understanding, and it is difficult to see how such an appreciation could likewise be reflected in its behaviour. This, it may be suggested, just goes to show that the problematic dimension, the appreciation of intention, is to some extent a luxury as far as the basic functioning of language is concerned. We can agree that the ability to send and receive messages is fundamental. However, to the extent that this occurs shorn of any appreciation of intention, to that extent an ascription of language ability will, of course, be without mentalistic implications.

How does the chimpanzee fare in the other role, that of communicator? When seeking to inform we usually seek to inculcate a belief, but this is not essential, being further to the aim of making something known to our audience. I inform you of my plans; whether or not you accept what I say is your affair; you may or may not, but you have at least been told how things stand. However, if the relevant species of communication takes place in the animal world, we should not expect it to be typically of this form, but we can suppose that the animal will be imparting information for the sake of the action which that will make possible, and this means action which manifests the belief induced. Can we make sense of this, and of the necessary intention to impart information?

Since getting another to know or believe will, for an animal, be getting that other to act, the issues would appear to be much the same as arise with requests. However, there is the possibility of some advance beyond this point with apparent 'naming' uses of signs. Savage-Rumbaugh reports that, initially, lexigrams for 'chase' or 'tickle' feature only in requests for these activities, but eventually the chimpanzee comes around to using them in apparent detachment from any request, interrupting activities of chasing or tickling to go to the keyboard seemingly to 'comment' in these terms before returning to the game. Or again, the chimpanzee may look at objects in a tray, walk back into the room, use the keyboard to 'announce' which object it is going to get, then give the teacher the named object (Savage-Rumbaugh 1986: 329, 334). There is the problem mentioned above of ensuring that the word is associated with just the object, and not a larger situation, but it would appear possible in principle to conclude that the animal does have an understanding of the word—that is, that it knows what, more narrowly, the word stands for.

Once more the difficulty arises at the level of intentionality. It is said that the chimpanzee could 'comment' or 'announce', but are these uses associated with the ancillary marks of a communicative intention? Such an intention might be one of getting an audience to know that something is so, or of making known that it itself knows, but so long as we have only behaviour to go on, there appear to be no grounds for attributing any such concern to the animal. Again, there are uses of lexigrams where it is suggested that the chimpanzee is making a statement about what it was going to do, had felt, or had seen (Savage-Rumbaugh, ibid. 328), but it would seem that, in so far as such a description applies, it does so without essential reference to an audience, and hence without any implications as to a communicative intention. Once more, this seems to arise only when getting someone to know is a matter of getting someone to act.

Still, there is at least this possibility, and it is one of some importance. Let us go back to examples of apparent deception. In the presence of its fellows, a chimpanzee acts as if ignorant of the whereabouts of a cache of fruit, but when it finds itself alone it proceeds to dig up the fruit and eat it (Cheney and Seyfarth 1990: 191). We might describe this in two ways. First, we say that the chimpanzee does not want its fellows to know of the whereabouts of the food. Secondly, we say that it does not want its fellows to take possession of the food. It might be held that the first constitutes a more demanding psychological description, perhaps the description which goes with deception proper, but it is surely clear that we are in fact dealing with just two different formulations of the same possibility, the relevant knowledge being explicable, at least in part, in terms of the ability to engage in the behaviour in question. Moreover, this is a case where, once more, the form of explanation which the behaviour calls for is straightforward enough: the chimpanzee has learned the benefits of not drawing attention to hidden food; and, once more, the crucial psychological capacity which this demands is one of being *able to tell*—in this instance, being able to tell when there is hidden food. More generally, when it is suggested that there would be an advantage to an animal in being able to recognize (supposed) mental states on the part of other creatures, the advantage in question is only as comes from anticipating the behaviour which would constitute a manifestation of that state.

Likewise with respect to uses of language. We are not asking of the chimpanzee, whether as sending or as receiving a message, that it should make an inference from outer to inner. It is not impossible to speak of it as making inferences—it develops certain expectations in certain circumstances—but these have as their 'conclusions' future behaviour, as the creature might come to treat the distressed state which goes with wanting as a sign of imminent behaviour aimed at making good what is lacked. But, then, it is not altogether appropriate to compare animals with human beings in this connection, and to see them as falling short by our standards. What I am getting at might be indicated in the following way. To the question, how intelligent is some species of animal, it is sometimes said: as intelligent as its typical circumstances require it to be. Similarly, just as we aim to induce beliefs in our fellow men in a way that is possible for, or particular to, members of our species, so animals may aim to induce beliefs in their fellows in the only way that makes sense for them, the animal acting in such a way as to bring about action from other animals of a kind which would lend itself to a characterization in terms of belief. All we are doing here is trying to apply consistently, and on a wider front, the concept of belief as tailored to animal capacities.

4.4 ANIMAL MINDS

In *Remarks on the Philosophy of Psychology*, vol. II, Wittgenstein describes an animal behaving in a way which, he suggests, would lead us to speak of it as thinking: 'It has been trained to fetch an object from one place and take it to another. Now it starts walking toward the goal without the object, suddenly turns around (*as if it had said* "Oh, I forgot . . .!") and fetches the object, etc. If we were to see something like this we would say that at that time something had happened within it, in its mind' (*RPP* II §6). It is no doubt tempting to view the animal's performance in this way, but it is not clear just what we should then be saying with talk of 'mind' or 'thinking'. It is not that wordless thought is to be rejected, but, if we look at the wider setting which makes this possible, we find that language looms large: it may be that the subject has to be able to address a question; it may be that the thought attributed to it presupposes a grasp of a concept which is not open to a non-language-user. If you can forget something you were meant to do, you have to be capable of meaning to do something, which in turn makes demands on your capacity to look ahead in thought. There is indeed the pattern of behaviour which is as of one who might suddenly say, out loud or to himself, 'Oh, I forgot . . .!', but, if, confronted by such behaviour, we say that the animal has realized that it forgot . . ., this seems to be a figurative way of speaking which is to be cashed in behavioural terms, not a hypothesis about an inner life. Nothing is made more intelligible by extending this characterization to the animal—for which, after all, nothing remotely like silent soliloquy seems a possibility; and, of course, it is not an extension which contributes to an understanding of how it is that the behaviour comes about. True, in the passage from which this observation is extracted, Wittgenstein's concern is in part to play down the significance of anything that might happen within a *person* when acting in the way described, the little that may then take place being no more important than what can proceed externally, through speaking, drawing, etc. But, however inconsequential it may be, with us there will be something to report where with the animal there is nothing. Nothing in its mind, that is. Something will doubtless have taken place within *it*, but it is the justification for taking the pronoun as referring to the mind rather than merely to the body that is wanting.

We have not found reason for saying that what is known about animals' capacity to acquire language advances their claim to enjoy an inner life. It is doubtful whether we have to do with a grasp of language sufficient to warrant Kenny's notion of having a mind, let alone the notion which applies when there is something which, failing its manifestation in behaviour, we might know of only if it were disclosed to us by the creature. What, then, *would* warrant us in going beyond behaviour and ascribing an inner life to an animal?

Let us suppose that a chimpanzee could use signs in a way that entitled us to speak of it as thinking or believing that *p*; we have, let us say, a regular association of the sequence of signs with circumstances in which the creature's behaviour alone invites a characterization in these terms. Suppose too that now, with a recurrence of these circumstances, the chimpanzee is prevented from signing. Could we not conjecture that it had none the less had the relevant thought, formed the belief? If to have the thought were just to have a disposition to behave and/or sign in a certain way, then we could readily make sense of this suggestion, but this would not capture the relevant notion of unexpressed thought: merely being disposed to produce a sign is consistent with having one's mind a total blank. I do not wish to deny that there is *a* sense of 'think' which may apply even when nothing occurs to the subject; we have already seen illustrations of this possibility, but the sense is not one that concerns us at present. It is, I suggest, only with the development of a more reflective capacity, the capacity to report a thought or belief, that we should be on firm ground in speaking of the animal as enjoying states and episodes which might occur without our knowing in the way that is characteristic of the mental. Or, rather, it is only with the kind of report of which reports of beliefs are a particular case. There are also thoughts reportable as questions or wishes, as well as dreams, daydreams, imaginings, recallings, and so forth.

But, if an animal were to make such disclosures, it would have to do more than simply mouth the relevant words, make the relevant signs; it would have to use them with the meanings which we attach to them. How could this be recognized? Very roughly, we should look for an extension to a linguistic practice that had already earned its credentials as such with respect to the more straightforward contexts of the kinds we have been discussing. As an indication of the patterns we should then seek, consider how language used by a person in reporting auditory 'images', as with a tune running through one's head, might be recognized for what it was. Here we find the vocabulary associated with perception and its objects, but with certain features of its use cancelled or modified. Most strikingly, the language of a report is invoked when nothing relevant by way of a public sound is to be heard. The 'sounds' are never said to deafen or grate, seldom to disturb or to calm; they are subject to the will to a greater degree than are public sounds, there is no wondering as to what course a tune in the head might next take; the tune is not thought of as having unnoticed features, as continuing when the person is no longer aware of it. And so on. We could continue to elaborate a series of characterizations, positive and negative, which might serve to test our subject's capacity for enjoying this experience. His invocation of the appropriate descriptions, refusal of those inappropriate, would reveal to us that what is called 'imagining a sound' was going on, or at least that he had a grasp of that concept, and so *could* report an experience of this kind, even if on the given occasion he was attempting to deceive us. Clearly, variations are possible, as with differences in the degree to which we have subjection to the will: 'voices imagined' may cover both voices heard by a schizophrenic and a speech we imagine ourselves delivering. However, none of the variations is within the reach of the known capacities of animals.

Let us now summarize the main theme of the last two chapters. Philosophical views on the mental capacities of animals are often sharply divided. On the one hand, there is a tendency to dismiss psychological ascriptions as being, in view of the animal's lack of language, no more than extended or figurative uses of the vocabulary in question. On the other hand, it may be insisted that a large segment of that vocabulary carries over to animals without undergoing any significant alteration in sense, and that we may justifiably speak of animals not only as seeing, fearing, and so forth, but even as pretending and hoping. The position I have endorsed need not take issue with either party, but it is more concerned with the commitments of any such ascriptions as regards the mental character, in the sense here indicated, of the acts or states in question. In some cases the literal applicability of the descriptions may be indisputable—as with perceptual verbs, and perhaps even with the central notion of *action*—but, whether literal or figurative, the pattern is one of a redescription of the observable; or, if we can speak of an explanatory hypothesis, this will be of a kind for which observation can bring final confirmation. With respect both to belief and to concept possession, the recognition that something different is involved with animals risks being distorted into the claim that something quite unfamiliar, perhaps unknowable, is at issue, when it is a matter of something different only in the sense of something *less* than what we have in the familiar case—a subtraction from the cluster, not a problematic addition. We are never, I submit, confronted with behaviour which obliges us to postulate underlying mental happenings; a fortiori, we are not obliged to find any place for mental causality in the animal realm.

5

Intention and Desire

If a place has to be found for mental causation in the explanation of human behaviour, we shall be departing significantly from what is required with animals, a departure which risks failing to take seriously the status of human beings as part of the natural order. On the other hand, since our superior mental capacities make for an undoubted gulf between us and the animals, with corresponding differences in the kinds of explanation possible in our own case, this departure need not be unwarranted. The principal question remains, not whether there is a difference, but where it is to be located; in particular, whether the causal origins of human action are to be found in our thoughts and desires.

Belief in such a causal role is often associated with the claim that what is needed is a satisfactory *theory*. This association is not surprising. The concept of theory beckons when mistaken assumptions or other errors result in an ever-increasing complexity needed to save the appearances, and causal accounts of desire and intention have had their fair share of difficulties with the problem of deviant or wayward causal chains: while seemingly flowing from a desire, a person's movements may none the less not qualify as intentional, the character which the causal condition is aimed at securing. Just how to specify the right causal chain does not find a ready answer, so the appeal to theory is understandable. By my lights, the appeal is misconceived—it is questionable whether we should speak of a *theory* when the relevant form of refutation is grammatical; certainly, there is nothing deserving of this title in any significant sense if it is just a matter of making explicit the understanding of the relevant language which our usage shows us to possess. Compare Wittgenstein's observation that our normal, naïve way of speaking does not show you a *theory* but only a *concept* of seeing (Z §223; RPP I §1101). However, until we have a more thoroughly worked-out alternative, it may be held that the advantage still lies with a causal conception. At all events, we shall now try to shed some light on the key concepts in this area in preparation for an account of practical reasoning and an analysis of action.

5.1 *SHALL* AND *WILL*

We begin by looking in some detail at the particular verbal forms with which intention is associated. The simple first-person future, as in 'I shall return', is sometimes taken to represent a statement of intention in its most basic form. More precisely, it is thought that the future form has one reading which entitles it to this status, though this exists side by side with a reading where, as with 'We shall be late', a declaration of intention is less likely, and in some cases—'We shall regret this in the morning', 'I shall need your help'—impossible. This thesis may ascribe two meanings to the single grammatical form, and we shall begin with this possibility.

The characterizations 'statement of intention' and 'prediction' are occasionally invoked in making the contrast, a sentence such as 'We shall be the first to arrive' being a possible subject of either. However, whatever the character of the distinction, this cannot be the way to draw it, since prediction is in no way excluded from the statement of intention. Moreover, we should not be too hasty in looking to the sense of specifically future-tense verbal phrases to find the difference, since other constructions, such as the past conditional, are equally capable of raising what is essentially the same issue. So, consider 'She would have incurred the debt'. This could be a matter of: faced with that situation, that is how she would have proceeded, the step she would have taken. On the other hand, it could be a matter more of what supposedly would have befallen the person. Intentions are, of course, for the future, in that a statement of what one intends looks to a future action, but there is also the more general characterization, 'a specification of an intended action', and this can embrace statements of past intention.

Even with the present tense the same variability may be found. Take the sentence 'We are following a red car', where the activity reported may or may not be intentional. Since the given verb can present us with the two possibilities, there is no call to relate the matter of intentionality to the auxiliary 'shall' when we move to the future case. Is it then that 'follow' has two senses? A consideration which goes against this is that we turn to just the same happenings for confirmation or refutation in either case, here and with the many other examples that can be devised: 'We are weighing down the car', 'There will be no dinner for you this evening', 'He was exceeding the speed limit', 'They all started coughing'. There is room for clarifying what is being reported, but that need not be a matter of resolving a lexical ambiguity.

Since in both cases an assessment of what is said as true or false proceeds on the same basis—by having regard to how things turn or turned out—it might seem that the two characterizations relate more to the sentence in association with its different *grounds*. Certainly, while uniformity in truth conditions suggests constancy in meaning, there is a clear divergence in the kinds of grounds we have in the two cases. The appeal to such a difference is most tempting with respect to future-tense statements. With the past tense, as in 'I was blinking', one's grounds for the assertion will be overwhelmingly knowledge of what took place, irrespective of the matter of intentionality. With the future, by contrast, there is a difference in the way the putative desirability of the action provides a basis for the assertion in the one case but not in the other. Similarly with the 'unreal' cases, as 'If I had taken the other route I should have crossed the bridge'. The present-tense form stands somewhere in between, having a reportive character which it shares with the past tense, but looking to the future in so far as the event is still under way.

We may also note that the prediction of a non-intentional action can be based on grounds of the kind associated with intention. So, you assure me that you will not forget the appointment, that you will hear the bell, or that you will win the argument. There is intention here in so far as there are steps which you intend taking to ensure that that is how things will turn out, but, while your grounds may involve an assessment of the value of acting, together with beliefs as to ability and opportunity, what you actually predict is not an intentional act. Conversely, one's grounds for predicting an intentional act can be much as when the act envisaged is not intentional—namely, a basis in experience. This is particularly so when a qualification such as 'probably' enters. 'I shall probably get married some day' or 'I shall no doubt get married some day' could easily be a qualified prediction of an intentional act, but one that rests on considerations of the same general character as, say, 'I shall probably outlive my parents'. Again, with 'If I had taken the other route I should have crossed the bridge', crossing the bridge may be thought of just as something which taking the other route would have entailed, even though it would have qualified as intentional. However, while the difference in grounds takes second place to the question of *what* is predicted, reported or hypothesized, this question does not present us with a choice as to how to interpret the verbal phrase. The sentence 'We left the luggage behind' does not bear two meanings depending on whether it describes an intentional or an unintentional act.

If we do not make the difference in grounds crucial in distinguishing the two cases, it would seem that all that is left is the different character, as intentional or otherwise, of what is predicted, reported, or hypothesized, but, if this difference is not one in the meaning of the verbal phrase, to what is it to be traced? I suggest that the difference is one that bears upon the *manner* of acting: 'He exceeded the speed limit' means the same whether the act was intentional or unintentional, just as it means the same whether it was done willingly or reluctantly. In either case the common verbal form can cover two distinguishable cases; it is the further qualification that embodies the difference. In so far as different grounds are relevant to this distinction, it is because of their relation to the manner of acting. Compare the statement that someone has died. A very different matter if it is suicide or murder, not a natural death, but such diversity does not leave 'died' ambiguous. It is just that there is room for distinctions among the possibilities which warrant its affirmation.

These considerations, however, do not do justice to those predictions of intentional action which are also to be reckoned the *expression* of an intention, the overwhelmingly likely reading with first-person uses when the verb specifies an intentional act. I *decide* that I shall enter a competition, visit an aunt, or learn to fly, rather than simply conclude that these events will come about, and in uttering 'I shall feed the birds' as an expression of intention I announce a current preparedness rather than predict a future preparedness to act. With the expression of intention it is hardly in place to speak of grounds or evidence, though there will be a distinctive pattern of underlying reasoning, involving an assessment of advantage or the like. However, I do still predict an action in the sense of saying something that will be true only with my future feeding of the birds. It is important to hold to the predictive element, since relinquishing it may leave a gap which is then filled with alternatives which, like imperatival or performative readings, may be suggestive, but are at best supplementary, and usually plain wrong, leading, for instance, to a severance of vital links with the concepts of truth and falsity. However, we should not settle on this characterization until we have examined 'shall' and 'will' more closely, since certain of their uses appear not to favour this simple parsing.

The problem arises with questions. If I state 'I shall resign', then you may contradict me with 'No you won't', which looks forward to a contrary development, and it is equally a future happening, a failure to resign, that may be said to falsify the declaration. With 'Shall I resign?', on the other hand, the questioner is seeking not reasons for thinking it true or false that he will resign, but reasons for acting. The form 'Will he resign?' is not parallel in this respect, reasons of the first kind being very much the concern, and the reply 'Yes' to 'Shall I resign?' constitutes, or would at least normally herald, the proffering of advice—'It would be a good thing'; not 'That is how you will act'.

It is understandable that the interrogative form should receive this reading. If it is entirely up to the agent whether he Vs or not, then only the question of desirability, not that of success, is at issue. However, this shift is not one which arises unless we forsake the declarative form 'I shall V'. Even when this is used in putting a question, the shift does not occur. That is, it is possible to form a question by retaining the word order of the declarative form but varying the intonation, as 'He is ready' becomes 'He is ready?'. However, with 'Shall I resign?' such a variant is not available in the required reading. The response 'Yes' to 'I shall resign?' cannot be reported as 'He advised me to resign', but is wedded more to the (inappropriate) predictive use, 'I will resign?'. Even the reply 'Yes, you shall' tends to take 'Shall I resign?' in the wrong, predictive, way. Compare 'Yes, you shall' as an answer to 'Shall we expect you for dinner?'. This question enquires after the reasonableness of harbouring such an expectation, whether there is anything that licenses it, whereas the answer represents the person as asking whether such expecting will occur.

We have now reached the two main points of importance to us. First, 'I shall V' is rightly construed as making a prediction, and so to be assessed as true or false in accordance with that role. Secondly, notwithstanding this construal, the corresponding interrogative form is to be understood as raising the question of the desirability of Ving. If anything, it is the first reading that is basic, and there is even a case for refusing to lose sight of this reading with the interrogative contexts. Perhaps it is not so much that the predictive element is alto-gether lost to the interrogative form; more that the matter of what will happen simply reduces to the question of desirability when the main verb specifies an act that is fully within the agent's power. Consider 'I think I shall finish this book'. This may express a decision: I have—perhaps with some diffidence—chosen this course from various options: 'I think that's what I'll do.' On the other hand, it may have the force of 'I think I shall succeed in finishing this book'. The choice has already been made, I am not concerned to adjudicate between options; my course has been set, the question is whether I shall arrive. When a tentative decision is involved, the speaker hav-ing not quite made up his mind to finish the book, the action is thought of as one within the person's power: it is up to him to finish the book, if he chooses. With this as a given assumption, any uncer-tainty shifts to the matter merely of making up one's mind, though without negating the future reference channelled through 'shall'. Likewise with 'Shall I resign?' or 'Shall I deal?'. The only real issue is non-predictive, the speaker seeking reassurance on the wisdom or propriety of the action contemplated, not on the likelihood of his car-rying it through. Once uncertainty enters, the act not being some-thing one can do at will, the more likely form is given by 'will'. So, with 'Shall I beat him at draughts?' the speaker represents himself as one for whom winning is unproblematic, whereas 'Will I beat him?' is appropriate if he is in doubt about the likely outcome. (At least in my usage. I must grant that for some speakers the patterns are dif-ferent—even to the extent of being the exact opposite. However, it is the contrasts that matter rather than the choice of auxiliary favoured in drawing them.)

Note that, when the action is thought straightforward, then, while 'certainly' may be invoked—'I shall certainly speak to her'—the cer-tainty is the certainty that goes with determination, with firmness of purpose, not—as in 'I am certain that I shall speak to her'—with the elimination of doubt from a hypothesis. With the latter, the speaker may be confident that the event will take place, but it is thought to some extent out of his hands whether it does or not. This is the kind of contrast that is useful in characterizing the difference between expressions of intentions and mere predictions, but again without denying the predictive element in the former. In passing, we may also note the parallel contrast with respect to statements about one's feel-ings: 'I certainly feel dreadful' as against 'I am certain that I feel dreadful'. The latter would, quite inappropriately, require the speaker to have resolved any doubts he may have had about how he felt, whereas the former has a genuine role in giving his audience an assurance that he feels that way: 'You can be sure' rather than 'I am sure'.

Are analogous peculiarities to be found with 'will'? Surely the question 'Will you speak to her?' has primarily a present focus, the sense being that of, roughly, 'Are you willing to speak to her?'. First, it may be said that the use of 'will' just introduced is not 'will' as a future-tense auxiliary. Compare 'Take liberties with my wife, will you?'. In one major respect this is, of course, in striking contrast to 'Will you speak to her?'—the person addressed is not, on the more humanly likely interpretation, being *requested* to take liberties with the speaker's wife—but, whether willingness or wilfulness is in question, perhaps we have only a homonym of the future form.

I am happy to allow that 'will' does not invariably have a straight-forwardly future reference. We have one illustration in 'He'll spend hours glued to his computer', and another, more relevant, with 'He won't eat his greens', taken as a report—'He refuses to eat his greens'—not as a prediction. What of the form 'Will you speak to her?'? Are we dealing here with a simple future? Suppose first that there is no intention to make a request, but that the speaker is simply curious. Curious about the person's intentions, no doubt, since these are all-important in determining what will come about, but it is still these that are his concern. If that concern also extends to an interest in having the addressee act, so that the words give voice to a request, then this makes for a further difference from a query about a non-intentional act, but, while the addressee's present willingness comes into focus with that interest, the question of what the future holds retains its relevance. In so far as there is an allusion either to present willingness or to present intention, it is not such as to preclude what the general grammatical form indicates in terms of future reference. That, rather than anything that occurs at the time of utterance, is of overriding concern when it comes to assessing the truth of the corresponding declarative form.

Furthermore, it is again important to take the main verb into account, as we see from the comparison with 'Will you be speaking to her?'. Is it not because a presentation of the action as intentional is better served by 'Will you speak?' than by 'Will you be speaking?' that the former is more readily invoked in making a request, the

auxiliary falling into line in either case? That is, 'Will you be speaking to her?' goes with the case where one envisages the person *finding* himself speaking with the woman in question, whereas the
non-progressive form looks forward to a time when one may take a
decision to speak. Still, not only does this shift the issue away from
'will', but it is a matter only of the one form being better geared than
the other to presenting the activity as intentional, rather than of an
invariable association of the forms with the intentional and the non-
intentional respectively.

However, while it is important not to abandon the superficial
grammar too readily, the interrogative form once more provides us
with a context in which, for parallel reasons, the future reference has
become subordinated to a present concern. With 'Will you speak to
her?' the question of the person's willingness comes to the fore, since
this is all that it takes for the action to be engaged upon. That this
has taken over to the extent of excluding a predictive query seems
apparent from the possibility of adding 'please': 'Will you speak to
her, please' makes excellent sense if the 'please' extends a request; not
if it joins with a query about what will take place. However, while
with both 'shall' and 'will' these departures from a predictive concern
have to be acknowledged, that concern remains dominant outside
these limited contexts, which are in any event to be seen as growing
out of this central case.

5.2 INTENDING

In speaking of 'I shall V' as the expression of an intention, we are
not usurping the role of 'I intend to V', which is geared more to
reporting an intention. Clearly, while the two may cover much the
same ground, 'I intend to V' may be significantly weaker. You ask
me whether I shall go to the meeting. If I reply 'I certainly intend to',
I avow a preparedness to take steps to this end, but at the same time
convey a reservation about actual success that is absent from the
blunt 'I shall be there'. Similarly, 'I don't intend standing idly by' can
survive inaction in a way that, as far as truth is concerned, 'I shall
not stand idly by' cannot. With 'I intend to V', the speaker gives us
to understand that, if Ving does not come about, it will not be for
want of a favourable disposition on his part, though, while perhaps
nothing more can be asked of *him*, this does not guarantee the truth

of 'I shall'. In this contrast, the character of 'I intend to *V*' as a report of how one is minded or disposed, and of 'I shall *V*' as a prediction—with the supposed desirability of *V*ing as the agent's reason for making it—is very much apparent. This analysis mirrors what was said for thinking or believing that *p*: in uttering the unqualified *p* we give expression to our belief without reporting that we have it, whereas 'I believe that *p*' may be explicit in just this respect. The likeness extends to a parallel with Moore's paradox, as discernible in such a conjunction as 'I shall get in touch but I don't intend to'. The source of the paradox is plain from the consideration that to intend to *V* is to be in a state of mind expressible by saying that one will *V*. Once more, the characterization is built around the notion of a direct expression: with 'I shall *V*' we may have the intention taking shape, whereas it generally falls to 'I intend to *V*' to have the derivative role of reporting the intention which dates from this initial expression.

It is sometimes claimed that one cannot intend to *V* without holding a belief that one will in fact *V*. This would make it puzzling why we should stop short of saying 'I shall be there' when prepared to say 'I certainly intend to be there'. Of course, if the latter expresses a determination to do something which it is simply up to the speaker to do, should he wish, there will be no shrinking from the form with 'shall', but in general only a belief as to the possibility of success is presupposed with 'intend'. A fortiori, we may note, intending to *V* is not a matter of believing that one will *V* *because* one desires to do so.

The verbal forms associated with intention are of interest for the diverse ways in which they involve report, prediction, and expression. Suppose there is no question of the kind of uncertainty that leads us to retreat from 'I shall' to 'I intend'. Finding the prospect of *V*ing overwhelmingly attractive, you simply say 'I shall *V*', and such is your power to act, you have no need merely to announce an intention, rather than simply tell us what will come to pass. Use of the simple future, as in 'I shall ask for my money back', is likely to represent a decision taken there and then rather than express a more long-standing intention, so, even if we were certain we should not undergo a change of mind, or meet with obstacles to carrying our action through, should we not have a use for 'I intend' in indicating that our mind was made up at an earlier time? That is, the circumstances envisaged do not remove the need to settle on one course of action rather than another, and 'I intend' could be enlisted in indicating just what future action had been elected. Perhaps, but the phrase to which this role more naturally falls is 'I am going to V', the form favoured when we have already settled on a course of action, so do not wish to suggest that we are only now taking a stand, but have no reservations about carrying the action through.

Whereas 'I shall' and 'I intend' have an unambivalent future and present focus respectively, matters are more complex with 'I am going to', and certain other verbal forms which offer the opportunity for vacillation between the two temporal poles. Here it is useful to consider contradiction and insincerity. If a person does not intend to V, then he lies if he says he does, whereas, if he says 'I shall V', then, while he is certainly insincere, he is less readily accused of lying, since he may not yet know of the falsity of what he claims. There is some scope for speaking of lying, in so far as the speaker gives one to suppose an intention that is in fact absent, but with 'I am going to V' the present form of the verb makes it easier to think in terms of there being something to which the affirmation can be false as it stands. Note too the use of the progressive form, as in 'We are leaving on Sunday'. Without the intention to leave, a person can perhaps be said to have lied, though again there is a possibility of contradicting him by pointing to the impossibility of the action, rather than imputing insincerity. Slightly differently, and enjoying a more limited use, we have the form illustrated by 'We leave on Sunday'. Here 'No you don't' contradicts the implication that this is what *has* been arranged, though it is perhaps also possible to regard a denial that the departure *will* take place at the appointed date as a form of contradiction.

In one respect, 'I am going to V' has the present reference of 'I intend to V': despite a failure to V we may still insist that we were going to do so. On the other hand, the former embodies enough of a future reference for our declaration to be greeted with something like 'Oh no you're not', seemingly in contradiction of what we say, but without necessarily imputing insincerity, and its use matches that of the plain future in being appropriate to the case where failure is not thought to be a real possibility. Overall, the correlation is more with 'I shall V' than with 'I intend to V'. 'I shall V' is used when we have just come to a decision, or are making an initial commitment. You ask to borrow a book and I say 'I shall bring it along tomorrow'. If there is uncertainty, that is still not enough for 'intend' at this initial stage, but 'I shall try . . .' is more appropriate. The lack of doubt which goes with 'I shall . . .' is retained when at a later point one says 'I am going to bring the book to him tomorrow', and where 'I shall . . .' would be suggestive of a decision just taken, a commitment just engaged upon, and 'I intend . . .' would strike too cautious a note. Again, as closer to 'I think I shall write', 'I think I am going to write' is more acceptable than 'I think I intend to write'.

In going over these various distinctions, one of our main aims has been to show that they are distinctions which can be drawn within a certain framework. There may be important differences separating uses of one and the same form of words, as with a statement of intention and a mere prediction, and with respect to uses of 'know' and 'think' with either, but the differences are within the general categories which the surface grammar presents, with no call to forsake such notions as those of reporting, predicting, and asserting for a quite different range of speech acts. Consider 'I'll do it', uttered by someone volunteering to act. Such a use appears remote from one where the notion of *predicting* identifies the core act embodied in the words, the present willingness of the agent, not the future realization of the action, being what comes into focus. However, once we take in the broader picture, one encompassing relations between the declaration and other linguistic moves, the words are found to bear the marks of a prediction, rather than to take us outside that scheme. This is revealed in the way, for example, someone who says of the volunteer 'She'll never manage it' can be described as contradicting what was said. It is not just an accident that the future form lends itself to a use in volunteering, as well as to that in a mere prediction, but we can *explain* how it is that the predictive element then ceases to be to the fore: if the ability to act is not in question, interest shifts to the matter of the person's willingness, but it is only because such willingness ensures the likelihood of the future happening that it has the importance it has.

The general question at issue had an earlier illustration when the language of sensations was under discussion (§2.2). Here, too, there was the threat that an expressive interpretation would make it a mystery how one and the same linguistic form could, seemingly without change of meaning, be endowed with such differing uses; how, for example, uses of 'pain' in first-person and third-person ascriptions could be comparable. Hence our reservations about making the expressive use central. A further instance is to be found in the way Wittgenstein dismisses the suggestion that such broad linguistic categories, as those of assertion, question, and injunction, might allow of a uniform characterization. His attachment to the motto 'I'll teach you differences' may be a prophylactic against a procrustean regimentation of language, but there is also the risk of swinging to the other extreme, of failing to do justice to the uniformities, the general patterns, to be found in the language (cf. Rundle 1990: ch. 5). It is, I suggest, through an appreciation of such patterns, not buried in mind or brain, but not always on the surface of the language, that we can often hope to find our way through the philosophically puzzling areas of our language.

5.3 WANTING

If 'I intend' is weaker than 'I shall', 'I want' is weaker still, though agreeing with both these in involving a commitment to action. Or, typically, a *qualified* commitment, 'want' being a verb to which we often turn when we are thwarted in some way. I wanted to catch the chairman's eye, to speak to the meeting, but unfortunately I was unable. I want to move my queen's pawn, but it would be unwise at this stage. Again, if I am confident of having the opportunity to speak to my wife, there is room for a decision or intention which might be expressed with a simple future: 'I shall raise the matter with my wife this evening.' Seeing my way clear to acting, I have no cause to invoke the more cautious form, 'I want to raise the matter with my wife this evening'. Similarly, a possible hitch in the action proposed is suggested with 'I want to pick up the groceries on the way back' rather than simply 'I'm going to pick up the groceries on the way back'.

However, it is important to see what is responsible for this feature of the use of 'want'. Clearly, there is nothing amiss with using the verb when no obstacles are in view: she wanted to have a swim, so in she plunged. Rather, if we do not believe that there is an obstacle to an action we propose, then, preferring the stronger, more informative form to the weaker, we shall opt for 'I shall' rather than 'I want'. On the other hand, if an obstacle is envisaged, 'I want' is still available when 'I shall' is not. Hence, the overall effect of these considerations that, in the relevant contexts, we tend to use 'I want' if and only if we take there to be an obstacle to successful action.

While a retreat to 'want' is in order if one has reservations about carrying through the action, there is usually the supposition that at least nothing insuperable stands in one's way. So, if you have a use-less chest taking up useful space, you may declare 'I want to get rid of that chest'. If whatever obstacle there is to removing the chest is one that might reasonably be overcome, there is room for this degree of movement towards a commitment to action, but, if there is no real possibility of doing anything, then a form of words which does not so readily lead us to expect action of the speaker is accordingly more apt. So, 'I should like to get rid of that chest', or 'It would be so nice to be rid of that chest'. And, of course, 'I wish I could be rid of that chest', 'wish' being suited to the case where what is thought desirable is also thought to be out of reach.

That wanting involves a (qualified) commitment to acting seems plain enough. If x is what someone wants, it cannot be simply that it is considered that x would be enjoyable or satisfying; there are many things which we suppose to have these virtues but which we do not want, since we find nothing uncongenial about being without them. Rather, to say that one wants x is to imply that one is with-out x, and that one minds the lack of x sufficiently to do something about it, other things being equal. This latter proviso is, of course, necessary—the steps needed to remedy the lack may make it not worth the effort, or there may be other more pressing demands upon us—but, the implication that we shall seek to do something in the absence of such contrary considerations is apparent. I say that I want to visit the local museum, but although opportunities present them-selves often enough, I never get around to doing anything about it, *any* rival activity proving to be a superior attraction. Here, surely, the profession of a want has become quite empty.

The preparedness to take steps which 'want' implies is evidenced by the awkwardness of the verb if, for temporal reasons, there is no conceivable action to look forward to. Think of the tycoon's idiotic 'I want it done yesterday!'. Granted, there are such contexts as 'I want to be released from the contract', where what takes place may be, and be thought to be, quite out of the speaker's hands, but even then the question of the degree of dissatisfaction implied by the use of 'want' remains important; this would be assessed precisely as what is or would be sufficient to lead one to take steps, if possible. If the idea of a preparedness to act does not give the best rendering, this is because it is not sufficiently emphatic as to the commitment to action—perhaps, indeed, the person is already engaged in action to the end in question, whence it is no longer a question merely of being *prepared* to act. However, since it is wanting at its broadest that we are trying to capture, this does not leave it too far off the mark, and, if the action is already under way, what the person is doing can be said to give concrete proof of a preparedness to act.

Because 'want' implies a willingness to take steps, its use is at times a shade brusque or peremptory—'I want to see you at noon' may hint at a possible exercise of authority to enforce one's will; as if the speaker had just to make known his desires and the person addressed would act upon them—or else. Even to ask 'Do you want a cup of tea?' may be felt impolite, through threatening to ascribe this demanding stance to the person addressed. But why look to an implication that one is prepared to take steps for this suggestion? Is it not enough that in saying 'I want to see you at noon' one is making known a goal ostensibly of benefit to oneself without regard to the wishes of the person spoken to? But I can announce that it would give me great pleasure to see you at noon, which is also silent on the addressee's wishes, and it would seem that it is because this does not threaten action that its tone is less demanding. The peremptoriness of 'want' is, of course, diminished when what is wanted is for the benefit of another, as with 'I want you to know how sorry we are about your loss', and it is in no way hectoring if the speaker is not so much announcing a preparedness to take steps as indicating what he is aiming at with an action already under way. We shall return to this important case.

In giving a negative slant to our characterization of wanting we follow Locke—'an uneasiness of the mind for want of some absent good' (*Essay*, II. xxi. 31)—but with the link to action made explicit: it is a matter of minding the absence of the good sufficiently to act. While such an addition is called for, to speak of minding the lack of something to such a point that one is prepared to act can mislead with its possible suggestion that one acts on recognizing that this point has been reached. That may be so, but it may also be that there is no proof of sufficiency, for the agent or for us, short of the action itself. True, one may *decide* that this point has been reached, though, once more, in many cases it will be a matter of deciding *with* one's action.

With such cases in view, we might approach the characterization of wanting in the following way: among the things we lack and which we mind being without, there are some which we take steps to get, and these we single out as things which we want. This connects with the point made above that there is more for 'want' to do when the agent is thwarted. *Want* can then acknowledge a persisting preparedness in the face of an obstacle. Otherwise it simply draws attention to character as an action. Suppose you had the task of creating an autonomous robot, one capable of initiating action. How might you design it so that this could come about? It is of no use to say: build in desires—as if there were such components to be introduced into the robot, like a power supply. Rather, you would seek to ensure that the robot's circuitry was such that it could be counted on to engage in certain goal-directed activities when various conditions were realized. We could then leave it to the world to provide the obstructive circumstances which would make it appropriate to speak of wanting. With this approach we reverse the commonly accepted priority of wanting over acting. I have mentioned the view which would have us dismiss desires and beliefs as figments of a discredited folk psychology. It is not a view which could coherently be argued for, but we should be on firmer ground with the suggestion that desires are transformed into entities with no real existence when they are called upon to provide the moving forces in a mechanics of action.

True, as just acknowledged, we do not need frustrated behaviour in order to speak of wanting; all that matters is that intentionality, or at least purposiveness, should be discernible. But, so long as this is all we have, there is nothing distinctive for *wants* to do. We could just as well say '*x* is avoiding *y*' or '*x* is going to *z*' as '*x* wants to avoid *y*' or '*x* wants to go to *z*'. If, when prevented from proceeding, the creature does not simply shift to a totally different pursuit, but reveals a persisting preparedness to act, then we have something which *wants* can usefully mark. We see something more of this aspect if we consider the question why, given their goal-seeking behaviour, we none the less do not speak of guided missiles as wanting to hit their target. It was suggested above that distress was of secondary importance *vis-à-vis* the action which manifested a desire. However, if there is no reaction on being thwarted or impeded, if the lack of the end desired is in no sense felt—as signs of distress make plain— then a significant element in our conception of wanting—that of sensibility—is lacking.

Differences over the use of 'want' often revolve around the question of the degree of separability of wanting and intending. Can one intend to do something, or actually engage upon an action intentionally, without wanting to do it? So the father who punishes his child, not because he wants to, but because he feels he has to for the good of the child. This contrasts with action which the man really, without qualification, wants to perform, action which he wants to perform for itself—because, for instance, of the pleasure he thinks it will give him. Similarly, the man who hands over his wallet at gunpoint may be acting intentionally, but not doing what he really wants to do.

However, to exclude altogether talk of wanting in such cases would be uncalled for. Ideally, the threatened man does not want to part with his money, and of course he wishes he did not find himself in such a situation. But, given that he is faced with the choice of handing across his wallet, or else suffering the consequences of refusal, then, it could be said, what he wants to do may indeed be the former in preference to the latter. Certainly, his behaviour may have all the marks of purposiveness, of determination; in particular, his concern if his action threatens to be thwarted—if, through nervousness, he fumbles when trying to extract his wallet—would show clearly enough that this is what he wants to do—wants to do more perhaps than anything else. It is true that it is a matter of wanting only in preference to the alternative, but this qualification does not license a flat denial that he wants to perform the action; rather, the qualification is appropriately channelled through an 'adjuster' such as 'ideally' or 'really'. If anything, it is the desire to refrain from acting that is the more problematic in such cases. After all, the fact that the person did act can be set against his declaration that he did not want to. Given that we often have overriding reasons against the pursuit of something we desire, we cannot say that wanting x is simply a matter of being prepared to aim for x, if we are able. We may add 'other things being equal', but, since this clause may introduce reference to other desires, the formula does not furnish a satisfactory definition. What is needed here is an appeal to comparative judgements: x is wanted by A if it is something A will aim for if he can, or which he would aim for were it not that he judges something else both more desirable and such as to preclude the attainment of x.

In this discussion I have been concerned to do justice to 'want' in its broadest sense, the sense in which an ascription of a want follows on characterization as an action. This is not to exclude the possibility of other uses. We have perhaps the core idea of lacking or being without in 'This wants another coat of paint', and, even when used of human beings, the verb may fail to connect with intentionality, as when we say 'He wants to serve more to his opponent's backhand', or 'You want to be more careful with that knife'. Again, feeling a sneeze coming on, perhaps uncontrollably, I may say that I suddenly wanted to sneeze. Nothing intentional about it, no end in view which might be met by sneezing; indeed, I do my best to stifle the sneeze. But I did want to sneeze.

This last example brings us to the familiar and important distinction between 'want' as it correlates with 'act' and a more circumscribed use of the word, or more especially of 'desire', in which we have to do with something which we might speak of as experiencing or feeling, where we might often also speak of *urges* or *cravings* (cf. D. Locke 1974; Kenny 1975: 49–52). I may want to purchase a postage stamp or check a reference in Kant, but I am unlikely to speak of experiencing a desire to make the purchase or of being seized with an urge to check the reference. A desire as an urge may be a desire for something recognized to be quite undesirable, as we might experience an insane desire to touch a live wire. Acknowledging such a desire need not amount to an indication as to how one is minded to act, need not give expression to one's will in the way we have argued for *want* in its very general use.

With the narrower use, the question why someone has a certain desire is much the same as the question why he has a certain like or dislike, with in both cases ignorance of the answer being likely to be ignorance of a cause. Why do you have such a strong desire (liking) for spicy foods? No idea, you reply. That is just the way you are made. By contrast, the question why you want a particular dish invites specification of what it is about the dish which makes it attractive to you. Wanting in the more intellectual sense involves *belief*. You see a curious object on the table, and go to take a closer look. On seeing that it is just the teapot, you lose interest, not bothering to examine it further. On learning what you have learned you lose your reason for further investigation, whereas urges and cravings do not in the same way evaporate with a change in belief. Of course, if you want to do something which you cannot—you want to paint the roof but it is raining—you will not accordingly cease to want to do so. It is typically a change in view as to the desirability of the end sought that results in the wanting ceasing, not a change in beliefs about its achievability—though this, too, is possible. At all events, this is the sense of 'want' in which it has everything to do with reasons, whereas the other is one in which it has much to do with causes.

Since action detached from wanting, in its more general form, occurs only at the fringes of what qualifies as action, an explanation of action in terms of bare wanting is somewhat empty, any substance coming only with a specification of *what* is wanted. There is an apparent exception when 'Why did you V?' is answered by 'I just wanted to', but this just means that nothing beyond the Ving itself was aimed at. In getting across the idea that the activity appealed to the person in some measure, it at least gives a more intelligible explanation than would 'I just intended to'. Moreover, the tendency towards vacuousness which 'want' shows in this use points up its unsuitability as denominating a cause of action. If wanting to succeed, say, is simply a matter of being prepared to direct one's efforts to this end, if it is something of which those efforts can give trivial proof, then it does not appear to qualify as their potential cause. Nor, a fortiori, is a desire to be thought of as something, the proper function of which is to help cause its own fulfilment (Millikan 1986: 63). The value to an organism of its desires resides in the value of the actions they are desires to perform, or in the persistence in trying to perform these in the face of adverse conditions. We may postulate neural networks subserving patterns of behaviour, but these are not desires. Desires are not inner items having to be postulated, but may be secured by the behaviour itself, as with the movements of the cat which lead us to say that it wants to catch the mouse, or the expectant state of the dog which occasions the comment: it wants you to throw the stick.

Indeed, for philosophical purposes, it would often be less misleading to drop talk of wanting altogether and speak just of the end for the sake of which a person acts. This is especially so in the critical case of action already engaged in, where it is no longer a matter of a mere readiness to act. So, Kate is standing on the seat because she wants to get a better view; that is, she is standing on the seat for what that makes possible—namely, a better view—or it is because she believes that she will thereby get a better view that Kate is standing on the seat. That suffices to explain Kate's action, any introduction of wanting being made redundant by the fact of action. And before the event? It occurs to Kate that she could get a better view by standing on the seat, and she does so. That was all that entered her head, the wanting coming with the acting—I do not mean: as something accompanying the acting; rather, given the action, and the thought, we may say that Kate wanted to get a better view. Again, consider unreflecting replies to such questions as 'What are you doing?' and 'What is your name?'. If someone, not hearing the question, asks why you spoke your name, you may conceivably reply that you wanted to inform another of it, though simply 'To tell the enquirer what it was' would be more natural. At all events, wanting finds its way in with the response rather than as a condition antecedent to it, the response giving, trivially, proof of a willingness on your part to answer the question. It is with desires of the felt variety that we seemingly move closer to psychological causes, but, even if they can qualify as such, we have no assurance of their presence when what is done is done for a reason. Certainly, as we shall see in §6.2, it is only with the wanting which can become absorbed into the action that we have something deserving of a place in a characterization of the latter.

We have, then, a spectrum of cases, 'I want', 'I intend', and 'I shall', which differ progressively in the confidence implied that the action in question will come off. 'I shall' is suited to the announcement of an intention at the point of its inception, whereas 'I intend' usually reports an intention as an established state of mind, and is, of course, explicit as to the state in question. Here there is a clear parallel with belief. To make such a pronouncement as 'There is a job going at the bank' is to express a belief, though an explicit mention of the (enduring) state of mind, namely, one of believing, may be given with 'I believe there is a job going at the bank'. In merely indicating the state of mind, 'I intend' and 'I believe' make less of a commitment than 'I shall' and 'There is . . .', though of course 'He intends' and 'He believes' are suited to reporting utterances in these terms. 'I want' also reports a preparedness to act when it is necessary to retreat from the two stronger forms because of supposed obstacles to carrying through the action in question. In being a form to which we have to retreat when our power is in question, it is akin to the use of 'believe' as an appropriately weaker verb when actual knowledge is in doubt.

It is useful to draw attention to this pattern—representing various psychological verbs as distinguishable through the different associated beliefs as to the likelihood of successful action—since it may offer a corrective to the idea that, for example, desiring and intending are revealed by their phenomenology to differ greatly from one another, much as, equally erroneously, a state of mere belief is supposedly revealed to differ from one of true knowledge. It is not as if, on noting one mental state, you declare, 'I want to get rid of that chest', whereas on noting a different such state you report a mere wish to get rid of it. Compare our parallel observation that phrases such as 'I expect', 'I suspect', and 'I am sure' are dictated by *evidential* considerations. On the view being opposed, it may be thought appropriate to characterize intentions as being more *potent* than desires. After all, a desire can exist side by side with a realization that action is impossible, whereas action can more readily be expected from one who has progressed beyond desire to intention. As befits matters of causation, this way of looking at desire and intention treats them as phenomena whose characteristics are learned of by experience: we come to appreciate that the states which we identify as intentions can be counted on to lead to action more readily than those that merely qualify as desires. But the source of the commitment distinctive of intention, denied to mere desire, is nothing over and above the consideration that it is proper to speak of intending only when the relevant commitment has been made, and that a belief that action is out of the question logically requires that we speak of what we merely want rather than of what we actually intend to do.

Appreciation of this pattern may also point us in the direction of an alternative to a causal construal of the relation between desire and intention, as in this passage from Davidson: 'If a person intends to steal some Brussels sprouts, then whether or not he executes his intention, the intention itself must be caused by a desire to possess some Brussels sprouts and a belief that by stealing them he will come into possession of them' (1982: 293). If, at a certain time, a person wants to steal some sprouts, but has not as yet formed the intention to do so, this will be because he sees some impediment, real or apparent, to the action—he regards it as dangerous, impractical, or whatever. Just as the notion of wanting comes in to mark a state of one who *would* act, but for certain impediments, so too the notion of intending characterizes the state of mind of one who would act, were the time ripe. If the matter of choice or preference has been resolved in favour of action, and all that is required is that the time for action should arrive, we shall speak of intending. If there is thought to be a more significant obstacle, something which the mere passage of time will not remove, then we may be able to speak only of wanting. The difference being one in the constituent beliefs as to what is practicable, it would be nearer the truth to say that the intention comes from the desire by definition, rather than by causation: with one belief giving way to another, we have a transition to a state which qualifies as one of intending rather than of mere wanting. More succinctly, in many cases we can speak indifferently of a desire or of a conditional intention, of wanting to steal some sprouts or of intending to do so when the opportune moment arrives. With all obstacles believed removed, the conditional intention becomes unconditional, with no need of causation to effect this transformation.

The causal account has a close relation in an 'instrumentalist' conception of intention: we form an intention as a *means* to achieving our ends. This, too, is in error. Wanting to steal some sprouts, and having no scruples about theft, you decide to take steps to that end on seeing your way clear to doing so. The intention which comes into being with the decision is an intention to take the relevant steps, but is not itself one of them. If conditional, an intention to act awaits the availability of the means, antedating a belief that the time is ripe; if unconditional, the intention follows on a decision to act once it is thought that the means are available; as subsequent to such a belief, the intention cannot itself figure among the conditions believed to be in place for successful action.

It is suggested that, wanting to go to a party, Judith forms the intention of walking to the taxi rank to take a taxi; she forms this intention for a reason, namely, in order to get to the party in the quickest and most convenient way, the intention being part of the means of getting to the party (Harman 1976: 438). It can indeed be said that Judith forms the intention to take a taxi in order to get to the party quickly, but the final clause, 'in order to get to the party in the quickest and most convenient way', extends 'to take a taxi', giving the rationale for the step which this specifies; it does not qualify 'forms the intention', as if it might give the rationale for this act.

5.4 INTENTION AND REFERENCE

Suppose I startle someone unintentionally. This may be an unintended effect of an action that was intentional in some other respect. What exactly does this mean? 'In some other respect' is sometimes taken to equate with 'under some other description'. Thus Davidson suggests that, while spilling the contents of one's cup may be intentional, and while the very same act can be redescribed as one of spilling the coffee, the act is no longer intentional as thus portrayed. Again, while Hamlet intentionally kills the man behind the arras, he does not intentionally kill Polonius, even though Polonius is the man behind the arras, and indeed Hamlet's killing of the man behind the arras is identical with his killing of Polonius. There is accordingly, claims Davidson (1963: 46), no class of intentional actions, for that supposition would compel us to say that the same action was both intentional and unintentional.

On this way of looking at the matter, it is no doubt correct to hold that there is no class of intentional actions. Indeed, it is no doubt true that there is no such thing as an intentional action. If an action really is intentional as described in certain terms, and is not simply made out to be so, then another description of that action can only fail to bring out that feature; it cannot deprive the action of its intentional character. It has to be that something different is being described, and, since one and the same action can have a variety of effects, this seems to be the place to turn to if we are to find suitable subjects for the two characterizations. Davidson, however, refuses to allow us to draw the necessary line between an action and its effects: 'We might not call my unintentional alerting of the prowler an action, but it should not be inferred from this that alerting the prowler is therefore something different from flipping the switch, say just its consequence' (1963: 4). Davidson is, I believe, right to claim that 'flipping the switch' and 'alerting the prowler' are equally valid descriptions of the same action, so, if what the one picks out is intentional, the same goes for the referent of the other. However, the consequence or result of the action (under *either* description) is, say, *that the prowler is alerted*; clearly not an action but a state of affairs. Equally clearly, it is not the same consequence as is given with *that the switch is flipped*. There is no inconsistency in holding that the latter is intended, the former not—intended, note, not intentional.

Supposedly, spilling the contents of my cup may have been intentional, yet spilling the coffee in my cup need not have been, despite the identity of coffee and contents. If the possibility which Davidson wishes this to illustrate is genuine, there must be better examples of it, since normally one could quite happily say 'His spilling of the coffee was intentional' without implying that the person even knew it was coffee in his cup—ignorance which is being supposed to rule out this formulation. Again, consider 'His timely exposure of the thief was intentional'. This can be read in such a way that the qualification 'timely' does not enter into a specification of the intention: his exposure of the thief—which was, as it happens, timely—was intentional. Likewise, we may say that someone's foolhardy gesture or tiresome fidgeting was intentional, without implying that character as foolhardy or tiresome was intended.

There is no need to exploit a distinction between action and effect in dealing with such examples as these, where the speaker intrudes his own comment with a description like 'timely' or 'foolhardy'. Moreover, there is no need for *any* restrictions on substitutability, but, here as elsewhere, Leibniz's Law asks for nothing more than a careful formulation in order to withstand any apparent counter-examples to its validity (cf. Rundle 1979: §§19–21, where the topic is discussed at length). Perhaps the commonest error is to mistake conditions for aptness in the choice of referring expression with conditions for their correct application. More subtly, there may be a failure of substitutivity due to a failure of the term for which substitution is made to be referential in the required sense. Suppose I play, intentionally, the card I am holding. Then I intended to play that card; and, if that card is the Ace of Spades, then I intended to play that card, the Ace of Spades. This elaboration is not forbidden, even if, had I realized it was the Ace of Spades I was holding, I should not have played it. Suppose now I intend to pick up the first card that is placed before me, and that card turns out to be the Ace of Spades. Then again it can be said of me that I intended to pick up the Ace of Spades, with reference to the time when I acted. However, it cannot be said that I *had* intended to pick up the Ace, with reference now to the earlier time when I formed, rather than executed, my intention, since my intention was merely to pick up *whatever* card was laid before me. 'He intended to pick up the Ace of Spades' is legitimately inferred from 'He intended to pick up the card placed before him', given the requisite identity, only if 'the card placed before him' can be read as 'the card which had been placed before him', not if it expands to 'whatever card would be placed before him'. If the latter rephrasal is in order we are not dealing with an identifying reference—a reference made with knowledge of identity—but the identity of the card, in a sense which is made definite by giving its value and suit, is still open. It is only in the former case that Leibniz's Law applies.

Compare 'She remembered that Kate was Tim's cousin'. On its more likely reading, 'Tim's cousin' cannot be varied freely, but on that reading its use is not symmetrical with that of 'Kate', which can. No identifying reference is to be associated with the description, but

we could equally have said 'cousin to Tim', just as we might switch
between 'She thought he was the owner of a yacht' and 'She thought
he owned a yacht'.

To take a more well-worn example: if Oedipus intends to marry
Jocasta, then, since Jocasta is in fact his mother, that—his mother—
is the woman he intends to marry. There is nothing amiss in putting
it this way, no commitment to saying that Oedipus realizes that
Jocasta is his mother. On the other hand, if Harvey intends to marry
the first girl who will have him, and that description comes to apply
to Kate, it cannot be said that Kate had all along been Harvey's
intended. Not, patently, a failing on the part of Leibniz's Law: we do
not have in 'the first girl who will have him' a referential term in the
requisite sense; a fortiori, there is no question of varying the mode of
reference by substituting 'Kate'.

It was indicated in §3.3 that the considerations which govern
choice of referential term have to do with the communicative
demands of the situation of utterance, not with a need to remain true
to the terms which the person whose thought is being reported used,
or was in a position to use. I say, 'It was feared she would not pull
through'. To your query 'Who is "she"?', *any* answer that correctly
identifies the person in question will do; it is just that some will, in
view of your own knowledge, be more or less apt. In so far as it is
thought that the original thinker's formulation furnishes a constraint,
this will be because that person was not able to offer variant forms
of reference, there not being at that time anything that *might* be variously identified. So, we are not at liberty to vary the mode of reference in 'Harvey intends to marry the first girl who will have him' for
just this reason—there is no reference in the requisite sense—and for
just this reason it is misleading to speak of such contexts as 'referen-
tially opaque', if by this is meant that what matters to truth is the
particular way reference is achieved.

The distinction between the two uses of descriptions is at work,
though less readily discerned, in the following variant way of avoiding paradox in intentional contexts. Suppose that Harvey overtakes
a bus, thereby exceeding the speed limit. It could well be that he over-
took the bus intentionally, but exceeded the speed limit unintentionally. The possibility of speaking of different aspects or outcomes of
the action makes for one means whereby ascriptions of *intentional*
and *unintentional* may be reconciled, but there is a more subtle way
in which we can continue to find room for these opposing predicates.

As an analogy, consider the notion of predictability. We may say of Harvey's action that it was predictable, but mean only that it was predictable that he would overtake the bus, not that he would break the speed limit. Clearly, there must be some variability in our interpretation of 'Harvey's action', despite the apparent constancy of its reference. And indeed, I may predict *that* action, the action Harvey took, but only in so far as the action is what is required to make the prediction true, not 'that action' as it embraces everything that falls to the historic action in all its concrete detail, including the excessive speed.

I say 'Harvey will dive into the river', and he does. Did I predict the action that took place? I did not predict that Harvey would perform that particular dive in just that way and at just that moment. Had he dived in some quite different manner, that would still have been the action I predicted in the sense that it would still have been true that he did what I predicted he would. But, if that is so, then 'I predicted his action' must be explicable in a way that does not tie it too closely to the dive that actually took place. 'Predicting what he did' is to be a variant only as concerns tense of 'predicting what he will do'—that is, with no more to be read into the former than can be read into the latter, made from the earlier perspective of ignorance of the character of the verifying event beyond what is required for fulfilment of the prediction.

Expanding 'That action was unpredictable' as 'That he would exceed the speed limit was unpredictable' does not present us with even a prima facie contradictory of the proposition 'It was predictable that he would overtake the bus', since 'that action' has given way to something different. But is it not the same action that is predictable under the one description, but not under the other? The actions are the same if and only if to overtake the bus is the same action as to exceed the speed limit, and, in the sense in which we are talking about the actions *predicted*, this is not so. In that sense we were talking not about an action whose criterion of identity was that of the concrete action that in fact ensued; rather, 'that action' was to be understood more generally—the highest common factor of whatever counted as making true the prediction 'He will overtake the bus'.

The analogy here with intention is closest with the verb 'intend', as when it is said that Harvey intended to overtake the bus, and did so. Again, what he intended to do would equally have come about even if the character of what he did had been different. Within certain limits, of course, but limits which allow for a difference in speed. So, in the sense in which what he did is what he had intended to do, 'what he did' is not interchangeable with phrases which designate the historic event, the event in all its actuality, known and unknown. The constraints on interpreting 'He intended to do what he did' are set by the truth of particular instances, such as 'He intended to overtake the bus'.

Since talk of an intention or intending to V tends to place us at a time before there is anything describable as someone's intentional Ving, or someone Ving intentionally, there is the possibility of differences in what the agent knows when the one rather than the other way of speaking is appropriate. We saw one example with respect to the knowledge needed for an identifying reference, and we find another with respect to unforeseen consequences. We may be said to be Ving intentionally if our voluntary action produces Ving as a known consequence, but it need not have been at any point our intention to V. More on this in §8.1.

Again, though somewhat differently, while both intending to V and Ving, a person may not V intentionally, since he may not have intended to V in the way he in fact did. I intend to embarrass someone by disclosing a confidence about him; I do indeed embarrass him, but by making a fool of myself in speaking out. The problem here is not one of finding a recipe for excluding a 'wayward' or 'deviant' causal chain, but what is required is that the intention be specified more fully: I intend to embarrass Smith by *revealing something to his disadvantage*, not by some other feature of my utterance.

There are, finally, more puzzling contexts in which questions of means to an end come to the fore. We have already noted that the agent need not feel assured of success in Ving in order to have the intention to V, though there must, as far as he is concerned, be some available means to the end sought. If this latter condition fails, we may speak in terms of an *aim* rather than an intention. So it may be an aim of yours to become rich and famous, even if, not knowing how you might, you have not formed the intention to do so. Perhaps the most you can do is seize any opportunities which offer to advance your aim. If it is a matter of intending to V by doing x, it must be believed that doing x stands a good chance of providing a suitable means to that end. So, if A is a poor shot, he hopes rather than intends to hit a distant target. On the other hand, if he succeeds, can he not be said to have hit the target intentionally so long as he considers that his efforts, engaged upon with that end in view, stand some chance of success?

But if that—some chance of success—is all that is required, *A* could surely claim to have thrown a six intentionally if he threw a die hoping for this outcome. This would not appear acceptable, but now suppose that throwing the die will have a certain consequence— *B* will be ruined financially if a six is uppermost. Then *A*, wishing to ruin *B*, may throw the die in an attempt to bring about this consequence, and, if he succeeds, he can be said to have ruined *B* intentionally.

To reveal the order in our apparently inconsistent intuitions we must see how the various possibilities fit into a pattern of means and ends. A person may throw a die intentionally, but not throw a six intentionally, since, while he did indeed throw the die in such a way that a six came uppermost, and that throw was intentional, there is not a specific way of throwing the die which raises the probability of a six and which he intentionally adopted. For the six to be the intended outcome, there has to be something he did to produce that number rather than another, but while he knows no way of favouring the one outcome over the other, he does have a means, unreliable though it is, for producing a six—namely, throwing the die. Here, where the choice is between throwing the die and not throwing the die, the former does raise the probability of getting a six over the latter. So, suppose the task were to make a pattern of six dots to be visible on the table. There are various ways in which this might be achieved, including throwing a die with the requisite face uppermost. This is a state of affairs which *A* can be said to have brought about intentionally if he throws the die with this aim and is successful. Unreliable though it is, throwing the die has the advantage over not throwing the die—as, indeed, over many other acts—as a means to the desired end. Compare: there is a device which flashes six dots when a marble is dropped into it, but does so on average only once in every six occasions. If I drop a marble into it, hoping to elicit six dots, and do so, can I not be said to have produced the pattern intentionally?

Again, consider the man who, eager for riches, buys a ticket in a lottery. May it be said that he became wealthy intentionally? We could not say that *A* intended to get a six as against another number, since he knew of no way of favouring that outcome, but we could say that he intended to ruin *B*, since he did have a way of raising the probability of that event. We cannot say that the man who enters the lottery intends to get a winning rather than a losing ticket, the means once more being lacking, and here it is less readily said that he intended to get wealthy by purchasing a ticket, since the chances of success are so remote. If the person does succeed, it would be less misleading to say that he had achieved one of his *aims*, though perhaps the pattern of means–end reasoning is sufficiently in evidence to warrant *some* talk of acquiring a fortune intentionally. He adopted a means to that end which was most unlikely to pay off, but it did in fact serve to bring about the end desired.

This discussion of intention has been largely negative, the aim being to remove some of the misconceptions on which contemporary treatments founder, and which lead to unneeded complexities in analyses of the concept. Likewise with our examination of the future auxiliaries and the verb 'want'. With these preliminaries behind us we shall be better placed to stay on course when we embark on a more positive account of action, practical reasoning, and intention in the next two chapters.

6

Action

A natural—perhaps naturalistic—perspective on action began to take shape with our observation that with animals, as well as with human beings, we have a contrast between reflex movements and such purposive activities as those displayed by a creature as it explores the world about it. To characterize the latter category of *action* we might accordingly look for a common denominator to both the more primitive and the more sophisticated instances; a matter, perhaps, of a complex state of mind, manifested with animals only in their behaviour, but manifested with us in what we say as well as in what we do.

This general perspective has the merit of taking us away from a Cartesian picture of actions, whether conceived of as movements of the limbs directed by a spiritual being at the helm within, or as movements having psychological events as their inner causes. However, our alternative needs more support than mere divergence from these positions affords. Consider the following, seemingly simple, issue. Most acts of blinking are pure reflexes, acts of which we are not even aware. But we can also blink for a reason. What differentiates the act in its two forms? The desire to blink which marks the latter is most readily taken to explain the difference through what it contributes to generating the occurrence of the blink. If it is not a matter of the desire's figuring as cause, what might its role conceivably be? When, conversely, the blinking is of the unthinking variety, it is surely the indifference to its occurrence of any psychological happenings that makes for involuntary character. We have seen reason to query this analysis, but it is not yet clear what shape its rightful successor should take. Putting thought and desire where they belong in an acceptable account will be the task of this chapter.

6.1 MARKS OF ACTION

What is essential to action, it may be said, is its purposive or goal-directed nature. Essential, perhaps, but not sufficient, since this feature takes in reflexes as well. Peristalsis serves a purpose, but does not engage with agency in the requisite way. It is not a purpose which a creature has, just as the reason it takes place is not describable as the *creature's* reason for contracting the muscles of its alimentary canal. What is needed, on most accounts, is a further condition of a psychological character. Intention is nowadays the most commonly favoured, but other conditions have been thought worthy of inclusion in a definition of action, and we shall first give some of these our attention.

Traditionally, a central role has gone to willing, to acts of volition; notoriously, these do not appear to answer to anything which our ordinary explanations of action make familiar. It would appear, rather, that we have to do with happenings imagined to occur under the pressure of a suspect analogy with action proper. Your shaking of the clock is an observable act with, you hope, an observable effect: the clock will start to tick. If the shaking itself is to receive a comparable explanation, then it will in turn have an antecedent, but now in the shape of a mental act, an act of willing. This is naturally thought of on the model of issuing commands, as in Locke's characterization: 'a thought or preference of the mind ordering, or as it were commanding, the doing or not doing such or such a particular action' (*Essay*, II. xxi. 5). However, in so far as there is anything in our experience that might answer to this description, it arises when we *cannot* act, as when someone might say, 'Move, damn you!', to something which refuses to budge. Willings which are addressed to our limbs, rather than to what we are trying to effect with them, are even less commonly resorted to, though equally vain.

There are, of course, many uses of 'will' with which we should have no quarrel—'where there's a will there's a way', 'with the best will in the world'—and even with 'will' as a non-auxiliary verb it may be that we can call upon less questionable terms, as 'try', 'decide', and 'wish', to furnish variants. There are numerous conditions over which we may have no control and on which the success of our actions depends, but the originating act of will is entirely up to us. So it is claimed for willing, but it may also be claimed for *trying*, another notion thought to mark the point of contact between the mental and the physical.

Setting aside possible misconstruals, trying is at least something we know to have a reality and a relevance where either is dubious with willing. Could it be what distinguishes action from non-action? First, whether or not trying signifies a mental happening, a common objection to invoking the notion in such generality has to be met—namely, that there is no trying with respect to a totally effortless act, as speaking, chewing, nodding or waving may all well be. This we may grant, but not as a point of great substance; it is simply that, if an action is thwarted in its early stages, we shall speak of trying with respect to those stages, otherwise not. However, while we may withhold 'try' when everything proceeds smoothly, the action engaged upon when it is invoked may be identical: it is just that it receives a description in these terms only if it breaks down. So, if Rachel attracts Rebecca's attention by waving, there need be no call to invoke this description, though on another occasion an identical act will count as no more than trying if, say, something comes in front of Rebecca to block her view of Rachel. Again, if I try to reach you by telephone and fail, I may do just what I do when I try and succeed, the only difference residing in what you do or don't do—namely, pick up the receiver. Of course, in many cases we introduce 'try' because of the *efforts* needed to overcome obstacles, but these will be cases where 'try' will apply when we have success as well as when we have failure. Here we may recall the similar pattern with 'want', this verb being favoured when we foresee a possible hitch to carrying through our plans.

This suggests that any extension of trying to cover action generally will not take us to an antecedent of a different character—mental rather than behavioural—but we are directed to nothing more than the initial stages of the action in question. Trying, thus extended, could then provide us with a criterion for action, though one which would, of course, be very much parasitic on a prior understanding of the latter. Trying is not an act with a distinct identity which occurs as an antecedent of action generally in any sense other than this: every action has an initial phase. If there is anything beyond the very beginnings of the act, it involves a *grammatical* shift, not a move to an anterior mental event. Thus, if 'I was unable to' does not report a failed attempt, this may be because the action is one I cannot even try to perform, as making my finger glow. Here the 'cannot' is logical: for me, nothing even counts as trying to do this, since there is nothing in my repertoire of actions which I believe to stand any chance of having such an outcome.

It may still be felt that 'try' has no place unless there is some question of effort expended, that we should say only that A *went* to V if an effortless action fails. Very well, but, as far as the supposed involvement of the mental is concerned, the conclusion is the same. So, I went to raise my arm, but it stayed put; I went to speak, but not a word came out. It would seem that, for 'I went to' to gain any purchase, there must again have been the beginnings of the act. After all, if we are to speak of being thwarted, of meeting with resistance, even just of failure—as 'I was unable to' would normally report—it is necessary to have something under way, something to be checked. How otherwise might our powerlessness be brought home to us? If one's arm is totally paralysed, with not even the very beginnings of movement possible, then the situation is as wiggling the ears is for most of us. That is, there is then no going to move, no trying, in the sense of getting at least the first stages of the movement under way, but only experimental muscular flexings, flexings which are not known to have the desired outcome, but which, it is hoped, just might do so. This point is important. It is sometimes thought that even total paralysis of a limb does not exclude an attempt at moving it, but, if even the very beginnings of the relevant movement are beyond our powers to initiate, it seems we must turn elsewhere, to other muscular flexings, however futile. And, if even this desperate expedient is excluded, then, indeed, willing is no doubt all that remains, but only as an ineffectual command to unheeding limbs.

But if action does not require an anterior mental happening of this kind, does it not at least require intentionality? Is that not indeed its hallmark? Possible objections to making intentionality necessary for action might rest on certain of the confusions exposed above, as when it is erroneously said that Oedipus, in marrying his mother, performed an action, but did not marry his mother intentionally. However, there are other considerations. First, the term 'action' presents a difficulty, in that everyday speech does not align it exclusively with the use which interests us, and even letting ourselves be guided by the usual illustrations of that use does not exclude all uncertainty. The difficulty arises with movements which are not to be grouped with such reflex acts as ducking an unexpected missile, or clutching one's chair to avoid falling, yet which need not occur together with an appropriate intention. Thus, cupping one's head in one's hands, absently drumming one's fingers on the desktop, or running one's hand through one's hair—even whistling or humming as one walks or works. Think too of the various expressions and movements displayed when talking or listening to another: raising one's eyes heavenwards, curling one's lips in contempt or disbelief, moving the head to one side, gesturing with the hands, laughing, and so forth. Add to this the category of things done from habit, as with the movements involved in getting dressed or brushing one's teeth, and it becomes even more unclear just what is to be reckoned an action. Many of these are things we could do in our sleep, so little do they require our attention; indeed, many of them are things we *do* engage in when asleep, as the example of sleepwalking shows.

Whether or not an intention is necessary to action, it can be deemed sufficient, and this allows us to assign much habitual or automatic behaviour to the category. Recall the example of being engrossed in a book, where the intention behind our turning of the pages is brought home to us when we turn two by mistake. Or again, when getting dressed we perpetrate a mismatch of button and buttonhole. We may not be able to speak of *forming* an intention, but that does not mean that 'intentional(ly)' is excluded. However, this leaves many cases where any talk in terms of intention is unreal, even though *action* still seems applicable. Many of the things we do we do for no particular reason, or indeed with little knowledge of their occurrence, but we might none the less consider those of them actions that appear to be the same whether or not accompanied by any intention.

Note that when 'intend' is used there is generally a greater distance from the action than with 'mean', the latter being better suited to the case where we are offering an explanation of an action. So, 'I meant to put it in the drawer' is more readily said than 'I meant to become a lawyer', though 'intend' will do for either. 'I meant to become a lawyer' suggests that becoming a lawyer is something one can achieve in relatively few steps, like signing a document, the speaker either denying that he achieved this accidentally, or asserting that, while he had had it in mind to perform the act, he somehow did not get around to doing so. Because 'intend' may set a distance between thought and action, between plan and execution, it is not the best choice if the act is one to which no thought is given.

We should certainly narrow the concept of action excessively if we required that an intention to act have taken shape previous to the

acting, but, even with 'intentionally', or with 'mean', there is another
restriction, both being suited to acts which have an effect—as already
noted for the adverb. It is useful to consider this in terms of doing
something unintentionally, as when we unintentionally startle someone by suddenly entering the room, or when we unintentionally
knock over a vase when waving our arms about. Here what is unintended is quite plainly an *effect* of our action. Consider now 'I unintentionally sniffed'. Coming straight after such examples, this may
sound odd, since it suggests the unlikely event of my somehow coming up with a sniff when I had intended to bring off something else.
It would be like speaking of a sniff as 'accidental': if there is nothing
I might do *to* sniff, then I cannot sniff accidentally. For the same
reason, it would be strange to ask someone who spoke whether he
had meant to do so.

Clearly, if acting intentionally is a matter of acting to bring about
a certain effect, the notion of action is being presupposed. But is there
not also sniffing intentionally in the sense of sniffing with some intention? It may be questioned whether the latter is a sense of the former,
but, if there is sniffing with an intention, there is also sniffing with
no intention, and I am inclined to reckon both as actions for the
reason mentioned—it is a matter of behaviour which would appear
to be the same whether or not an intention can be cited, behaviour
which in either case is under our control.

But there is also intending *to* V, as intending to sniff or to speak.
That is right. You can intend to do such things; that is, it makes sense
to speak of intending to do them, and that proves something which
the fact that you may want to sniff or speak does not. You may want
to V even though you know Ving to be impossible, whereas a belief
in its possibility is required for the intention. Once more, however,
the notion of action is being presupposed. An action is something it
makes sense to say one intends to perform, since it is something over
which one has control, something which it is up to the agent to perform, when circumstances allow.

Rather than 'intentional', the epithet best suited to actions generally is 'voluntary'. I may insult someone intentionally—that was the
effect aimed at and achieved—and there is no redundancy in this use
of the adverb, but, since one does not find oneself involuntarily giving voice to a string of offensive remarks, 'I insulted him voluntarily'
has a pleonastic ring—at least when taken at its broadest: the claim
rebutted could be that the insult was performed under duress.

'Voluntary', taken thus broadly, focuses more directly upon the character of the action—to its character, I should say, *as* action—whatever its effects, whereas 'intentional' directs us to the latter, to the specific outcome. Moreover, whereas intentionality is something which may or may not be imposed upon an act without there being otherwise any difference, there is a quite different 'feel' about, for instance, a voluntary as against an involuntary cough. There may also be no doubt in our minds that what we did was a voluntary act, something within our control, though we can still be at loss for an answer when asked why we did it, what our intention was.

While 'voluntary' is the preferred term, there may still be doubts whether it applies to the various idle or unthinking acts instanced, the main question for decision being whether behaviour which we *can* control is to be reckoned voluntary, even though on the given occasion no control is exercised, as with our unthinking smiles and frowns. I am inclined to regard behaviour as voluntary if it is of a *kind* which one can control, can choose to perform, even if on the given occasion one does not. More accurately, I am inclined with this proviso: it is to be of a kind which one can *directly* control—that is, where it is not a question of an effect of anything one does. So, we can increase our pulse rate by running, and by shifting our gaze from a near to a distant object we know we shall alter the focus of our eyes. If these changes are to be considered voluntary, it is only in a secondary sense—namely, because they are voluntarily brought about, though they differ from, for example, the movements of one's hands, in that the latter still remain under one's control once under way. We cannot vary our pulse rate at will, as we can move our hand this way or that as we please. Again, it may be correct to describe a sneeze or a yawn as involuntary, though it is not entirely out of one's control—we can stifle a yawn, or even prevent the sneeze from coming about, though neither yawning nor sneezing itself has, in my view, the character of a voluntary act.

Here we may note that, when an action is spoken of as voluntary, it may not be clear in which aspect it is being thought of as having this feature. A fully voluntary action will be one where the agent has direct control of its inception, continuation, and termination, as with whistling: we can choose when to start whistling, together with the variations in the whistling from then on until the point where we decide to stop. With blinking, on the other hand, we can choose when to start, but once started it may be over and done with in a trice, leaving no room for variations to be introduced. With laughing, by contrast, we may not choose to start, but we can usually stop if we try.

Suppose you are fast asleep. Is it too outlandish to suggest that, when you pull the bedclothes up around yourself to keep out the cold, what you are doing may be set alongside, rather than against, instances of action? Such movements bear the marks of purposiveness: they are geared to the attainment of an end, they adapt to local conditions, and they terminate when the end has been achieved. But you do not, we shall suppose, have any awareness of what you are doing. The persistence in a pattern of goal-directed behaviour, but with a degree of flexibility in coping with resistance to one's efforts, makes for a marked contrast with plainly reflex behaviour, as when our leg suddenly jerks whilst we sleep, or with such involuntary performances as snoring. Even if we are awake when we make a reflex movement, such a movement lacks the deliberateness, the control, of the sheet-adjusting manœuvres. Perhaps the main reason for distinguishing these from fully conscious actions lies in the different relation to responsibility. When asleep, a person cannot be remonstrated with, asked to take others into account, and of course has no idea of the consequences of what he is doing. But it could be that in other respects what we are dealing with is essentially the same as the action of someone wide awake. At all events, whether or not this is accepted as action, even conscious belief is too strong a condition to impose in general, but what we have to do with is more by way of a *type* of movement. By that I mean that a movement engaged in will count as an action if it is of a type or kind with which a belief is in general associated, rather than that the condition is required to hold on any occasion on which we can correctly speak of action.

To sum up this preliminary, it would seem that actions are not identifiable as such through being the upshot of an originating mental act which trying or willing might furnish. It would seem, too, that the concepts of intention and action are linked only to the extent that an action is an item of behaviour which it makes sense to think of as performed with some intention, not that there must be one. It makes sense to think of it in these terms, precisely because it is in our power, within varying limits, to perform as and when we wish. We possess a repertoire of acts over which we exercise control and which we can enlist in pursuit of our goals. What is important is that they can be thus enlisted, not that they should occur only in this capacity.

6.2 CHARACTERIZING ACTION

A movement counts as an action, then, if it is voluntary. What does that mean? Wittgenstein suggests: 'Anything we can *order* a child to do we call voluntary' (*LPP* 36). But an order may prompt a frightened reaction. It has to be a matter of acting for a reason—which an order indeed provides. An action, for human beings, is the kind of movement that can be engaged in for a reason, something it makes sense to speak of deciding or choosing to do. What does it mean if we are speaking of an animal? Our earlier discussion focused on distinguishing animal action from purely reflex acts. Both forms of behaviour can be described as having a purpose, but with the former we find greater flexibility, greater adaptability to changing circumstances, whereas reflex reactions are over and done with rapidly, and allow minimum variation from occasion to occasion. Take the activities of preening and grooming. Unlike reflex acts, these are not an all-or-nothing affair, but may be carried on for a greater or a lesser time, being brought to completion if nothing intervenes, but being interrupted if more pressing demands arise.

It would seem that reference to some psychological condition should enter into a fuller characterization, and this is most readily achieved, in a way that maintains continuity with the human case, by regarding as action behaviour which can manifest a belief or a desire through the variations introduced into it, as preening and grooming are varied according to the needs of the circumstances. This is intended as a verbal elaboration of our earlier formulation, not a substantive addition. A matter of: you can, should you wish, redescribe behaviour which qualifies as action as a manifestation of belief and/or desire; it makes sense to give a description in these terms. It is the more basic attributes of the behaviour, the plasticity which the contrast with reflex movements highlights, that secures the possibility of this further characterization. We shall now try to elicit what is comprised in this common denominator of human and animal action, exploiting the links between knowledge, perception, and action which we have already touched upon.

Observation of an animal moving about its environment may yield much the same patterns of behaviour, deserving of much the same psychological descriptions, as observation of a human being: things are recognized and approached, examined, pursued, disregarded, avoided, and so forth. Perception, clearly, has a central place in any such account. Equally clearly, perception involves knowledge: the animal learns of the presence of something at a certain location, it recognizes it as of a certain character. Moreover, we cannot detach perception from action. The behaviour that gives proof of perception is behaviour that testifies to knowledge or awareness, behaviour which is geared to the location and character of what is perceived; in short, purposive, adaptive movements which qualify as actions.

In making this connection we favour knowledge over the more usual condition of belief. Is this in order? It is true that belief may apply where knowledge does not, but there is a respect in which it is the less problematic case of knowledge that is fundamental, thought and belief being, as noted, concepts to which it is appropriate to retreat only in special cases. Thus, we have a pattern of behaviour which allows us to say that the bird knows where its nest is, and it is when it engages in such behaviour even though its nest has been removed that we may say, if with some awkwardness, that it thinks or believes that its nest is in such and such a place. But there had to be the pattern licensing talk of knowledge before we could have the entitlement to speak of mere belief. It may seem all one whether we speak of getting belief by subtraction from knowledge or of arriving at knowledge by an addition to bare belief. But this symmetry is deceptive, since without relevant instances of knowledge we should often not be entitled to specify the belief in the given terms.

In so far as either knowledge or belief is at the heart of action, there is no calling upon either to explain action, but they enter only at the level of redescription. In terms of knowledge, the basic case will be one of behaviour which testifies to an awareness of the where-abouts of something, the kind of behaviour which gives proof of per-ception, as when, in flight or pursuit, a creature shows its appreciation of the location of pursuer or pursued, and, at the same time, a desire to escape or to pursue. If we wish to speak of think-ing, it will be a matter of thinking that is done *with* acting, that is manifested in immediate responses to the surroundings, rather than thoughts that have already formed when the agent comes to the scene of the action. Clearly, whether animals or human beings are our con-cern, a characterization of action is better served by eschewing talk of thought in favour of talk of knowledge, wherever possible, given how the former so readily suggests a silent soliloquy, ruminations and deliberations *in foro interno*.

Since behaviour is being held to provide a direct ground for invoking the psychological description, the explanatory value of the latter *vis-à-vis* the former will, as indicated, be nil. We do not, for instance, explain how the bird is able to find its way to its nest by saying that it knows where it is situated, if this latter just rings a possible change on the former. If a substantive step is to be found, it is in verifying the credentials of the behaviour to be so described. Thus, behaviour which shows knowledge has to conform to an established pattern, as when the bird shows over time a knowledge of the whereabouts of its nest, such regularity being needed if coincidence is to be excluded. It is also a matter of behaviour which is a part of an extended performance, such as getting about the environment, a particular item of behaviour qualifying as action because it can be seen to have a part in a larger such pattern. If a fleeting segment of such a performance is considered in isolation, there may be no way of knowing whether it is to be classified as action or as a mere reflex or tropism.

Although our observations have been directed at animals, it is clear that we could equally have been speaking of human action. Here too we may give a central place to movements which are under the control of perception. The account which was in fact proposed—in terms of the voluntary, of movements under our control—appears to invoke quite different concepts, and it is of interest to see how the two approaches may join up. To characterize human action in these terms is hardly enlightening; the characterization steers us clear of a mistaken emphasis on intention, but otherwise does no more than isolate the concepts which need to be elucidated. We shall find that the more primitive conception of purposive behaviour furnishes a more substantive analysis.

We start, then, with the idea of purposive behaviour, identified through its contrast with a mere reflex—behaviour in which a creature is often found to *persist*, as well as which it may vary, behaviour which invites description using such terms as 'knows', 'believes', and 'wants'. Consider further how this psychological vocabulary may be justified. Our concern is with knowledge and belief as these relate to action. With human beings there are innumerable beliefs which do not engage with anything we do, and, even with those which figure in practical reasoning, some are more closely bound up with action than others. In the present connection the most important are beliefs that such and such is a means to a certain end, as when you know or believe that you can open the door by turning the handle, or clean your glasses by wiping them with a cloth—that is, you believe that a certain sequence of movements will have, or is likely to have, a certain upshot. Against the assumption of a relevant desire, it is not difficult to regard such activities as *manifesting* knowledge or belief. When the knowledge is of this practical variety—knowledge how to do something—extension of the notion to animals is not unreasonable. There is, of course, a dimension absent with animals in that they cannot be said to know why they are doing what they are doing, but the notion of a practical ability none the less has application, and is readily enough formulated in terms of knowledge. Belief, as we have seen, is more troublesome, but, if understood as no more demanding than knowledge, can be accommodated.

What of desire? If we are looking at the more primitive instances, we shall not want behaviour which *follows on* a desire or intention, since this would surely require the agent to formulate the desire or intention in thought as a prelude to acting upon it. It strikes you that it would be pleasant to sit in the sun, so, when you finish tidying your desk, you make for the outdoors. For an animal unable to look ahead in thought in this way, we are obliged to find a feature of the actual behaviour at the time which warrants use of 'wants'—a possibility also, of course, with human behaviour. As already indicated in §5.3, we frequently act intentionally even without giving the matter prior thought, as in habitual or in spontaneous behaviour. All we have to make use of is the purposiveness already presumed, but this appears adequate: the creature's ability to persist or persevere in a pattern of behaviour, coupled with its ability to modify a current pattern in such a way as to cope with changes in circumstances, perhaps even an ability to discard a strategy and to adopt an alternative—such behaviour is rich enough in marks of *wanting*, whether our subjects be human or non-human animals.

My principal concern is to suggest that action can be equated with purposive behaviour identifiable as such without hypotheses as to knowledge, belief, intention, or desire. Whether any of the latter may enter into our description non-hypothetically is secondary. Consider a bird dropping a shell onto a hard surface to break it open. We may say that it knows how to break shells open, that it knows or believes it can break them open in this way. These descriptions are progressively less apposite, and we may prefer to go a stage back and settle for saying that it is *able* to open shells by dropping them onto a hard surface. This gets in the idea of purposiveness via the implication of a successful accomplishment, so of something aimed at—given the part perception plays: the bird is also able to digest what it extracts from the shell, but that is not action.

The flexibility and adaptability we are envisaging may also provide us with grounds for saying what would have happened with a change of circumstances. For instance, had certain other obstacles been placed in its way, had there been other variations to cope with, the creature would have adjusted its behaviour accordingly. This variability underlies the notion that there are other things that it could have done had it wanted to. Once more, the behaviour which wasn't, but which might have been, is not envisaged as having been preceded by thoughts as to desirability, but here too it has to be a matter of a description tied to the action, a matter of there being other things such that, if the creature had set about doing them, it would have succeeded. A foundation for the notion of voluntariness, to be built upon in Chapter 9, is given with such a consideration.

This linking of action to purposive behaviour, without presumption as to thought, appears to be necessary if we are to give an account of action when there *is* thought, since the notions of belief and desire presume action, in a way we shall now show. Human behaviour can be allowed to testify to a belief only in so far as we can say that it is directed to an end the agent wants. Thus, if *A* is V*ing*, we reason that *A* must believe that V*ing* leads to something he wants, otherwise he wouldn't be doing it. And this approach, surely, presupposes that we have to do with action. That is, it is a matter of something which *A* can do or not do, depending on his desires. But desire makes a similar presumption. We argue: if *A* V*s*, knowing or believing that this will lead to *E*, then—with certain provisos—*A* must want *E*. In this case, the behaviour can indeed be a criterion for the wanting—we do not require an independent test—but the argument is sustainable only if the movement is under *A*'s control, is an action. These points bring out the way beliefs and desires are commonly appealed to in *explaining* behaviour, when the basic case, as indicated in §3.3, is one in which a more direct description of the behaviour is being offered.

The point of the preceding considerations is to show both the possibility and the necessity of elucidating action in terms which make no presumption of an ability to think—as is to be expected, if intention presupposes action—but these last observations also reinforce an earlier objection to reckoning a movement an action if and only if it is caused in the right way by beliefs and desires. We have first to secure action before we can make sense of wanting. To think of wanting as given independently of action, of the action as then discovered to be produced by wanting, is surely an error. Indeed, at this basic level, belief and desire become absorbed into the action, vanishing altogether as potential causes of movement.

While essentially the same concept of action would appear to be available for animals as well as for human beings, with us the relevant desires and beliefs may also be expressed verbally, or formulated in unspoken words. A position which the present approach may be used to counter is one that elevates this latter aspect to a definitional status. Thus, when attempting to characterize human action, we are inclined to see occurrent thoughts and associated behaviour as providing the factors to be put together in our characterization, where the thoughts comprise both thoughts as to desirability and thoughts as to means. Take the formula 'Thinking it desirable to V, A Vs'; so, thinking it desirable to cough, you cough. Suppose we cancel any implication of action which V may suggest. How can this implication be restored? Here is one possibility which our discussion to date might be thought to favour. With some kinds of movements we find that a different assessment of value goes with a different pattern of behaviour: thinking we shall be more comfortable if we turn over, we turn over; having no views about the desirability of a change in position, we stay put. With other kinds of movement this is not so, the same bodily changes taking place whatever we think. Hiccups, sneezes, yawns, slips, and shiverings occur regardless of our thoughts, and, of course, things which act upon us are no respecters of our wishes. Actions, we might say, are happenings of the former kind, and the reason for one's action just is the reason *with* which one acts, an accompanying rather than a causative relation.

This account is, I believe, on target, but only so long as the thought component is correctly construed. First, while desire may be considered the central notion around which that of action is built, the behaviour involved will typically manifest a belief as to means as well as a desire, and the desire itself may be identified via a thought or belief. There may, for instance, be nothing to choose between 'wanting to turn over' and 'thinking it desirable to turn over'. Wanting as experiencing a desire may be at some distance from believing, but wanting as thinking something worth pursuing is another matter. This is, after all, the kind of wanting which, unlike an urge or a crav-

ing, can completely vanish with a change in belief. It is with the introduction of thoughts that we are likely to take a false step, construing
these not as beliefs which may be manifested in what is done, beliefs
which may be attributed to someone whose action is automatic, but
as inner sayings to oneself, thoughts running though the agent's head
at the time of acting.

A preoccupation with thoughts as inner speech episodes preceding
or accompanying behaviour is undoubtedly one reason why a causal
account is taken to have the right general shape, action being viewed
as behaviour caused by, rather than behaviour which expresses or
manifests, a desire and/or belief. To enlarge upon these differing view-
points, let us go back to the problem of distinguishing a voluntary
from an involuntary act, as with a cough or a blink. In seeking to characterize acts of the former variety, we naturally seize upon associated
thoughts and desires, and, looking for a relation between these and the
behaviour, are tempted to invoke that of causation. However, if, as is
also likely, these thoughts and desires are thought of as verbalized,
even if only inwardly, we are left with a truly impenetrable relation
between the psychological and the behavioural. How could saying to
oneself such things as 'I must blink', 'Let me blink', or 'Now is the
time to blink' be of any consequence for action? No one would suppose that actually uttering these words might be what sets an eyelid in
motion; how, when said to oneself, might they acquire such a power?
But it is not that thought has no place here. It is simply that it is a
matter of thought as a belief which may be revealed in what we do, as
well as in what we say, whether out loud or to ourselves. The behaviour is on a par with the latter, not its mysterious upshot. True, we
may be reluctant to speak of thought in any literal sense unless the
agent is also capable of putting that thought into words, but even then
it is not necessary that words, spoken or unspoken, should precede the
behaviour. So, the doctor asks you to cough and you cough. Nothing
whatsoever need run through your head as you comply, but the only
formulation of the thought may be after the event, when you give a
verbal expression of the rationale to which occurrence of the cough has
already testified. Again, suppose a belief as to means amounts to
knowledge. You know, and do not merely believe, that you purl by
doing a plain stitch backwards, but, while your knowledge may be
evident from your knitting action, there appears to be no way of making sense of the claim that your fingers are moved by your knowing
what you know. It was suggested above that our primitive idea of

cause is to be explicated in terms of one thing acting upon another. Primitive it may be, but it is the idea that is relevant when mental causation is thought of as involving a generative cause, and it is an idea that is seen as unserviceable when knowing how or knowing that are the relevant psychological conditions.

We may also call upon the notions of choosing and deciding to make the point. An action is something you can choose or decide to do. If this were to be interpreted causally, actions would be understood as items of behaviour which choosing and deciding set in train, and it would make sense to say that one might speak *by* choosing to do so, whereas it is clear that the relation between choosing to speak and speaking is more intimate than the separation required for causation would allow. To give our alternative analysis, we note, first, that choosing may itself be an action of a specific kind—namely, one of selecting: you choose a chocolate from among those offered. The connection with action is more general when it is a question of choosing *to* V, as choosing to speak; here it is a matter of Ving after having considered the alternatives, weighed up the merits of the available options. This—opting for one's preference—is choosing as it interests us: a matter of an action, but not of an action as specific as that of selecting. We do not have to think in terms of something *interposed* between the deliberating and the acting, but we may, given the antecedent deliberations, speak of choosing to V just on the strength of the Ving. An action is indeed the sort of thing you can choose to do, but in the sense that choosing can enter into our description in this way. The analogous point in terms of deciding will be developed in the next chapter.

Finally, while it is to the thought or belief describable as a state or capacity that appeal has been made, we noted earlier that thought as something episodic had to be acknowledged. Moreover, when we consider the mental antecedents of action we naturally fasten on the unmistakably episodic happenings given with a decision, say, or with the realization that something is so. How to fit such happenings into our scheme is also a question for Chapter 7.

6.3 ACTION AND PURPOSE

We have suggested that human action be approached through a conception of action that is sufficiently basic as to apply equally to animals. However, it is not always apparent how ascriptions of purpose to animals may be justified, and we shall now give further consideration to this topic. To offer a behavioural analysis of a psychological concept may be thought to be taking the easy way out. However, if there is any plausibility to such an analysis, it may well be because it is *purposive* behaviour that is being invoked, and this is not a feature which is either crude or simple, not a feature to which a notion of 'mere bodily movement' can hope to do justice.

We may not hesitate to invoke such notions as those of doing x for the sake of y, of having y as a goal or aim, even of doing x in the belief that it will lead to y, but it may not be entirely obvious what it is, for example, for a creature to have y as its goal. It seems innocuous enough to say that the bird is collecting twigs in order to build its nest, but, if it is not capable of envisaging its goal in thought, as we can, what does this amount to? Are we not confined to saying that it engages in activities which simply *have* a certain outcome, activities which, as it happens, serve a certain purpose, rather than that the purpose, in any sense, gives the creature's reason for acting thus?

There is one case which might be thought straightforward: it is not necessary to envisage the goal as before the creature's mind, since it is right there in view. So, the purposiveness displayed when one animal is pursuing another presents nothing like the same problem as when an animal embarks upon an apparent search for something outside its present environment, as with the squirrel which goes off to retrieve its hoard of nuts. It is, of course, just such behaviour that invites talk of a capacity to form an image of what is sought. How otherwise might there be any question of an end desired, anything other than blind behaviour?

However, it is not clear that we can deal so simply even with the allegedly straightforward case, since the animal's goal is more accurately specified not as x—its prey—but as *getting* x, and that is not something in view. Again, in some cases it may well be that we simply cannot say what the creature is aiming at. Not because it is difficult to tell; rather, in complicated cases it may simply not be defined. On the other hand, it seems apparent from the way a creature comes back on course after deviations that it is bent on getting to a certain destination, whatever the problems other patterns of behaviour may pose.

Recall our earlier observation that the completion of one stage in an activity may be the cue to move on to another stage. This requires the ability to recognize when the successive stages have been reached, but not necessarily a conception of an overall plan into which they enter. What is necessary—to warrant talk of an aim or purpose—is that the creature should show a degree of persistence in its behaviour, enough to confer a pattern on its responses; it is to display an accommodation to its changing surroundings in such a way that the probability of such and such an end state's ensuing is maintained, ideally, at as high a level as the creature's circumstances and ability allow.

Consider a dog which is yelping, its paw having been trapped. How are we to decide whether its behaviour is to be reckoned action? Once more, it is not sufficient that the yelping should serve a purpose. So, too, do sweating and salivating, but these are not actions. On the other hand, there are certain purposes which, if a case can be made out for discerning them, will make for such character, purposes evidenced in behaviour which is more plastic, which does not always follow the same course, but which adapts to circumstances. Such behaviour is to be found simply in the fact of variability, of its sometimes going this way, sometimes going that, sometimes terminating at a certain point, sometimes continuing beyond that point; not, of course, in a directionless way, but geared to the attainment of an end, as with avoidance and pursuit.

If, for instance, we can establish that the dog is yelping in order to secure help, that will identify its yelping as something more than a mere reaction on a par with shivering, as already noted with respect to the question of a communicative intention behind a cat's mewing. Unfortunately, the pattern of behaviour here may offer no basis for deciding between action and mere reaction. That is, if the dog starts yelping when its paw gets trapped, and ceases yelping once it is released, we may consider that we have simply witnessed a distressed reaction which the trapping of its paw induces and which its release brings to an end, yet this is the pattern we should also expect if the yelping could be considered purposive in the relevant sense.

Is the way the behaviour is initiated critical? Purposive behaviour of the requisite kind is behaviour which, figuratively speaking, is sensitive to information gained through perception, so perhaps a condition reflecting this should somehow be accommodated with respect to the beginnings of the behaviour. However, such a condition would not appear to be sufficient: involuntary responses associated with fear may be traceable to the informational value of a stimulus. Is such a condition necessary? With human action in mind, we tend to emphasize the point of inception: we choose to act just when we do. With an animal it will be the general character of the movements once under way that we look to, and even with human action all that is critical *vis-à-vis* the initiation is that the action should be of a *kind* for which a coupling with choice is possible; not that there need have been choice in anything beyond a behavioural sense. Think, for instance, of the movements involved in eating. As you dip your spoon into the soup and transfer the contents to your mouth you may have no thoughts of any relevance, but this is just the kind of behaviour which we might advance in illustration of the voluntary.

At *Philosophical Investigations* §628 Wittgenstein remarks: 'voluntary movement is marked by the absence of surprise.' The identification 'those that don't surprise me' is one he appears to regard as appropriate to those of our voluntary acts—and this means the general run of such—that do not proceed from a decision (*LPP* 305). If a voluntary movement were to be understood as one which a desire brought into being, one might well be surprised at one's good fortune in finding one's limbs moving just when and how one wanted them to move. Here the wanting is envisaged as falling short of the acting, and linked to it by a connection that might well fail. Wittgenstein goes on to say: 'And now I do not mean you to ask "But *why* isn't one surprised here?" ' (*PI* §628). Perhaps the question is symptomatic of the misconception just mentioned (cf. *RPP* II §267; *Z* §586), but there is, I should say, something to be learned from addressing it.

One may be surprised that a voluntary act is successful in its outcome, but, at the level of movement, the level sufficient for the identification of action, and where what takes place is up to the agent, we are not surprised by what we do. At this level, the lack of surprise is itself not surprising, failure here being largely unfamiliar. But this does not look to be the more relevant consideration. That concerns, not so much lack of surprise on succeeding, as lack of surprise on engaging in the action at all. If I fear I am paralysed, but try to get to my feet all the same, I may be surprised when I succeed, but, if I know that my ability to execute the initial phases of the act has not been impaired, I shall not be surprised on managing this much. After all, if I want to do such and such and know that I can, a failure to go ahead and act would cast doubt on this description. But suppose that the desire comes with the action, that the latter gives the rationale for speaking of the former. Then what is done has no substantive explanation in terms of desire, so the lack of surprise remains unexplained. But then, if there is no antecedent desire to call upon, what is being described is an impulsive, spontaneous, action, and in that case it is surely possible that the subject should surprise himself with what he does. A timid man, I none the less come out with a daring remark, surprising myself as much as anyone else. Whether we set about Ving normally depends on our views as to the desirability of Ving. Indeed, it is precisely the variability of one's behaviour on this score that brings it, at the point of initiation, into the range of the voluntary, whereas an impulsive act is only on the fringes of that range, even if its continuation and cessation mirror one's changing assessments. So, I may well surprise myself on blurting out an unthinking comment, especially if this is out of character, but if I should continue in this vein, the other pattern will take over; I am then doing something I want and am able to do, so it is no surprise to me either that I continue or that I succeed.

With an animal, the notion of voluntary character may appear to have no application at the point where behaviour is initiated. What grounds could we have for saying that the dancing of a bee—which serves to indicate the whereabouts of a source of nectar—compares, at its point of inception, with an item of voluntary human behaviour? If the bee is found to set about dancing even when none of its fellows is in the hive to witness its performance, we should take this to tell against speaking in terms of a communicative intention, but, if the presence of some of its fellows is necessary for the performance to take place, this simply obliges us to say that the conditions which prompt the behaviour must be taken to include this further circumstance. Our specification of initiating conditions may meet with refinement upon refinement, but without, it would seem, tending towards the point at which voluntariness will be identified. Or consider blinking. For us this is nearly always automatic, unthinking, but we can also blink to order, blink at will. How could we conceivably draw such a contrast within animal blinking?

Let us focus on this last example. Suppose that we somehow manage to teach a chimpanzee that, if it blinks, it will be rewarded. Then we shall find—this is what success in teaching means—that in certain circumstances it will engage in blinking, and in such a way that it can be described as adopting a strategy to get a reward. The circumstances, along with the further behaviour of the creature, are all-important. We could not describe the bee as attempting to communicate if it was indifferent to the presence of its supposed audience. Likewise, the only animal blinking which we should accept as having the suggested purpose would have to occur in the company of other responses, as showing expectant behaviour, closely following the trainer's movements, giving attention to the area where the reward tended to come from, and so forth. The circumstances would also include triggering conditions; for example, the chimpanzee takes its cue from the appearance of the person who trained it. It is, of course, no objection that its response is caused in this way. Having an environmental cause is something its blinking has in common with blinking induced by a bright light, but the difference is that the beginning of the purposive blink is also the beginning of a period of expectancy, and other relevant responses; it marks the point where the chimpanzee has learned of something—namely, the presence of its trainer. It is also true that the more manageable aspect of its behaviour, the extended pattern subsequent to the blinking, is subject to causal constraints, but again this in no sense negates a voluntary/involuntary distinction. What matters is the pattern which the creature imposes on its behaviour in response to what it perceives. Characterization of the blinking as an action rather than a reaction requires consideration of what ensues because only in this way can we say that the animal started to blink on learning of the presence of the relevant person.

Similarly with the dog's yelping. This too requires us to take in the wider circumstances. The situation as described may offer no help in distinguishing the possibilities—action and mere reaction—but suppose we find that the presence or absence of a being who might come to its help results in a correspondingly different pattern of behaviour. If the dog continues to yelp so long as there is someone present to help, ceases once the potential helper goes, starts up anew when the person returns, and so on, then, while the initial trapping of the paw may have set off the yelping, its subsequent variations may be explicable in terms of the end suggested. It has been learned that a certain end can be attained by a certain strategy, and, because the yelping can be viewed in this light, we can regard it as a purposive action—even if the intentionality involved is intentionality at its most primitive. We may note, finally, that, in laying emphasis on the circumstances in which a response occurs, we are echoing Wittgenstein's emphasis on the importance of the *surroundings* of a movement to character as voluntary (*RPP* I §776).

6.4 ACTION AND CAUSATION

It was suggested that voluntary responses as much as involuntary reactions might have causes external to the agent. This, it might be said, is acceptable if we are speaking of animals, but it is not consistent with the peculiar autonomy which human agents enjoy. We shall now make some remarks on this topic as a preliminary to our discussion of freedom and determinism in the final chapter.

Consider 'Why did you cough?'. This may or may not invite specification of a reason; it depends on whether or not 'cough' signifies an action. But, even when an action is at stake, the question 'What caused your coughing?' is surely legitimate. Not, of course, to be answered by the person's giving the reason why he coughed, but presumably, even though the coughing was voluntary, it was the upshot of physiological happenings. Whether voluntary or involuntary, coughing, breathing, crying, and nodding surely belong with the many other happenings for which there is every expectation of finding a cause.

Again, suppose you are trying to keep a moving object in view. The movements of your eyes will then track those of the object, but you will not naturally think of the movements observed as causing your own, though they of course give you a reason for moving the way you do. But that is all it is: you do not *naturally* think in these terms when, for example, offering an explanation of your behaviour. That is just not a concern when giving your reasons for what you are doing. It is not that the object's movements *cannot* be a cause of yours in that situation. True, we may be led to think otherwise by reflecting on the consideration that it is up to us to move or not, as we please; given the undoubted truth that it is we who initiate the movement of our head or gaze, the causal role is, we might suppose, already spoken for.

An undoubted truth it is, but again, not one of a causal character; a fortiori, not one which requires us to deny a causal role to the things with which we interact, or to find a place for the special category of agent causation. According to this conception, if it is entirely up to us whether we move, it cannot be that our movement has any cause other than ourselves. Even if it should be our beliefs or desires that generate the movement, that would take it out of our hands. The distinctive feature of causation of this variety is that it stops at the agent—in contrast to event causation, where the chain of causes extends indefinitely back into the past (cf. T. O'Connor 1995: pt II).

However, it is a mistake to say that causation of one's movements either stops or starts with the agent. To say that we moved our head or shifted our gaze is normally no more to state a causal proposition than if we were to say that our head moved or our gaze shifted. When 'I shook my head' differs from 'My head shook', it does so not in what it implies as to the causation of the movement, but in its (non-causal) relation to belief and desire. Contrast shaking one's head as this normally occurs, and as it would occur if one took one's head in one's hands and shook it. With the former, but not the latter, we lose the division between action and effect which would give substance to a causal role for the action. Agent causation is a familiar and intelligible concept when based on our familiar and intelligible concept of an agent, a person seen acting upon things by tugging, twisting, or whatever, but, since there is no causing that is not itself an instance of shaking, pulling, raising, or whatever, there is nothing for 'cause' to do if all such acts are excluded.

Admittedly, we keep company with the upholder of agent causation in that we do not look to beliefs and desires to get actions under way, and it could be that one of the central aims of this view is to do justice to the notions of acting in the knowledge that p and out of a desire that q without construing these as causal conditions. Moreover, if we consider a series of changes set in train by an agent, we can acknowledge a special place for the originating act. It is special not because it is the first link in the causal chain, but because it is the first *act*, the first thing done for a reason. But, while the agent may do nothing to bring about his own movements, there is no expectation that those movements should prove detached from all previous happenings. No escape, then, from causation, but nor is there anything that can be said to take your agency from you when you do such things as poke the fire or lower the blinds; it will be *your* desire that informs the act, *your* will that is being put into effect. Your special place as an agent is amply secured by such considerations; it does not need you to do something to bring about your actions, so does not need you to stand outside the causal network to do so.

But, if I close my eyes, don't I bring it about that my eyes close? The answer is once more No if 'bring it about' means 'bring it about by some means'. On the other hand, by closing my eyes I can be said to have made it true that my eyes are closed. This outcome is now a *logical* consequence of what I have done, as is found with *making true* more generally. What makes 'pi is irrational' true is pi's being irrational, or certain facts about pi; facts in which pi's irrationality consists, not facts which *cause* this to be so (cf. Rundle 1990: §8.2). Similarly, what I do—close my eyes—has as a consequence that my eyes are closed, but this is not an independent effect; it is a logical, not a causal, consequence.

The point can have a less trivial application when there are temporal complications. When we act, there will be preceding physiological states or happenings which are necessary to the act's occurrence, along with such states or happenings simultaneous with and subsequent to the act. What we do—raise our hand—can unproblematically lead to the subsequent changes, but can we not also, by our action, bring it about that the accompanying physiological happenings take place, and even those earlier happenings without which there would have been no movement?

We do not do anything that causes the relevant physiological events to happen if these just *are* the micro-events constitutive of our act. Even more evidently, nothing earlier can stand in the relation of an effect of that act. However, the notion of making it true that *p*, or even that of bringing it about that *p*, can be detached from any implication of a temporal ordering. If event *E* is necessary to my raising my hand, then by raising my hand I make it true that *E* occurred. The causal overtones of 'make it true' may suggest that some mysterious agency is at work, one that defies the usual causal ordering, but no more is being asserted than with 'Since I raised my arm it follows that *E* had then come about'. I shall not raise my arm unless *E* has occurred is like 'I shall not raise my arm if it is paralysed'. If I succeed in the act, it follows that *E* is a reality, and that my arm is not paralysed, but there is no more backwards causation than if I make your prediction true by acting to fulfil it.

But if our actions have originating causes external to us, if they are part of a causal network sustained by the workings of our nervous system, how can it be said that they are truly *our* actions? So long as external causes operate, so long even as the causation comes from the largely unknown system of physiological happenings, from below rather than above, as it were, it seems impossible to credit the agent with the executive role which his autonomy, indeed his personal responsibility, demands. At the very least, we must be *ignorant* of the physiological causation of our movements if we are to see them in this light.

However, I do not believe we have any reason to give in to either demand—that external and physiological causes should be wanting, or at least that we should be ignorant of their operation. Consider first the physiological processes which occur with our acting. These do not have somehow to escape from the physical realm for their gross manifestations to earn the title of free actions, of actions under the control of the agent. Talk of neural causation may conjure up a picture of trying and failing to resist or thwart some superior causal agent, but if our movements, whether as of resisting or otherwise, count as an expression of our will, then they are in no way at odds with the underlying neural happenings, whether those involved in the movements at the time of their happening, or those which generate these. There is nothing remarkable or untoward in the supposition that there should be a neural condition which unmistakably presages action; its invariable occurrence could simply reflect a role in conferring voluntary character on what is done. Neuronal activity is, after all, what makes possible the movements involved in acting for an end; the causation provided is not constraint; there is no question of our coming up against such activity as if grappling with an opposing force; we are not pitted against ourselves. The notion of agency is being misconceived: a matter of an intervention, on our part, from outside; as if it required that we act upon our nervous system, that our status as free and independent agents depended on our being sufficiently distanced from the workings of our own body. Similarly, there is no inconsistency in saying that voluntary actions are to be found among the ways of behaving that our genes determine. As we shall see in Chapter 9, 'determine' does not mean 'render inevitable'.

But, if our dependence on our own physiology poses no threat, there is still causation upon us from outside to consider. Suppose that, engaged in what you would describe as looking for your slippers, you make movements which have some external agent as their cause, an alien force of which you have no inkling. You insist it was because you wanted your slippers that you went to the wardrobe, but it is surely because of the intervention of this agent that you did so.

The shift to a very different use of 'because' is readily perceptible in the transition from the familiar to the fantastic account, but even at this stage it may still be felt that a conflict is possible between the two forms of explanation. And indeed there could be. This would be brought home to you if at some point your movements diverged from their intended course without a corresponding change of mind on your part; or, more emphatically, despite a contrary state of mind. The causation would then be of significance through casting doubt on the applicability of a description in terms of *action*. That doubt would extend even to your movements up to the point of divergence, if it gave reason for supposing that, had you sought to do something different, you would none the less have found yourself doing what you have just done. Your belief or desire would not be the reason for your action because there would not have *been* an action. But, so long as action is assured, the reasons can continue to have their customary explanatory role; causal considerations are not of themselves of any account.

This is a key point of difference between the present analysis and one centred around causation. Consider what is required for someone to have acted intentionally. The causal view is not alone in insisting that the agent should have acted *because of* the relevant reasons, but, on this view, it could not be that, while having the reasons in question, the person was made to act by being pushed, for instance, since the pushing would then pre-empt the causal role which 'because of' supposedly signals (cf. Davidson 1963: 87). However, it is enough to appeal to the simple consideration that a person cannot be made to *act* by being pushed. As argued above, intentionality *presupposes* action, and this is what needs to be assured at the point where the appeal to causation is thought mandatory; it has to be, on the present account, that we have to do with a movement that is voluntary, that is of such a kind that, if A chooses to V, he can V; not only that, but if he chooses not to V, he is able to refrain. That these are not causal conditionals will be argued later (§9.3).

This complementary ability holds a crucial place in the present account, and it is worth going over the central point again. Let us suppose that, quite generally, I want to avoid injury to myself. It does not follow that a movement of mine which achieves that end, as when I withdraw my hand from something hot, is done for that reason. The movement has to be voluntary for this to be so. Even if I withdraw my hand, intending *thereby* to avoid injury, it is still true that action is presupposed if this is to give my reason. That is trivial, if the reason is to be a reason for *acting*, but I believe it can also be said that I did not withdraw my hand in order to avoid injury if the *movement* was not voluntary. Note, once more, that causal considerations are not to the point. It is enough that I act *with* the intention to avoid injury for this to give my reason. No further connection is needed; it is just that it has to be that I do indeed *act*, that I could have desisted from, as well as engage in, the movement.

The possibility which led us to these observations was, of course, quite unreal, but there are others, less fanciful. One source of doubt as to the role of our reasons comes with certain empirical investigations into choice. R. E. Nisbett and T. D. Wilson report an experiment in which passers-by, invited to choose which garment in an array of similar articles was of the best quality, made a significantly greater number of choices in favour of the rightmost article in each case. With stockings, for instance, they found that the rightmost stockings were preferred over the leftmost by a ratio of more than four to one (Nisbett and Wilson 1977: 243). However, not only did subjects not mention position when asked about the reasons for their choices; they denied that this had any bearing.

This result is on first acquaintance more disconcerting than, say, the finding that subjects, asked to think of a number, tend to favour certain digits over others. Numbers would appear to be much of a muchness in terms of their desirability, so there is ample room for causes to operate which do not connect with features which the person rates along this dimension. Here such replies as 'I don't know why I chose 7', or 'It was the first number that came into my head', are very much to be expected. Again, I may choose what and when to write, but *how* I write—the manner in which, for example, I slant and space my letters—is a matter of unthinking habit. However, if the request is to judge on the basis of perceived quality, it is unclear where *position*, a feature detached from anything relevant to quality, is to be located *vis-à-vis* indices thereof. If there is little to choose between the objects in an array, then perhaps it could become as with numbers: no really good reason for preferring one to the other, so we look for some other form of explanation. Thus, the authors suggest that the position effect might be explained by a habit of 'holding off on choice of early-seen garments on the left in favor of later-seen garments on the right' (ibid. 244). In such a case the person is not preferring one thing to another in the face of what would otherwise decide her choice. If it comes to that, if position comes to dominate despite the presence in the rejected object of qualities which the subject's behaviour in other circumstances shows her to rate more highly than those in the object selected, we shall have to ascribe a greater contribution than we

should have credited to some extrinsic feature—a feature detached
from the qualities, but one which, like the order of sampling, is none
the less relevant to our assessment of them. Position sounds ludi-
crously irrelevant, and to reduce choice to a nonsense, but, if, for
example, the article most recently contemplated makes the greatest
impression, it becomes possible to see how position could be an operative factor. It is not as if being on the right somehow presents itself
as a rival attraction to being well made, or of an agreeable colour—
as though we might have to choose between it and them. It is, rather,
that—on the authors' suggested explanation—judgements made on
the last-viewed, and therewith rightmost, objects will favour these.
We may have to concede that our avowed reasons may in such circumstances be unsure guides to our true preferences, but only because,
in effect, we forget, are unable to survey our reasons, give full value
to our successive judgements. This would reveal a respect in which we
had to be on our guard in making a choice which we should be prepared to stand by, but it would not reduce the whole procedure to one
in which our rationality had deserted us.

6.5 THE SKINNER SCHEME

The notion of action undertaken for the sake of an end is most readily understood in application to human beings, beings capable of
envisaging a goal in thought, and hence of giving verbal expression
to their aims. Indeed, although it is legitimate to speak of animals as
acting purposively, the danger remains that we should read too much
into such descriptions, as though a conclusion that the dog's yelping
was genuinely an action meant acknowledging that the dog appreciated the rationale of what it was up to, when it is *just* a certain pattern of behaviour that has been identified. It is not as if, wanting x,
the creature thinks of a means of getting x, and acts.

If we wish to give an account of purposive behaviour purged of all
unwanted psychological implications, it is tempting to turn to a
simple Skinnerian scheme in which purposiveness is explained in
terms of 'learned behavioural contingencies', a matter of action
engaged in because of consequences which it has had in the past,
rather than, as is the norm for human beings, a matter of behaviour
engaged in because of consequences which it is believed it will have
in the future (cf. Skinner 1953: ch. V).

That this scheme has a claim on our attention is in many cases undeniable, but it offers a different style of explanation from one in terms of reasons, even when animal behaviour is the object of the explanation. Our interest here is in elucidating what it is to be acting for a certain goal. What is it for a bird to be collecting twigs in order to build a nest? With the Skinnerian formula we are addressing a different question: how has it come about that the bird is collecting twigs? More accurately, since the scheme is geared to a recurrent pattern of behaviour, we are offering an explanation as to how that pattern comes to be favoured more generally, rather than seeking to explain its occurrence on a particular occasion. An analysis along these lines does not give any direct specification of a cause, but it presents us with a schema for an explanation which we could expect to fill out in causal terms: because a certain form of behaviour has had certain beneficial consequences, any causal mechanism which facilitated such behaviour could be expected to persist.

As another example of the Skinnerian pattern, consider Konrad Lorenz's limping dog (1954: 169). When Lorenz cycled in the direction of the military hospital, where the dog would have to remain tied up for hours on end, the dog would limp, but if Lorenz went in the direction of the Army riding school, with a cross-country walk in prospect, the limp would vanish and the dog would run normally. It is natural to describe such behaviour in terms of pretence or dissimulation, implying that the dog has adopted this strategy in an effort to get its master to hold a certain belief—that its leg is injured—and to act accordingly—take it out into the country rather than to the less welcome location. However, no such assumption is necessary. The dog has simply learned that a certain mode of behaviour has certain desirable consequences; it is not also required that the animal conceive of itself as pursuing the end in question.

Although it has rivals to contend with, the Skinner formula enjoys a broad application, being of service with respect not only to actions, but to other behavioural and non-behavioural happenings as well. Prima facie, an explanation of a reflex will involve investigating its causation in a way that makes for a difference from the explanation of an action, but even with a reflex there is a question which such investigation will not answer—namely, what the function of the reflex is. The characterization of a reflex movement as occurring because of the consequences which it has yields a plausible way of defining this invaluable concept: to say that the function of the heart is to pump blood through the body is to say that it is because it does this that we have a heart (cf. Rundle 1972: ch. 3). Clearly, in so far as we are supposing that the behaviour to which the Skinner formula is being fitted can already be recognized as an *action*, we shall not be looking to that formula to find an analysis of this notion. It is again the plasticity of the behaviour that matters, its modifiability in the light of perceived changes in the environment. Moreover, there is one psychological notion which it seems must be invoked in giving an account of action, as opposed to mere functionality, and that concerns, once more, the matter of recognition, the possibility that the creature should be able to recognize the state of affairs ostensibly aimed at. An outcome which fell quite outside anything of which it could become apprised is disqualified as its goal.

Consider the frantic movements of a fly trapped in a spider's web. If this is a mere reflex, it is questionable whether we should say that the fly is doing what it is doing for the sake of an end—that it is struggling to escape. The reason why contact with the web triggers this reaction may well have much to do with what that reaction has made possible in the past, so a broad functional explanation applies, but there is not, I am supposing, the plasticity that would make it appropriate to speak of action. There is accordingly, we may note, some danger of confusion in using the term 'teleological' to apply to the two patterns, difficult though they may be to distinguish.

In its application to behaviour, the Skinnerian scheme has been strenuously resisted by many—with some reason, when it has been held not merely to be in competition with explanations in terms of reasons, but even to show the latter to be misguided, a vestige of a primitive folk psychology. However, this misunderstanding should not lead in turn to a dismissal of the scheme. Its disregard of questions of belief makes it ill suited to take over in contexts where just such questions are paramount, but this neglect is a virtue when it comes to its application to uncomprehending animal behaviour. (Compare our suggested analysis of the chimpanzee's feat with the slotted sticks, where the real possibilities are reduced to those offered by chance and learning from past consequences, with no need to introduce mentalistic considerations.) Where we might have hoped to find a place for the notion of a goal envisaged, what we in fact have is in all likelihood just an instance of the Skinnerian pattern of behaviour which occurs because of the consequences it has had in the past—perhaps in the past history of the species, rather than of the given individual.

It was mentioned in §4.1 that, while intelligent animal behaviour could not be explained by an appeal to reasoning, in any literal sense, the explanations which are in place are psychological in form, making use of such notions as those of *learning* and *recognition*. Can we further smooth out the transition from the animal to the human case by making use of the Skinner formula? Are we, in invoking this formula, dealing with a primitive form of intentionality?

Laying emphasis on the belief as to future consequences which intention involves seems to make a negative answer unavoidable. Clearly, it will be at best an extended use that goes with the ascription of intentionality to, for example, the blue tit which gets at the milk by pecking away at the foil on the milk bottle. However, it is important not to set too great a gulf between the deliverances of the formula and an explanation in terms of *expected* consequences. There is an innocent enough reading of what is going on in such cases which suggests that a legitimate characterization need not represent the regularity learned as one terminating with its last experienced occurrence. It may be more arbitrary to incorporate in our description an explicit cut-off than to specify what is learned in a more open way, a way which makes talk of intentionality, while still an extended usage, more acceptable.

Thus, the bird is said to be pecking at the foil because this has enabled it to get at the milk in the past, but it would be legitimate to elaborate this as: the bird is pecking at the foil because it has learned that this enables it to get at the milk. In using the form 'enables', we do not restrict what has been learned to past successes, as we should have with 'because it learned that this *enabled* it to get at the milk'. It is not that we are obliged never to advance beyond the past-tense description, but the present-tense form is warranted in the light of the habitual character of the bird's activity. It might be said: it is one thing knowing what has happened when certain activities *have* been engaged in; it is another thing to believe that the same activities *will* have that consequence on this occasion. There is indeed this distinction, but our suggestion is that we may also invoke a description which does not sharply distinguish the two possibilities. The bird has learned that pecking the foil brings such and such results; or, the bird has learned that, if it pecks the foil, it will get at the milk. Its behaviour shows it to have learned the broader lesson.

Does the Skinnerian scheme provide a challenge to explanations in terms of the agent's reasons? Suppose that for an explanation of *A*'s present behaviour—seeking out a certain foodstuff—we follow Skinner in turning to the consequences which such an activity has had in the past, concluding that what has served to reinforce that behaviour has been the acquisition of trace elements of value to *A*'s well-being. The pattern is one we might enlist whether we are speaking about a person or an animal, though in the former case there is also the mode of explanation which the agent himself might offer, and this may make no mention of the reinforcing factor. If, let us say, an agreeable taste is cited, and this is in some way linked to the presence of the trace elements, the two explanations can happily coexist.

Suppose, now, that a Skinnerian explanation can be invoked to account for the unexpected pattern of choices discussed by Nisbitt and Wilson: in some way choosing the item last viewed has had beneficial consequences, consequences which have led to a favouring of this alternative. There is, as before, ample room for this scheme to operate if the subject confesses not to know why she chose as she did, but, even if the person is emphatic as to her reason, the applicability of the Skinnerian explanation would not mean that the reason then given was not acceptable as such. That this is so is, on our scheme, somewhat trivial: in the situation as described, position simply does not feature as a rival *reason*, though it may, as a cause, be instrumental in dictating what comes to figure as a reason. We shall return to this relationship in Chapter 8.

To end this chapter, and to recapitulate our account of action, let us return to the topic with which we began—namely, that of the will. In the *Notebooks 1914–16* Wittgenstein wrote:

At any rate I can imagine carrying out the act of will for raising my arm, but that my arm does not move. (E.g., a sinew is torn.) True, but, it will be said, the sinew surely moves and that just shews that the act of will related to the sinew and not to the arm. But let us go farther and suppose that even the sinew did not move, and so on. We should then arrive at the position that the act of will does not relate to a body at all, and so that in the ordinary sense of the word there is no such thing as the act of the will.   (*NB* 86)

Wittgenstein blocks the conclusion which threatens by affirming: 'The act of the will is not the cause of the action but is the action itself' (ibid. 87). The same identification is apparently endorsed, if less forthrightly, even as late as the *Philosophical Investigations*:

' "Willing, if it is not to be a sort of wishing, must be the action itself. It cannot be allowed to stop anywhere short of the action." If it is the action, then it is so in the ordinary sense of the word; so it is speaking, writing, walking, lifting a thing, imagining something. But it is also trying, attempting, making an effort,—to speak, to write, to lift a thing, to imagine something, etc.' (*PI* §615). The assimilation of willing to acting appears to be no less paradoxical than the conclusion it is aimed at avoiding. An appropriate next step would accordingly be to refine the identity, but Wittgenstein moves off in another direction, the discussion culminating in the suggestion, already considered, that voluntary action is marked by the absence of surprise (ibid., §628).

By contrast, the strategy we have adopted has been, in effect, to straighten out the grammar of the crude identity. We are not to think of willing and acting as one and the same, but it is enough that our movements should give proof of wanting. Or, perhaps, bodily movements are to be taken to constitute actions so long as their purposive, adaptive, character allows them to be reckoned *expressions* of the will. Since the term 'will' hovers uncertainly between naming a mythical mental act and providing a variant of our innocent 'wanting', we do better to forsake it for this latter, and, since the pattern of movements will also be shaped in accordance with what we know and think, we may broaden our account to embrace these conditions as well.

The key to a fuller analysis is to be found in an appropriate construal of the psychological components. In formulating our account we cast our net widely, taking in animal as well as human action, and the thoughts we focus on are not the thoughts that unfold in an interior monologue—sayings to oneself—the desires are not the urges we experience. In these forms, it is difficult to see thought and desire relating to behaviour in anything other than a causal way, but we see another possibility when we turn to the broader notion of thought as an enduring state or capacity rather than an episodic act or activity, a state which may be made manifest in words or in deeds, together with the broader notion of wanting which is grounded on behaviour rather than on feeling. The right conception represents action as behaviour that is informed with thought and desire, not behaviour which remains opaque so long as the mental, construed in Cartesian terms, cannot be readily thought of as brought into a relation with the physical or the behavioural. True, the plans which we put into effect with our actions may be highly complex, with no real possibility of reading off our behaviour beliefs as to ultimate goals, but the movements we engage in, commonly under perceptual control, can be recognizable as purposive, and indeed as manifesting our knowledge, whatever the larger projects into which they enter. It is a matter of the purposiveness which we can discern in the behaviour of animals, or in that of young children even before they can speak.

Much of the problem in getting clear about action stems from our understandable tendency to take as central movement which *follows on* a desire, where the desire is conceived of as an urge experienced, a 'separate existence' which asks to be placed in a special relation to the movement if this is to count as action—and what relation, if not one of causation? True, we are looking here at a distinctively human trait. That is, our powers of thought enable us to appreciate that we lack something desirable, and we can look ahead to its attainment. The ability to envisage future possibilities creates a space which can be filled with longing or yearning. None the less, for our purposes we do better to consider the desire at the time of acting. This is of greater importance, earlier desires being of relevance only so long as they are subsumed under the current desire; they may, after all, be forgotten or abandoned. Before the action, the desire may be at the centre of consciousness, but when action is under way there is the desire for x just in so far as the agent is working towards this end. It is the character of the movements as purposive that now comes into focus.

Although we have been sparing in what we credit, psychologically, to animals, our account of action has the virtue of leaving animal behaviour less mystifying than is possible with the Cartesian causal approach. So, the dog is watching expectantly, waiting for a sign that it will be taken for a walk, and enthusiastically heading for the gate when its expectations are fulfilled. If there are no thoughts which pass through its head on such occasions, then, it might be supposed, there is nothing that might explain its behaviour in the way such thoughts explain human actions. However, the real difference between us and the animal lies in the reasoning and deliberating of which we alone are capable and which may issue in the expectation or belief. The belief/desire scheme of explanation does not require that the belief have such antecedents, and the belief itself is, with us as well as with the animal, a state which has the behaviour as its manifestation rather than its effect.

7

Reasoning, Deciding, and Intending

Practical reasoning is reasoning undertaken with a view to determining what to do. But it is often seemingly more than that—a matter of reasoning which in some way *issues* in action. Can we say that such reasoning is then like theoretical reasoning, differing only in having action rather than truth as its goal? Given the gulf between words and deeds, we might expect to find the procedures which have these disparate outcomes to be themselves dissimilar. Is it, indeed, a matter purely of reasoning in the practical case, or at least of reasoning in the same sense? In pursuing these issues we shall make *decision* the focus of attention: how is a decision related to the reasoning which culminates in it, and how in turn is any subsequent behaviour related to the decision? Answers to these questions will help us enlarge upon the relation between thought and behaviour which emerged with our characterization of action.

7.1 PRACTICAL REASONING

You wish to pay a bill. Knowing that you may do so by making out a cheque, you make out a cheque. A rational enough way of proceeding, but suppose some other means is available to the same end, as with using cash or a credit card. Suppose, too, that you are aware of these options, and have no reason to prefer your chosen method of payment to either of them. In such a case, where a means chosen is sufficient for, rather than necessary to, a given end, there appears to be an insuperable difficulty in applying any deductive scheme. If the given means is adopted simply because *some* such procedure is called for, there may be no way of expanding upon the agent's reasons so as to generate a deductively valid argument to the desired conclusion. What are we to make of this circumstance? Is the logic of practical reasoning perhaps different from the theoretical variety?

An affirmative answer is defended by Anthony Kenny, who

proposes the following as the commonest pattern displayed by practical reasoning: '*G* is to be brought about. But if I do *B* then *G*. So I'll do *B*.' This, he claims, shows an important difference *vis-à-vis* theoretical reasoning, where the pattern '*Q*. If *P* then *Q*. Therefore *P*' is simply fallacious (Kenny 1989: 43). We might query the comparison, with its failure to distinguish '*G*' and '*G* is to be brought about', but, even with a more accurate formulation, deductive validity seems to escape us.

By the canons of Kenny's logic of satisfactoriness (1975: ch. 5), the following example of a practical syllogism, advanced by Aristotle, is valid:

I need a covering
A cloak is a covering
I need a cloak

(De Motu Animalium 701ª17–18)

However, such an assessment surely throws doubt on that logic. The syllogism invites comparison with other arguments in the same area, as:

> I could do with a covering
> A cloak is a covering
> I could do with a cloak

That is, any covering would serve my purposes; a cloak is a covering; therefore a cloak would serve my purposes. Aristotle's syllogism would appear to come off rather badly in the comparison, being no better than 'I've got to have a covering; a cloak is a covering; therefore, I've got to have a cloak'.

Kenny's solution to the problem posed by the divergence between the two species of reasoning involves treating the conclusion of a practical inference as a disguised imperative. There is, we may note, more than one form that such an analysis might take. We have already remarked on Locke's idea of issuing commands to one's body: 'This, at least, I think evident, that we find in ourselves a power to begin or forbear, continue or end several actions of our minds, and motions of our bodies, barely by a thought or preference of the mind ordering, or as it were commanding, the doing or not doing such or such a particular action. This power which the mind has . . . is that which we call the *will*' (*Essay*, II. xxi. 5). An alternative which stands a better chance of being taken literally is that of a self-addressed imperative, as in this proposal from Kenny: 'My claim is only that in so far as "I will do A" is an expression of intention it can be expressed in a philosophically less misleading way as "Let me do A"; and in so far as it is a genuine report, it is tantamount, on the imperative theory, to "I have said in my heart 'Let me do A' " ' (1975: 34). Issuing an imperative to oneself is an advance on commanding unhearing limbs to act, but the notion of a self-addressed imperative is still out of place, given that the person enjoining and the person enjoined are of the same mind. True, there is such a thing as being in two minds, and it has some application here: we can, as it were, cajole or goad ourselves. But this is clearly not the standard case, and, while the notion of a *commitment* has a part to play in explaining the role of 'I will . . .', it is much more plausible to acknowledge at the same time a predictive role for these words, rather than model them on a form whose principal use is in issuing a directive to another, often unwilling, party.

True, it is tempting to enlist some such reading in order to set a suitable distance between the use of, say, 'I shall make him angry', as an expression of intention and the use of the same words as a mere prediction. We may grant that an imperative gives a natural expression to a desire for action, and, as noted above, it is suited to the less usual case where, however ineffectually, one wills something to happen. Moreover, since 'Shall I V?' is closer to 'Am I to V?' than to an enquiry about what one will in fact do, an imperative might appear to be more in keeping with this reading. However, while the interrogative use is thus detached from a query about what the future holds, the assertoric use, as we have seen, keeps us within the category of predictions. The words may give truthful expression to the speaker's intention, to his determination, but that is not enough for their truth. For that the same demands are to be met as for the mere prediction—which as far as the actual words are concerned may, if I am right, have the very same meaning. In shifting to the imperative we sever the links with truth and falsity common to both uses, and we lose sight of the relationships between the different verbal forms, as 'I shall' and 'I should have'. To Kate's request, 'Will you contribute?', Harvey replies, 'I shall indeed', continuing with the grammatical form which Kate used rather than invoking one which dispenses him from claiming truth for what he says. A further query from Kate, 'Are you sure?', takes Harvey up on just this point, and Harvey may express uncertainty with 'I think I shall contribute'. As we have noted, certainty as to how one will act differs from certainty about the truth of a hypothesis. In like fashion, as a statement coming from one who has not quite made up his mind to act, 'I think I shall break the lock' is distinguishable from the use of the same words to voice the speaker's fears as to what may happen. But the difference is not one between indicative and imperative. The pattern of relations under threat when the former is abandoned for the latter is extensive.

The imperatival analysis is thought to cope with a style of argument which, by the canons of theoretical argument, would be judged unsound. My opposing suggestion is that the pattern in question may reflect a respect in which the action opted for is not wholly rational. To explain, the question 'Why did you make out a cheque?' can be thought of as covering two possibilities. First, we may be enquiring what end the action served, why there was such action rather than no action at all. Secondly, we may be asking why there was that action rather than some other serving the same purpose. It is quite plain why going ahead with writing a cheque is preferable to doing nothing, but, since the reason given does not answer the other question, there is a respect in which the explanation offered is incomplete. Indeed, there may be no reason, in the sense of reason the agent could advance, to the latter query. It is not that a special logic applies; rather, that the absence of an appropriate deductive scheme mirrors an incompleteness in the agent's reasons.

It would, however, be altogether too harsh to speak in terms of irrationality. After all, it is the choices contemplated which do not afford a basis for a relevant discrimination, and it would be only if the agent fabricated a reason, if he made out that there was a difference where none existed, that we might find fault with his procedure. You wish to have a grapefruit, and you are faced with two which you find indistinguishable. How could opting for one of them quite arbitrarily be a ground for criticism? The situation compares with that of a person trying to break a habit, as of smoking. There is no particular reason why the cigarette he is about to light should be his last. His aim of giving up can be achieved just as well by stopping with his first cigarette of the next day. To that extent a decision to stop with the present cigarette is not rationally compelling, but it finds adequate compensation in the consideration that, if he at no point resigns himself to taking such a step, he will never attain his end. In so far as the reasoning in such cases involves the belief that it is better to act arbitrarily than not to act at all, we may even hesitate to speak of an incompleteness in the agent's reasons. Certainly, the rationality may be as comprehensive as the circumstances permit.

The timing of an action may be similarly opaque, something we are at a loss to explain even though we have a reason for the action more generally. So, lying in bed in the morning, we contemplate getting up; at some point we stir ourselves, but why just when we do we may be unable to say—the reasons which hold good then need not have presented themselves as any more compelling than they had in the minutes preceding. Again, a mislaid object eludes you. Why do you give up looking for it just when you do? To the extent that we lack answers to these questions, they are questions in search of causes.

This is just a minor skirmish with the problems which practical reasoning poses, and it has not brought out the most striking respect in which the two forms of argument may contrast. As a more instructive example of an apparent inferential lacuna, consider the following. The gardener declares, 'I intend to spray the roses'. Coming after 'If I don't spray the roses, the greenfly will destroy them', this makes good sense, but it may be suggested that a further premiss is presupposed—for example, 'I intend to do whatever is necessary to protect the roses'. There could, of course, be a variety of premisses, but our problem lies not with these but with the idea that the initial remark might figure as the conclusion of an *inference*, in this instance:

> I intend to do whatever is necessary to protect the roses
> If I don't spray the roses, the greenfly will destroy them
> So I intend to spray the roses

We may detect nothing amiss with this sequence, but I doubt that we shall then be thinking of the speaker as drawing out the consequences of the premisses—as though it wasn't until he put two and two together that he realized what he intended to do. A more realistic pattern is this: the person has formed an intention to F; finding that it will be necessary for him to G, he has then to ask himself whether he is prepared to do so, whether in the light of this necessity he still intends to F; he does not *conclude* that he intends to G, in the sense of concluding that that is how things stand. The incongruity of this construal becomes particularly glaring if we imagine the person holding the general intention and being informed of the need to spray the roses, whereupon he *deduces* that he intends to spray them.

There is, if to a lesser degree, something of the same incongruity if the expression of intention uses the simple future, 'So I shall spray the roses'. Again we may see nothing amiss, since an expression of intention could occur at this point, but it is only as a mere prediction that it would figure as a conclusion drawn, a conclusion which had not been appreciated before. Seeing it in this light requires us to detach it from its usual role in announcing a decision then taken; restore this role and it then becomes detached from the premises.

It should be noted that cases in which talk of a *deduction* is inapposite are not confined to those where a decision or intention is announced, but a report of a past action may be comparable: she wanted some vitamin C, and she knew it was to be found in oranges, so she had an orange. This too is not to be represented as drawing out the consequences of what is known with a view to extending the range of the latter. After all, the conclusion is already accepted as falling within that domain. What is important is the distinction between (what we might call) a deduction and an explanation, the latter seeking to present a *given* fact as a consequence of appropriate truths, the former seeking to arrive at consequences whose truth has not as yet been appreciated.

While deciding is thus not the only alternative to deducing, the contrast between the two offers a possible test for distinguishing those judgements which do from those which do not amount to settling the major concern of practical reasoning—namely, what shall I do? So, although it is not in place to speak of *deducing* that one intends to V, there is not at all the same obstacle to speaking of deducing that one must or ought to do such and such—forms often taken as defining the goal of practical reasoning. And that is as it should be. Such conclusions are a prelude to a decision, but they fall short of the different step which the latter represents, and they fall short in just the respect that is distinctive of such reasoning. Deciding that it is time to get up and deciding to get up may well not be the same decision, diverging precisely when the former is merely deciding what one ought to do. Or, consider a judgement that some course of action is overall best. The comparison here is with *ought*, there being no difficulty with the notion of inferring or deducing a conclusion in either case. But might not a conclusion as to what is best and a decision to act be interchangeable? Not always, obviously. We have the example mentioned where there was no 'best', but a number of equally good alternatives, and there are many cases of impulsive action where we should not be prepared to say that the course of action decided upon presented itself to us as the best available; we simply did not address this—possibly complex—issue.

But my claim is not that a decision that a certain course of action is the best can never be one with a decision to act: when only non-moral considerations are at stake, it is more than likely that the two will converge. Rather, I am suggesting that the possible difference between deducing and deciding can show up a gap between the two. We may conclude that doing *x* would be best, yet still not be able to bring ourselves to take the decision to act. There is not the same inconsistency as found when, for instance, a person engages in an action having just declared, 'That is the last thing I'd ever do', or fails to act having just announced, 'That is what I want to do more than anything else'—with the obvious provisos concerning ability and opportunity.

Is there a difficulty here? The decision to act is not the conclusion of an inference, understood on the usual deductive model—as though one had worked out what was about to happen. Nor is it as with explanations of past decisions or actions, where these are supposed given. Since the decision is a matter of a step to be taken, rather than something awaiting discovery, it is beginning to look as if, in any interesting sense, there cannot be such a thing as practical reasoning. Yet there surely can be action-implying descriptions, as 'That is what I want to do more than anything else', so what is to be said?

An answer is already implicit, I suggest, in our description of what is going on when a decision is reached. A person comes to a situation with certain beliefs and desires, but, while he may be presented with the opportunity to follow up his preferred course of action, this may also be the occasion for him to decide that he no longer desires the end in question as much as he had. It is not that his beliefs and desires will furnish him with premises which could not conceivably be overturned and which make action inescapable. After all, there can be deciding in a full-blown sense only if there is a degree of uncertainty, in which case we have the correlative suspension of the premiss. This may represent the person's attitude to date, but it is not a truth fixed once and for all; on the contrary, it may fail the test of present circumstances. If, however, the agent does not change his mind, then his announcement 'I shall go ahead and do it' is not a deduction, but more by way of a reaffirmation of the relevant desire.

Similarly, while a previously formed intention to F may, in the light of what is subsequently learned, commit the person to an intention to G, this will be a *new* intention. On the other hand, while 'deduction' is inapposite, this does not mean that a deductive explanation of his action may not be open to him, in the sense that the premisses of his reasoning logically imply a preparedness to act on his part. It is just that it took the decision to secure those premisses; they were not beyond revision until that step was taken.

Or, at least, it will take a decision to secure the premisses if uncertainty arises. In many cases we have another pattern, one of action embarked upon unhesitatingly, with no consideration of possible alternatives, no resolution of uncertainties. The telephone rings, and you pick up the receiver. You might consider the pros and cons of doing so if, for example, you are expecting an unwelcome call, but in many cases no reason for not picking up the receiver will enter your head; there will be nothing for you *to* decide. While there may be nothing that deserves to be called reasoning, reaching a decision, or forming an intention, that does not mean that you do not act for a reason, it being sufficient that you are prepared to acknowledge something as your reason for it to count as such. Certainly, the likeness to instances of more explicit reasoning is closer than when you have no idea why you do what you do. It may even be possible to fit such action into a deductive pattern, to see it as an instance of something of this form: if a person wants *x*, and *y* is, as he believes, the only way of getting it, then, if he is able to do *y*, and sees no reason against it, he will try to do *y*. This schema may need some tightening up, but, however many loopholes are closed, we are not landed with a logical guarantee of action in any unacceptable sense. If the person does not act, we again reject one of the premisses, the supposition that *x* really and truly was wanted being the most likely to fall.

Even when it is in place to speak of deciding, there are many occasions when we simply arrive at a preference, take a decision, without having to consider the matter of consistency with prior judgements. So, you decide to accept an invitation, but there need have been no departure from previously held beliefs or preferences had you declined. If this makes for a greater difficulty in discerning a deductive scheme, that need be of no great significance. First, even when that model applies, the agent is not dispensed from taking the substantive step, making the commitment to action, which a decision involves. Secondly, the inapplicability of that model does not mean that the decision or action is without a reason. For *R* to qualify as a reason it is necessary only that action in accordance with *R* should be understandable, not that it should be inevitable, and, so long as *R* relates to some supposed virtue in the action proposed, it can have the relevant explanatory role.

To elaborate, we may note that a reason which suffices to confer rationality upon a decision may on another occasion occur without that decision, yet there be nothing irrational about this failure. It strikes us as a good idea to *V*, and we do so, yet on another occasion, while it again strikes us as a good idea, we do not act, without there being anything of which we are aware that makes for a relevant difference between the two situations. Of course, in the first case we can say that the appeal of *V*ing was sufficient to have us go ahead and act, but this description, while warranted by the mere fact of action, need not reflect a different state of mind prior to the action. The acceptability of an explanation in terms of reasons, despite this variability, makes for a notable divergence from what is required of a causal explanation: the admissibility of the former is not conditional upon finding an account of the difference between the two situations. There is scope for causal considerations in explaining why, for instance, activities which we once enthusiastically pursued cease to hold any attraction for us, but there is nothing exceptional about our ignorance with respect to such causal matters, since quite generally we have no inkling of what, causally, is involved in our voluntary actions. Nor, on the other hand, does any answer in terms of reasons make one in terms of causes otiose. They are answers to quite different questions.

According to Aristotle, the conclusion of a practical syllogism is action itself (*Nichomachean Ethics* 1147^{a}28, *De Motu Animalium* 701^{a}12). It is true that we may speak indifferently of deciding and acting as what the agent's reasons are reasons for, but to say that action is entailed by the premisses is only to say that the premisses logically imply *that* the person will act, a possibility which does not depend on any particular thesis about action, but holds equally for happenings of other kinds. We might interpret 'The conclusion is an action' in clausal terms—'The conclusion is that the person will act'—but there is surely no way in which an action might itself take on the role of a conclusion, no way in which the premisses might entail action as a spatio-temporal item, a subject of non-linguistic predicates such as 'clumsy' or 'took place indoors'. The nearest we come to bridging disparate categories is in claiming that an action may be a criterion for a psychological state, but even here the disparateness of the two is apparent only.

What of those expressions signalling relations of consequence which, like 'since', 'so', and 'because', have been thought to defy understanding so long as they are not allowed to be interpreted in terms of causation? Our understanding of 'because', say, is to be understood in terms of its introduction of a putative reason; whether or not a cause is at the same time specified is a further matter. Clearly, no cause is given with, for instance, 'The line does not scan because it has too few syllables', but, suitably filled out, the 'because' here is revealed as logically based. And with reasons as these concern us? Clearly, we owe an account of the relevant connectives if we are to provide an adequate alternative to the causal conception, and it may be wondered whether the only obvious alternative—one where a strictly logical inference defines the ideal—is available for patterns of practical reasoning.

It may seem paradoxical to claim that an action, an actual event, follows logically, given relevant desires and beliefs, but, as has just been argued, there is no question of premises which hold at a time antecedent to the action providing both an unshakeable given and a logically adequate basis for an inference to the action. Rather, it takes the action itself finally to secure the truth of the premises. At this point, clearly, the non-deductive practical reasonings with which we began become important. There will, of course, be no 'because' when there is no reason, as was supposed with respect to 'Why did you make out a cheque rather than tender cash?', but does not the simple 'Why did you make out a cheque?' prove an embarrassment?

I say that I made out a cheque because I wished to settle a bill. If this is to abbreviate a logically sound inference, we should be able to claim, assuming other premises held constant, that, if I had not made out a cheque, that would have meant that I had not wanted to settle the bill. And this, of course, need not be so, given that I might have adopted some other method of payment. However, it will be acknowledged that all I have an irrefragable reason to do is make payment in some way or other, and my reason to do that is as compelling, logically, as when, payment by cheque being the only possibility, the pressure to act is the pressure of logic. True, as just indicated, we are speaking of an ideal—there will often be some artifice in tidying up our unarticulated inferences in a way that would satisfy a logician—though we should surely resist the imposition of a 'because' which would demand a different rationale from that enjoyed when the inference can more clearly be seen to be logically grounded. What is more important, however, is the point that was made at the outset: a reason earns its title as the agent's reason through its place in a pattern of reasoning, however loose that reasoning may be. Any supposed virtues as a cause are as irrelevant as they are with reasons which support a belief.

7.2 DECIDING AND INTENDING

Practical reasoning differs from theoretical argument in that a substantive new step, a commitment to action, is taken with the decision with which the reasoning terminates. It is not a question of coming to recognize a truth. This difference reinforces earlier observations about the use of 'certain' in distinguishing an expression of intention from a mere prediction. To make the point now in terms of 'know', the announcement 'I'll get in touch as soon as I have any news' does not represent a deduction made, as considering the evidence, one might arrive at a prediction. Prefacing such an announcement with 'I know' forces it into another pattern, one where the evidence points unmistakably in the direction of the act announced, with this no longer thought of as something it is simply up to the agent to do, should he wish. If a causal account did justice to the relation between reason and decision, then, in the light of my beliefs and desires I might well infer that I should act as declared, and my declaration might well represent a deduction made; furthermore, the evidence of my reasons might be such as to warrant me in saying 'I know I'll get in touch as soon as I have any news'. The way the norm is thus misrepresented gives another reason for querying such an account.

A convinced causalist reflects: 'if it isn't literally true that my wanting is causally responsible for my reaching, and my itching is causally responsible for my scratching, and my believing is causally responsible for my saying . . . , if none of that is literally true, then practically everything I believe about anything is false and it's the end of the world' (Fodor 1990: 156). If what Fodor fears is so is so, this will not mean that, for instance, he never reaches for something because he wants to get it. There is no threat to anyone's ordinary beliefs in rejecting a causal analysis; on the contrary, a divergence from this conception is necessary if we are to remain faithful to the style of reasoning in which our beliefs and desires have their familiar explanatory roles; by exploiting only the content, the inferential potential, of reasons, we can make sense of behaviour which, on a causal explanation, remains opaque. Let us hope that this is enough to prevent Fodor's universe from crashing down about him.

However, perhaps even now it is not altogether clear how our reasons for acting relate to our actions. All that our introductory discussion yielded was the suggestion, doubtless deeply unsatisfying, that a mental dimension is required only for the justification of certain descriptions of behaviour, only for certain forms of explanation—not for the behaviour itself—to be possible. So long as thought is in no way instrumental in bringing anything about, so long as the behaviour can take place even when the agent's mind is a complete blank, any thought that does occur has been made to look a mere epiphenomenon. Is there no other way of finding a place for what is commonly seen as the overridingly important dimension, for finding something of greater substance for thought to do? Our discussion of action, and the way thought enters into its characterization, has moved us forward a little, but we have said nothing about the relation between specifically episodic thought and behaviour. Deciding is a central instance of such thought, and one which will now be considered along with the allied notion of intending.

Deciding and intending are concepts which appear to place us fairly and squarely in the realm of the mental, but, while that is no doubt in some sense where we find ourselves with them, this undifferentiated categorization is in part the source of our problem. To see through this classification to something more useful we may hark back to Ryle's distinction between task and achievement verbs, a distinction which, though sadly ignored nowadays, is to my mind as fruitful as any in providing a framework in which a number of troublesome psychological concepts can be investigated.

Ryle (1949: 152) noted that the supposed cognitive activities of seeing, hearing, and inferring have been found oddly elusive, but he held that the mystery dissolves once it is realized that 'see', 'descry', and 'find' are not process words, experience words, or activity words. None of them signifies a happening having duration, so not an experience, however brief; rather, they signify occurrences which occur *at* an instant. As such, these 'achievements' logically require for their application an extended state or process—a 'task'—of which they may signal the end point, but an end point which does not go on *for* a time. It is this durationless character that makes for the significance of an achievement. Whether it be the denouement of a preceding task—as in Ryle's use—or the first point of something that ensues— as we might also allow—its distinctive character *vis-à-vis* an enduring state is essentially the same.

It is the notion of an achievement in this extended sense that is the most useful for our purposes, an extension which Ryle came to acknowledge with his later talk of verbs which 'declare a terminus' (1954: 103). With this extension we may also drop any implication that the verb must signify something one can *try* to do. It is also important not to overlook the possibility that the same verb should enjoy both a task and an achievement use, 'see' being a case in point.

As an illustration of the utility of the generalized notion, we may consider its application to the concept of understanding, where it may sharpen Wittgenstein's treatment of the topic. Wittgenstein's observations represent understanding as akin to a capacity or an ability, a person giving proof of understanding by showing himself capable of making the right connections, drawing appropriate conclusions, offering satisfactory explanations, and so forth. Clearly, understanding is a state which may continue over the years, but there is also a use of the verb, as in 'Now I understand!', in which it appears to report an episodic event. Yet another elusive mental act, it might seem, but, whatever should pass through the person's mind with such a declaration, what is important is that these words should signal the dawning of understanding, where this is the extended state. The crucial question is whether the speaker has the ability, the capacity, to which he has laid claim with his avowal, the occurrence of any mental events at the time enlightenment dawned being of secondary importance. To echo *Investigations* (PI 218): no inner happening could have the *consequences* needed to constitute understanding, since no such happening could ensure that the requisite cluster of abilities had come into being. Think of our earlier example of Köhler's ingenious ape and its apparent insight into a problem. The Gestalt psychologist's appeal to insight does not tell us *how* a problem is solved; it merely highlights the suddenness of the transition from lacking to having the requisite ability to act.

My suggestion is that deciding likewise belongs with achievements, that 'decide' is a verb which declares a terminus. From the time when a decision is reached we can look back to a period when we were in two minds about a course of action, and forwards to a state of determination or resolution. The moment of decision is both the end point of the period of indecision and the initial point of a period of firmness of purpose. Unlike these extended periods, it does not itself have any duration—any reality, one might be inclined to say, but that would be wrong; still, the reality is primarily that of the period of which it marks a limit, much as with a surface and the body whose boundary it defines.

What can be said of the state which comes into being with a decision? Is it to be described as *mental*? The notion of a state of mind is most readily associated with various *moods*, as when one is troubled, gloomy, irritable, excitable, and so forth. Both here and more generally, however—as with suspicion, doubt, curiosity, or fear—a state of mind can embrace a disposition to *behave* in certain ways, and this is just what we have with a state of resolution, of firmness of purpose, or indeed with, simply, the intention to act which a decision initiates. Note that it is the intention as the intending, not as what is intended, that is at issue. Intentions may be characterized in various ways—as honourable, as ill-advised, as difficult to carry out—descriptions which may well make no sense when affirmed of a behavioural disposition, but it is only the intention as what is intended that collects these troublesome predicates. At all events, notwithstanding the term 'mind' in 'state of mind', the state of mind given with intending can be reckoned a disposition to act. Thought, in the form of decision, impinges upon behaviour through its non-causal relation to a behavioural disposition, the possibility that a state of mind can be at the same time of this character being what provides the bridge between the mental and the behavioural.

Some clarification of this conception will not go amiss. If 'state of mind' is taken to imply consciousness, the implication is one which will have to be cancelled; there is no question of an intention's having always to be before the subject's mind, the state being one we can be said to be in when sound asleep. The term 'disposition' fares better on this score, but 'being disposed to V' is misleading in its turn, suggesting a more habitual pattern of behaviour—as one person may be disposed to agree with everything another says—rather than the once-and-for-all response which the fulfilment of a particular intention may demand. Wittgenstein considers that an intention can be called a mental disposition, but that the term is misleading in as much as one does not perceive such a disposition in oneself as a matter of experience—it is not as if it eventually dawns on us that, when we intend to V, we generally find ourselves trying to do so when the opportunity presents itself. This is in contrast to the inclination to jealousy, which he regards as a disposition in the true sense. Experience teaches him that he has it (*RPP* II §178).

Certainly, if the decision is a decision to do something at a particular time, as a decision to catch the 6 o'clock train, something more than a disposition to act will succeed it. However, the notion of a disposition is more relevant when the time for carrying out the intended act is not specified, and with respect to acts which might further fulfilment of the intention. For instance, a person may have the intention to amass a fortune. He can be expected to take some of the opportunities to advance this aim which come his way, but some he may reject without our having to say that the intention has been abandoned, even though he may not have a clear reason for not taking advantage of a given opportunity. Not only may there be considerable variability in the extent to which someone who harbours an intention may be found refusing such opportunities, but there is perhaps even greater variability in the extent to which possible means to its realization are contemplated. Here too, however, we may speak of a disposition, the variability serving to define the degree of commitment, of determination, on the part of the agent, the extent to which the intention is firm or half-hearted. More important is the way an intention brings with it a systematic change in one's attitude to possibilities of action. It may not be a matter of a disposition to do what the intention is an intention to do, but we become liable to favour courses of action which increase our chances of success, which make it easier to carry out the intention when the time comes. Similarly, our reaction to possibilities which might frustrate the intention is different from what it would have been had we not taken the decision. With the decision our pattern of responses aligns itself with the intention, this redirection in many cases being effected without our taking further decisions: we simply act in a way appropriate to the demands of the situation and in the light of the intention. There is, then, a degree of indeterminacy, coupled with a shift in the pattern of our responses, which makes the notion of a disposition appropriate, a notion which has the merit of making perspicuous the relation between the mental and the behavioural and of helping avoid the bamboozlement which the typical philosophical queries may gen-

202 Reasoning, Deciding, and Intending

erate, as when it is asked how an intention can *influence* behaviour, or in what an intention might *consist* prior to the time when it is to be put into effect.

We noted earlier that wanting was of service in marking a preparedness to act pending the removal of obstacles, and intending has a similar role as a 'buffer' between decision and action, a buffer which contracts to vanishing point when action follows immediately on a decision. Here there will be no call to introduce reference to a disposition, though the person can still be said to act intentionally. Thus, in saying that you decided to get up, you may be alluding to something which happened *with* rather than *before* your getting up. An intimate link between decision and action was noted above with the observation that, when we have both, the reason for each will be the same. There is some awkwardness in saying that the deciding and the acting, or the beginning to act, are literally one. It might be suggested that the deciding is the acting in the sense that the preceding state of indecision terminates in action; the uncertainty is resolved by going ahead and getting up. However, it is questionable whether there *is* a sense in which the one can be said to be, literally, the other. Is it not safer to stay with the clear truth that the one may occur *with* the other? Yes indeed, but that is to be understood as something stronger than mere accompaniment. In the right circumstances, it would appear, we can introduce talk of a decision just on the strength of the action, action subsequent to deliberation being a criterion for there having been a decision.

To follow up this line of thought, let us suppose you are debating whether to go for a walk. It is a fine day and you could do with the exercise. On the other hand, you are not feeling particularly energetic, and the prospect of continued inactivity does not concern you greatly. At a certain point, we shall suppose, you get up and set off on your walk, but without there having been any words, spoken or unspoken, to mark the decision. In such circumstances—when the action follows on consideration of its pros and cons—we have enough to be able to say that you decided to go for a walk; we do not have to enquire as to what else passed through your mind at the end of your deliberations; it is just: you act, knowing what you are doing. With the thoughts which entered into these deliberations there will have been something which, in the light of the subsequent action, you can cite as your reason for acting. And this is true even though on other occasions the same thoughts may have been followed by inaction. It is, of course, not enough that the right *movements* should have succeeded your deliberations; there has to have been action. That is, the movements must have been such that you could have refrained from making them.

On this way of looking at deciding, it may be that the only indispensable mental state or episode separable from the acting is to be found in what happens prior to the latter, in the state of indecision which was to be resolved, the resolution coming with the acting itself, not with a further accompanying mental event. Or is this too frugal an account? Is there truly deciding if this is all we have?

There are two cases to consider. In the less contentious, the agent's deliberations terminate in a belief, a belief as to what is the most desirable thing to do, let us say. Supposing that action is immediate, the point of decision will then be a point which marks the beginning both of the believing and of the acting, the former assuring, at least to a degree, the rationality of the latter. Your deliberations culminate in the conviction that a brisk walk would be just the tonic your listless body needs. When you then set off, there is an evident harmony between your state of mind and your action, but this is in contrast to the sequence just imagined, when, having weighed up the pros and cons, the agent finally *just* sets off on his walk. In this, the second kind of case, it may be allowed that the agent has decided with his acting, but, to the extent that a settled belief as to what is most desirable is wanting, to that extent what we have will be less a matter of rational action. To this extent, too, we may share the misgivings which resting talk of decision on the more minimal basis may prompt, and which leaves us more in the sphere of the impulsive than the deliberate, and, in the extreme case, leaves us with something that is not even fully action.

These observations have some bearing on the possibility of akratic behaviour, behaviour which is contrary to the agent's better judgement. The phenomenon appears to be all too familiar. We often opt for something less than what we take to be overall best; not merely morally best, but even best in terms of nothing more than our own selfish interests. To those who deny such a possibility, it is natural to object that the final word as to what a person wants rests with what he does. If this means ascribing to him a preference for a frivolous short-term gain at the expense of a serious long-term loss, so be it. There can still be enough of a reason to make the action intelligible. However, to take actual behaviour as definitive of the person's preference surely presumes some accord between what he does and how he sees things. Even impulsiveness requires that the person be to some degree favourably disposed towards the act in question—in a way that would take his admission to establish—however quickly the act may be regretted. Otherwise, surely, there is no question of the kind of intelligibility which acting for a reason confers. Certainly, if we reach the point where the act is considered in no way desirable, but actually undesirable, we no longer have to do with voluntary action.

By itself, a disposition to act does not ensure an intention before the act. You may be disposed to greet your neighbour each morning, but, while your greeting may count as intentional, you need never form an intention to do what you habitually do. That more than a disposition to behave is required is also indicated by an earlier example: having abandoned an earlier intention to go upstairs, we none the less find ourselves doing just that; the behavioural disposition has persisted, but not the intention. Clearly, persistence of the latter also requires the survival of the thought component. More generally, your thoughts may revert to other concerns without detriment to an intention formed, but not to the extent of allowing that all memory of the intention should have departed when you are asked whether you still have it. To the extent that you have to be reminded of what you intend, the reality of your intention is in question. Such considerations, we may note, bring home the extent to which the concept of intention is stretched in its application to animals.

While I speak of a behavioural disposition, it would clearly be wrong to say that the act in question could never be mental. This would be so with, for example, a decision to think some matter over. And, of course, inaction may be decided upon or chosen, as when we decide to refrain from commenting, to stay put, or to ignore someone's advice. It is a matter of a disposition to do something in the broadest sense. The important example of refraining will come up again in §9.2.

Is deciding itself to be classed as a mental act? Its instantaneous character may be thought to leave it too insubstantial to merit this description, but 'mental' would seem to be in order to the extent that it applies to the state initiated. Consider other comparable achievement phrases, such as 'realize', 'remember', 'come to know', and 'begin to think'. Once more, and for the same reason, 'act' is suspect, and once more we should look to the ensuing condition to determine whether, and in what sense, we have to do with something mental.

But is it so clear that deciding introduces no more than such a limiting point? Isn't it more like saying to oneself 'I'll do it', something which (*a*) takes time, however short, and (*b*) accompanies the transition to a state of resolution?—in which case the question of its relation to that state has still to be settled.

Certainly, the impression of a gap between decision and action is likely to harden to a certainty if the decision is thought of as a subvocal version of the spoken word. As already remarked, such a conception, allied to a causal construal of thoughts, makes for a truly impenetrable relation between thought and behaviour. How could saying 'I'll do it' to oneself have the significance here claimed for a decision? Unless the unspoken words are understood, there need not even *be* the relevant decision and intention. They may be of no more consequence than a silent recitation of nonsense syllables. And even with this proviso, even when we have understanding, it is difficult to explicate a causal role for the thought which somehow takes its content into account, as would appear necessary. So great are the difficulties, our very conception of ourselves as human agents may appear under threat—a fear sometimes voiced by those who see the sustainability of that conception as waiting upon a satisfactory theory of mental representation.

If anything, the advantage would appear to lie with the spoken word in what it offers by way of possible roles denied to mere thought; in particular, we may seek something of substance for the words to do through the kind of speech act which they embody. Expressions of decisions or intentions are then naturally likened to promises, offers, or undertakings: in saying 'I intend to . . .' we are authorizing expectations of action on our part (cf. Hunter 1978).

However, both the conception of the utterance as echoing the same words spoken inwardly, and the alternative conception of it as allowing of no more than a quasi-performative, non-reportive role, are to be rejected. There is no call to deny that we can report our state of mind with 'I intend . . .', or with 'I have decided to . . .', no call to deny that we can express our state of mind with 'I shall . . .', but, of course, it is not enough to have spoken the words with understanding for a decision to be signalled. Nor, if we should say to ourselves, 'I'll do it', can this be merely a matter of a thought that crosses our mind, but there has to have been a decision with the thought. We become prepared to act, and we call upon such forms as 'I'll do it' to give expression to our preparedness. We must, of course, mean what

206 Reasoning, Deciding, and Intending

we say, but what that means in this instance is that the requisite state of mind must have come about, a state of mind which one might, or might not, express by uttering these words. And, if there has been a decision, it is not necessary that these words should have occurred inwardly. A fortiori, there is no problem of having to formulate a causal role for the words which somehow respects their content. Just as with 'Now I understand!', so what matters is that the words should herald the beginning of a state whose genuineness is verified by future happenings. And, as with understanding, so too any mental accompaniments to this change in state pale into insignificance when set against the question whether the shift has in fact occurred. Indeed, even the decision is not a necessity for the state, but, whether this comes about only once some uncertainty has been resolved, whether it takes shape only gradually, or whether the agent takes it as a matter of course that he will act in a certain way, is of no great account.

7.3 MENTAL CAUSES

The Rylean notion of an achievement takes us to issues closer to the heart of our concerns when, abstracting the more general temporal condition involved, we consider the inception rather than the termination of an extended state. The issues promise to be more central in that the episodes now singled out are likely to appear among philosophers' candidate causes of the happenings which follow. We noted earlier that a decision to V does not normally figure among one's reasons for Ving, so, even if reasons were causes, this gave no grounds for promoting decisions to that status. However, while my decision to cut back the hedge is not my reason for doing so, it is my reason for buying a suitable implement to carry out the task, so we are not entirely done with the causal question, and it is accordingly of some interest that the present analysis tells against construing decisions as causes quite generally.

Very roughly, triggering causes explain why an event of a certain general character took place, and took place when it did, whereas causal conditions or factors explain why the event caused was as it was. Deciding is a datable occurrence, and as such is inviting as giving rise to what follows; for some, indeed, its status as a mental cause with a physical effect is not open to serious challenge when we have to do with movements which follow on a relevant decision to move (cf. Mellor 1995: 2). However, as an occurrence which merely marks the point of transition from one state to another, the deciding is not capable of acting upon anything, of bringing anything about; it is no more the cause of the acting or intending than the beginning of wisdom is the cause of that state, or the onset of malaria is the cause of that illness. The difference between action that is, and action that is not, consequent upon a decision is not to be understood causally, but as the difference between action which realizes a pre-existing disposition, readiness, or determination, and action which is less deliberate and more spontaneous.

What of the intending? To take up one of the suggested analogies, the onset of malaria, while not its cause, is clearly the onset of a possible causal condition; is that the role of the disposition to act, and hence of the intention? Not only is the beginning of the disposition to act not a cause of the ensuing action, but the disposition itself is not suited to this role. Even if it is allowed that a disposition to act could be a causal *condition*, it would not as such explain why the action came about—any more than a tendency to put on weight may be cited as a cause of one's weight gain—which is just what interests us here. On the other hand, what a causal condition might explain— the character of the action—is surely not to be accounted for by a bare disposition to act.

Or is that really so? We know that by doing certain things we stand a good chance of eliciting a certain response from a person, a response which will differ depending on whether or not that person has a certain intention. In this scheme, the having of the intention has every appearance of constituting a causal condition. So, I know that you intend to put in for a certain job. I can thus reasonably infer that, if I inform you that you must act now to meet the closing date, appropriate steps on your part are likely. Or again, if I should tell you that the post has already gone to another, you will, given your intention, be disappointed. A voluntary and an involuntary response. We do not want disappointment to be the state which *ipso facto* follows when an intention is thwarted or frustrated—the disappointment of a disappointed intention—but there is also disappointment as something *felt*, and I may well consider that my disclosure makes me responsible for this reaction.

However, appearances may be deceptive. First, we are not, of course, speaking of an intention as this might be described as unrealizable, as inconsistent with other aims or intentions. Here there is no more question of a causal role than there is with an aim or an ambition. But even with the intention as the subject's intending the case is far from clear. Suppose I do not know of your intention to put in for a job, but happen to mention that the closing date is approaching. The subsequent pattern of events may still give me reason for saying that I was instrumental in bringing about your immediate response to my revelation, the steps you take to submit an application, but does it add anything to a *causal* account to say that you had the intention in question? It would add something if we introduced reference to a ground for the disposition, as a physical disposition may be grounded in molecular structure, but, while the intention forms an integral part of a reason explanation, it adds no more to a causal explanation than does the ascription of a probability or propensity with respect to inanimate behaviour. You blow out a candle. We readily put the extinction of the flame down to your action, but we do not fill out the causal story by adding that there was a strong likelihood that the flame would be extinguished if blown.

Belief presents us with further instances of the general issue, in that there are occasions when we are unquestionably responsible for a person's coming to hold a certain belief, and hence instrumental in bringing about the action that then ensues. So, by giving a signal I lead you to believe that I am stopping, and you accordingly slow down. It is your belief in the sense of your believing, your having of a belief, that I cause, and which in turn may have consequences for how you act, not the belief as, for example, something well grounded, or contradicted by another, which constitutes your reason. Moreover, it is the belief which may be manifest in action which I generate; whether there are also thoughts in the form of an interior monologue is by the way. You may indeed say to yourself, 'He is going to stop', but there can be the belief, and the explanation which invokes it, without these words. Such thoughts as cross your mind do indeed give us something mental, and something for which another person may be responsible, but there is no reason to regard them as in turn causes of anything. Thus construed, the mental drops out of any plausible causal chain; we simply bring about the behaviour which manifests the belief.

But that still leaves happenings less closely tied, in reason terms, to the intention or belief. Most notably, we have involuntary responses, as feelings of disappointment which a person experiences when informed that he could not now get something which he had set his heart on. In this case it may seem that, if I do not know of the intention, but note that what I say has this apparent effect, then the pattern of explanation is further elaborated if the intention is then brought to my notice. However, if it is causal factors that we seek, then once more, I should say, it is more in place to look to some aspect of the physiological state that people are in when they have an intention, rather than to the intending itself.

Many other examples come to mind. We can make people laugh by telling them jokes; we can make them cry by imparting bad news. In both cases we have to do, typically, with an involuntary reaction, and in both cases there is a psychological dimension to the causation. However, there are other pitfalls awaiting the identification of a cause in this area. Consider the following passage from Wollaston:

> Do we not see, in conversation, how a pleasant thing will make people break out into laughter, a rude thing into a passion, and so on. These affections cannot be the physical effects of the words spoken because then they would have the same effect, whether they were understood or not. It is therefore the sense of the words which . . . produces those motions in the spirits, blood and muscles. (quoted from Priestley 1965: 121)

That the words used should have the meaning they have may well be indispensable to their utterance's having the effect it has on a given occasion, yet meaning or sense is hardly suitable as a cause. How does it stand with the psychological notion which we should more fittingly invoke—namely, understanding, knowing what the words mean? Such understanding will be a prerequisite for the hearer's learning of something pleasant or rude from the words uttered, but it is a matter of a condition for our allowing this as a description of what has been learned from the utterance, not a causal condition.

Again, seeing a joke may be thought causally to explain subsequent laughter, but, in so far as the seeing is a matter of an achievement, the question of causation is more appropriately raised with respect to the state initiated. What about finding something funny? This does appear to involve causation, but perhaps not quite in the way we might first think. We find x funny if and only if x amuses us, which is indeed a matter of an effect induced by x, whereas we might have supposed it a matter of an effect brought about by the belief that something is funny. The two notions come close, but, as already noted (§3.2), we misrepresent finding a joke funny if we take it to be simply a matter of having a belief that the joke has a certain character.

In passing, there are possible a posteriori identities of note in this area. So, one may see a joke, find it funny, and laugh. These are all separable: one may see the joke without finding it funny, or find it funny but be no more than inclined to laugh. However, in some cases we may be able to think in terms of a single, if complex, state that begins with seeing the joke and which involves both being amused and expressing this in laughter. The difference between experiencing an emotion and merely holding a certain belief, making a certain judgement, may be approached in this way, the beliefs involved in fear and anger occurring now with, now without, the further affective elements which warrant talk of an emotion.

Emotions and feelings, as with feeling relieved, anxious, disappointed, and so forth, may also take us closer to a causal involvement of belief. Consider a state of worry or anxiety giving way to one of relief. We have, initially, reason to think that something unwelcome has happened or is about to happen. Our thoughts turn repeatedly to this prospect, we find it difficult to be light-hearted, but are tense, on edge, our mouths dry, our palms moist—various bodily aspects of the state which *feel* signals here. With a change in belief, our fearful expectations not being realized, the tension eases. To all appearances, believing or expecting the worst induces one set of bodily conditions which then give way to others on the cessation of that belief.

With such examples, a causal role for belief (as believing) may strike us as irresistible. However, there is more than this possibility to consider. To take a less complex example, suppose, first, that a person is frightened by a sudden unexpected movement. This may be a matter of a reflex, with no time for beliefs (as to menacing character) to form before the fright. Consider now the causation of feelings of fright which may arise on recalling the episode. One possibility is that both aspects of the experience, the perceptual and the fearful, are 'stored' together, and that in recalling the former we thereby reawaken the latter. Here a simple association is at work, with no need to call upon content to play a role. But what if the fright depends on the formation of a belief? There is a snake inches from your bare foot. If you immediately recognize it as a grass snake, you may not be in the least concerned; if you take it for an adder, you may be frightened out of your wits. Since it takes the belief for the frightened reaction to occur, that belief (believing) appears to have a causal role. Once more, however, it could be that you are activating a past association. If your current judgement that the snake is an adder brings the association into play, it may be in virtue of a link between the present belief and a past one of the same kind, the connection between belief and feeling then reducing to what was suggested for the first example. And if your feelings of fear arise when thinking merely of what might happen? Even here it would seem plausible to suppose that the main links operate within the network of beliefs, the possibility which you envisage being, say, of a type having other instances which have been associated in your experience with feelings of fear.

I am not concerned to offer these remarks as anything more than suggestions, but they do serve to open up a wider range of possibilities than philosophers engaged in a single-minded pursuit of the seemingly obvious causal relation tend to address. However, this has been a digression. It is the relation of belief to voluntary rather than involuntary behaviour that is our chief concern, and we shall now add to what we have on this topic.

7.4 THOUGHT AND ACTION

Examples of intentional action are familiar in which there is no uncertainty to resolve, no call to adjudicate between conflicting goals, values, or strategies, indeed no decision to have to take in any substantive sense. In so far as our concern is with the way a decision might relate to subsequent action, then, if there is no decision, that question at least does not arise. However, it might be said that another is quick to take its place—namely, the question of the relation to action of a realization, belief, or other form of thought that something is so. Note that it is not thought as reasoning that concerns us. Our thinking may take the form of turning over possibilities, considering the consequences of a supposition, weighing up probabilities, and so forth, but it is only once a conclusion takes shape that we shall have something we might then act upon. However, thought as reasoning comes to the fore when we consider the sense in which thought is necessary to action, and we shall finish this section with some observations on this topic.

When the thought or belief amounts to knowledge, a direct link to action is possible in a way akin to what was noted for understanding. Just as a person gives proof of understanding by doing certain things, so too our knowledge of, for example, the whereabouts of something may be clearly manifested in the way we unerringly find our way to that thing, and in giving proof of knowledge, the same behaviour thereby attests to a belief that the object sought is to be found at the location in question. But suppose that the object's location has changed without our knowing, so that we can be said *only* to believe that it is in a certain place. Merely holding that belief does not enable one to do anything comparable, except perhaps *try* to make one's way to where it is; that is, with that belief, something *counts* as trying.

Consider further the matter of explanation. We have schemes such as the one mentioned above: if a person wants x, and y is, as he believes, the only way of getting it, then, if he is able to do y, and sees no reason against it, he will try to do y. Extracting just the reference to belief, we may say that, against certain assumptions, a belief will make certain behaviour likely. Or, if the assumptions can more or less be taken for granted, then we can say that holding a certain belief makes the relevant behaviour likely, *tout court*, as when the belief is that something is harmful or dangerous and the action is action to avoid it. For reasons of indeterminacy, a logically incontrovertible truth represents a limit to which such propositions tend rather than their clearly defined status, but the way we treat them aligns them with conceptual truths rather than with empirical generalizations or predictive theories. In the face of inaction we adjust our descriptions, concluding that the person's resolution was less firm than we had supposed, that he couldn't be bothered to act, perhaps that we simply don't understand why he didn't take the opportunity offered. Any account of the relation between wanting and acting which insists on settling for a purely empirical relation, so finding reason to speak in terms of a predictive *theory*, has not carried the analysis far enough.

The appropriate comparison between knowledge and belief is to be drawn, I suggest, as follows. If, against certain assumptions, belief that p makes certain behaviour likely, then against the same assumptions, knowledge that p will also make that behaviour likely, but now with the added likelihood of *success*. So, if a person believes that the combination of a lock is given by a certain sequence of digits, then, under certain assumptions—he wants to open the lock, he has access to it, and he knows how to set about opening such a lock—trying that combination can be expected. If he *knows* that this is the combination, then, against the same assumptions, *success* in opening the lock can be expected. This does not, of course, serve to pinpoint knowledge, since the ability in question would associate equally well with correctly guessing. Knowing the combination enables us to open the lock, but correctly guessing it also makes the same action possible.

This approach draws knowledge and belief close to one another, and relates both to behaviour via desire. Although, in view of the need for desire, it is to some extent an accident that the beginnings of the belief may be at the same time the beginnings of its manifestation in behaviour, it is a possibility of some relevance if our concern is to specify an intelligible link between thought and behaviour. One attempt at drawing such a connection was alluded to above: thought is taken to be itself a species of covert behaviour, a matter of sub-vocal talk. As a way of remaining true to behaviourist principles, this is a cheat: there is nothing in unspoken thoughts which the behaviourist can recognize as behaviour, and adding 'covert', or some such qualification—'of very small amplitude'—cannot disguise the divergence. Moreover, the resulting picture is essentially Cartesian, the divorce between thought and the behaviour which it might be called upon to explain remaining every bit as absolute as when the sub-vocal talk is acknowledged to be mental. If any relation can be enlisted in bringing the two together, it must, presumably, be causal, but it is unclear how saying anything at all, whether out loud or to oneself, in a natural language or in mentalese, might bring about the movement of one's limbs. Hence, of course, the step taken by some behaviourists of simply dismissing any claim of thought to explain behaviour.

Our analysis has drawn the connection in a very different fashion. The relevant state of mind, or behavioural disposition, being assured by the relevant desires and beliefs, there will be no call to look beyond this assurance to a causal link. Having the thought and becoming prepared to act are not separate steps, as though, suddenly recalling where something one wanted at this moment was to be found, one only at some later stage became prepared to set off to fetch it. One becomes prepared to act *with* the realization, the memory. But a separate step *is* needed if we are to think of the relation between the thought and what follows as causal.

In passing, it is worth noting that a functionalist view of thoughts is vulnerable not only in its requirement that thoughts be causes, but even in its requirement that they be effects. This is not to say that they are never the latter; only, as indicated in §1.1, that the form of explanation into which thoughts typically enter does not cast them in this role. It is only when the usual kinds of why-question have been exhausted that we come to a causal query. This claim may seem perverse. Surely, if, on seeing the leaning chimney stack, I think: it is going to fall, that thought is caused by what I see. Perhaps, but, if the question is why we think what we think, then what we have first and foremost is a *ground* for our thought or belief. If you ask me why I thought that *p*, then, unless my memory makes matters uncertain, I shall not say 'I suppose it was because . . .'. It is not a *hypothesis* that I thought that the chimney was about to topple because it was leaning at such an angle off the perpendicular. But suppose I see a chimney. Don't I just think—but not infer—that a chimney is before me? I may, but, as already argued, that will be further to learning of the chimney's presence, and it is further to that precisely because with thought we move into the realm of classifying, judging, surmising, and concluding, where once more reasons are likely to be involved. As I say, when reasons give out, we shall have a causal question, but that is what our why-questions give way to, not the concerns with which they normally begin.

Where do we now stand on the question of epiphenomenalism? Consider Norman Malcolm's example of a man climbing a ladder in order to retrieve his hat from the roof. If, with the epiphenomenalist, we suppose that the behaviour on the ladder and the intention to climb it are the effects of a common cause, then the relation between behaviour and intention will be purely contingent. It may then be in fact true that we should not have encountered the behaviour without the intention, but it will remain conceivable that the intention should occur without the behaviour, or that the behaviour should occur with a contrary intention. As Malcolm puts it: 'Epiphenomenalism would permit it to be universally true that whenever any person intended to *not* do any action, he did it, and that whenever any person intended to do any action, he did not do it. This is a conceptual absurdity' (1968: 134–5). Our account, however, does not allow that the behaviour should be allied with just any intention, since a given intention *requires* a certain behavioural disposition, even if such a disposition is not sufficient for the intention. Likewise with animals. There is no pressure to ascribe undisclosed thoughts to the elephant that never forgets, but with those capacities which cannot be denied the creature, as with a capacity for remembering a route traversed, there is no question of dismissing a superfluous epiphenomenon: a state the reality of which is demonstrated by the creature's behaviour will survive the most determined efforts to prune inessentials. The possibility which Malcolm rightly dismisses results from construing the mental in Cartesian terms, an intention being conceived of as an inner event bearing only contingent links to behaviour. To rescue it from the idleness and inertia that threaten, the intention must, it is supposed, be given causal work to do; but the relation then introduced is not strong enough to avoid the absurdity to which Malcolm draws attention.

Epiphenomenalism is also thought to threaten the project of understanding how the content of a mental state can enjoy a causal role: it is difficult to see how meaning can be a property which determines the course of neuronal activity, but its status appears to be no more than that of an epiphenomenon. We have already found reason to query the assumptions which give rise to this problem. To recall our earlier argument, the dismissal of the cruder variety of materialism meant that there was no physicalist imperative to transfer to the brain any and every property of the mental, so, if meaning or content has application to the latter, this is no guarantee that they will resurface as properties of the former. Moreover, not only does it not make sense to locate these in the brain; their attachment to the mental is itself doubtful. Certainly, it is the belief as what is believed that has content, and constitutes a reason, and this is neither mental, nor suited to being a cause. What is to be said of the belief as believing? We cannot speak of the believing as itself having meaning or content, but believings can be differentiated depending on the content of what is believed. Let us then suppose that different believings reflect different neural states. Is this not enough at least for the project to get under way? Different beliefs will make a different causal contribution to behaviour depending on their content. Similarly, perhaps, with desires as desirings. If believing that p and wanting to V are somehow underpinned by physiological processes, we should like to know how the fact that the latter are associated with just this belief and desire comes to play a part in an explanation of what those processes are instrumental in bringing about.

Before tackling this question, we might mention two reasons why, more generally, the scope for the cognitive scientist's problem has diminished.

First, our rejection of certain determinations of what counts as mental narrows the problematic field. Consider desire. If an animal can show by its behaviour that it wants to V, and if it is only certain human desires that make the demand for thought—as a desire to master a foreign language—then there is nothing essentially mental about wanting. Perception is analogous. We may not know that someone can see or hear something unless he tells us, but this does not mean that what he then informs us of is a mental event. As we have insisted, a claim that perception is inescapably bound up with thought rests on attaching unwarranted importance to a distorting first-person perspective.

Secondly, once semantic properties have been acknowledged as out of contention, it is not easy to see how a physical event could have mental properties that were not at the same time physical properties in a straightforward way, as with such properties as being intermittent, lasting only briefly, causing or being caused by other events. The distinctively mental properties have distinctively mental subjects, so have no business characterizing relevant events. Compare 'experiencing pain' and 'pain', or 'dreaming' and 'dream'. Setting aside our reservations about sensations, we can take each of 'pain' and 'dream' to apply to something mental, and, if earlier arguments have been successful, it is no objection to physicalism that descriptions of dreams and pains, as, for example, lifelike or searing, do not attach to anything in our nervous systems. However, if the identity of the mental with the physical is being maintained at the level of *events*, then any applicable description must hold of the physical as readily as of the mental, a description which favoured the latter to the exclusion of the former simply showing the falsity of physicalism with respect to that instance of the mental.

Returning to belief and desire, it is important not to lose sight of the innumerable occasions when, notwithstanding their role in explaining an action, the psychological dimension is at a minimum. So, in response to a request to give your name, you do so. Did you believe you could comply by doing what you did? Certainly; indeed, you knew you could, though there was no sense in which you translated a thought into action. You simply spoke unthinkingly. Did you do something you wanted to do? Again, yes, but it is a matter of wanting only in the minimal way required for action: as your response so plainly showed, you were prepared to comply with the request; it was a matter merely of performing an act of a kind from which you might have refrained, but from which you did not.

Again, you hear letters dropping through the flap in the door, and you go to see what the postman has delivered. Did you think you could find out by doing what you did—getting up and setting off for the door? Yes, but the place of 'you thought that *p*' is not that of 'you had the thought that *p*', or 'the thought that *p* crossed your mind'. No thought as to what you could do need actually have occurred to you any more than when it can be said—as it no doubt could—that you *knew* you could do this. The 'think' is as consistent with as empty a head as when, but for something which unexpectedly thwarted you, it would have been true to say you knew. There are many background facts familiar to you—what the sound in question generally signifies, where the letter box is in relation to you—but doing something in the belief that *p* and for the sake of *q* need involve nothing as far as mental happenings of the moment are concerned; it may simply be: you hear the sound, you get up and walk. It is the action that makes the difference; in the circumstances, this may by itself be enough to ensure intention or desire.

The supposition is that the belief/desire complex underlying your response is associated with a neural state or process which produces that response. Let us suppose that there is indeed a neural condition effective to this end. It is the attachment of the neural to the *mental* that is now problematic, the dearth of any appropriate items of such character making for some embarrassment in fleshing out a causal sequence in which something mental, through its physical realization, might be responsible for a physical effect. It would appear, rather, that, if the neural happenings are to be correlated with anything, it is first and foremost with our *behaviour*. The things that pass through our head can be or not be as far as the truth of the relevant statements of belief and desire are concerned. Of course, if questioned, you will no doubt be prepared to say you thought that *p* and you wanted to *V*, but, while what you are prepared to avow truthfully is critical in determining how your behaviour is to be viewed, your words need not report occurrent mental episodes in order to fill this role. Here we might compare the way the mental was bypassed in the example of the motorist's signal bringing about behaviour manifesting the belief that he is about to stop.

Our original question now becomes: how is it that the behaviour in question comes to be generated by the neural happenings with which we have found it associated? This could be an extremely complex question. Not just a matter of a synchronic issue: just what is going on in the nervous system when the limbs move thus? More the kind of issue tackled in Dretske (1988): how is it that certain neural processes have been recruited to do the things they do?—a diachronic question. But, while the complexities here may be awesome, they do not require us to find a place in our explanations for mental characteristics of neural processes.

Perhaps we are going too fast. Occasions when there is a paucity of mental occurrences must not be overlooked, but there are also cases which present us with a much richer range of psychological happenings, as thoughts entertained, desires experienced, and it appears questionable to rest much on what is essentially just habitual behaviour. However, we may note that, when there is a flurry of mental activity which we might appear to have neglected, this will often be in the form of thinking which *leads* to a belief. You spend some time poring over a road map trying to work out how best to travel to your destination. The thinking you engage in does not connect directly with any subsequent behaviour, but that falls to the belief as to the appropriate route which eventually emerges. But now, the belief (believing) in question is not an episode, but a state or capacity which can exist when your thoughts are far away, and which makes itself known in a range of responses of a broadly behavioural character, as when you express the belief in words, seek to draw out its consequences, or act in accordance with it. There is no question of a belief conceived of in Cartesian terms, an inner item divorced from what you do and say, yet it has to be some such conception that is embraced for there to be any question of tracing a causal chain from the psychological to the behavioural. Our contrary suggestion is that any relevant physiological conditions will link directly with the state which is supposed to be merely the upshot of these inner events.

The picture we are presenting gains support from consideration of animals. Think again of a bird steering a course by environmental cues, and set this beside an analogous human performance. The scientific challenge is much the same in either case—to work out how the physiological events and structures combine with the perceptual input to yield the relevant pattern of behaviour. The common pattern of behaviour, along with the superfluity of any thought which does not amount to the shared belief, suggest that the data to be explained are essentially comparable.

We may take the point further in conjunction with one of the major problems glimpsed at the beginning of our enquiry. It is sometimes held that an explanation of action in terms of the agent's reasons coexists uneasily with an explanation which treats actions as movements to be accounted for in a more impersonal fashion— mechanically, electrically, and so forth (cf. Nagel 1986: ch. 7). Ultimately, it is feared, the latter, 'objective', accounts may come to supplant those in terms of beliefs and desires, thus destroying our conception of ourselves as autonomous agents. Physicalism does not provide an assured escape from this possibility: psychological states and events may constitute potential physical causes, but that is no guarantee that they in fact provide the sources of action.

Our own position is not necessarily immune to this objection. In urging a distinction between reasons and causes, our first concern was to keep apart the respective *concepts*: perhaps reasons are causes, but the familiar explanations of behaviour in terms of belief and desire do not depend on there being any such identity. However, if no *more* than the conceptual distinction can be sustained, beliefs and desires can be reckoned among the potential causes of behaviour, and this opens up the possibility that what the agent cites as his reason is quite unconnected with what turns out to be the actual cause. The embarrassment appears to be more than potential. Does not any account of action for which this is even a possibility thereby stand condemned?

I am filing away at a piece of metal, believing I may thereby remove some rust, but suppose that none of the neural happenings instrumental in producing my movements bears any significant relation to the holding of this belief. They correspond to some belief, we shall suppose, but, if it were the belief that there will be a general election in the autumn, would not my behaviour be unintelligible?

This seeming absurdity is made to appear consistent with our analysis only, I suspect, because an inappropriate conception of the causation of movements is being presupposed—a matter of neural events which will have done their work once the behaviour is under way. If a neural condition deserves to be called the condition associated with the given belief, this will be because it contributes materially to the *structuring* of the subject's responses; in this example, it will be a matter of a condition which exercises control over my movements towards their rust-removing end, a control exercised in the light of perceptual feedback as the task progresses. It is not a matter of a single causal happening which is as indifferent to the subsequent train of events as the throwing of a switch, and so which might be

associated with just any belief. Moreover, the neural activity underlying my efforts would surely qualify *automatically* as the physiological process associated with the belief/desire complex: it is precisely
through the behaviour for which it is responsible that it is identified
as such.

This last point is crucial. Think of the relevant psychological condition as paired—ultimately, as identical—with a neural state, and
linked causally to the behaviour which it explains, *when* it explains
it, and you may find that this last condition goes unsatisfied, thus
revealing the psychological condition to have nothing to do with the
way we behave. However, if the neural state associated with the condition is identified through the behaviour which manifests the latter,
there is no room for mind and behaviour to come apart in this way.
This consideration is surely a strong argument against the causal
Cartesian theory. Although that is commonly the framework in
which the cognitive scientist's speculations are lodged, the position
sketched here offers a more hopeful prospect to any programme of
making sense of physiological happenings in relation to behaviour.

How the relevant neural condition might be recognized as such
when there is no behaviour is, of course, another matter, and not one
that affects the claim that, when the behaviour is forthcoming, the
psychological condition, along with its neural substrate, are to be
identified in the way proposed. In this connection we may observe the
following. I have allowed, for the sake of argument, that we might
speak of *the* neural condition associated with (the having of) a belief.
The example considered may be thought favourable to this possibility, but there is no guarantee that this way of speaking can be sustained, even if everything we say or do has a neural history. Beliefs
can be enumerated or listed; we have a conception, however rough
and ready, of a single belief, perhaps of a belief as a unitary item—
based, no doubt, on the idea of a sentential unit. However, why
should the unity or singularity of a belief reflect anything in the brain
that could in any useful way be regarded as forming a single unit?
Perhaps, in so far as a person continues to believe that p, there will
be found to be conditions on which this continuation depends, but
they may not be unique to the belief, and they may well change over
time. As Wittgenstein asked, why should the *system* continue further
in the direction of the centre (Z §608)?

Does the *written* word perhaps count for something in shaping the
physicalist's more rigid conception of belief, hope, and the rest in

their relation to what goes on in the head? The written word presents us with reidentifiable items of some permanence, and it may be assumed that we can do justice to their abiding character only by pairing them with inner states possessed of their own distinctive identity—in contrast to the propensity to do and say a wide range of things which might also be associated with believing. Think of the diverse expressions of 'propositional attitudes' which come and go in the flow of conversation, as 'I suppose I'd better be off, then', 'I expect she'll find someone else', and 'I'm afraid I can't remember where I put it', remarks which are surely an unpromising starting-point for an excursion into mind *or* brain in search of suppositions, expectations, fears, and so forth. It would, of course, be wrong-headed to argue that, if there is nothing in the head that answers to the structure of individual beliefs and desires, this would show our folk psychology to be in error (Churchland 1989: 125). Such an argument is yet another example of the perils attending a causal construal of reason-giving explanations, or functionalism more generally.

Scepticism about basing anything of substance on such remarks as 'I believe we've met before' might be confirmed in the following way. We have allowed that, with belief as believing, the customary concerns about psychoneural relations appear to have some foundation, but this presumes that believing is a state in some substantive sense, an enduring condition of the believer which might compare with clearer examples of a state of mind, as given with, say, anxiety, resignation, or suspicion. With some instances of belief the comparison seems apt. Religious belief, for instance, may involve a consistent pattern of responses which allow us to give substance to the notion of a state of mind, and belief as involved in practical knowledge may be comparable. With belief more generally, however, and particularly with respect to the casual observations of the kind just instanced, it is less clear what there might be to any supposed state.

We noted earlier that belief as believing subdivides. Such beliefs may be firm or fervent, but they may also be surprising or unwelcome. In the first case it is the *manner* of believing that is in focus, and it is this use that may be said to introduce a state on a par with the clearer paradigms. In the second case it is a question of the *fact* of believing. No reference to a state is implicit, but it is simply surprising or unwelcome that the person should believe what he believes. The way one holds a belief is pertinent to, once more, religious belief, but more generally '*A*'s believing . . .' would appear to provide no more than an inconsequential variant on a form featuring 'A believes', any more ambitious attempt at matching up beliefs and neural states, via the notion of a state of mind, being doomed to failure (cf. Hacker 1992).

Consider again Malcolm's man retrieving his hat. Malcolm writes:

> We will recall that the envisaged neurophysiological theory was supposed to provide *sufficient* causal explanations of behaviour. Thus the movements of the man on the ladder would be *completely* accounted for in terms of electrical, chemical, and mechanical processes in his body. This would surely imply that his desire or intention to retrieve his hat had nothing to do with his movement up the ladder. It would imply that on this same occasion he would have moved up the ladder in exactly this way even if he had had no intention to retrieve his hat, or even no intention to climb the ladder. (1968: 133)

This issue, along with our response to it, is implicit in the preceding discussion. Since there could be the same pattern of behaviour, now with one range of accompanying thoughts, now with another, now with nothing much by way of thoughts at all, we can grant that the man's movements could be completely accounted for physiologically without taking into account psychological happenings, at least in a narrow sense. If there is a constraint, this will be because the behaviour itself forces a psychological description, now in a broader sense. That is, whatever the man's thoughts, perhaps his behaviour warrants the description: he is trying to retrieve his hat. If the activity was in fact preceded by the forming of an intention, the taking of a decision, then the behaviour has a place within a richer setting, being not merely purposive, but the execution of an intention which took shape with the decision to act, a decision which was perhaps the culmination of deliberations as to risks, means, desirability, and so forth. But this richer account is not more generous in its provision of causes, not one which obliges us to choose between a physiological and a psychological account of the man's movements. If our analysis has been along the right lines, we can make sense of decision and intention without casting them in the role of supplementary causes, let alone rival ones, and also without requiring them to give up their place in an explanation of the action.

Let us go back to our initial question about the contribution of thought to action, a context where thought as reasoning is as much to the fore as is thought in the form of belief. We claimed that there is nothing that is practically impossible without thought, since practicality requires only behavioural skills of a kind which may fall within the capacity of animals and machines. In so far as thought is indispensable, it is not for causal reasons, but because the pattern of explanation invoked, or the description of what is done, makes that demand; so nothing would count as debugging a computer programme or checking a disk for viruses unless the being supposedly engaged in these tasks possessed a considerable body of knowledge and could think in a way that involves the kind of reasoning in which alternatives are considered, consequences of suppositions are drawn out, and so forth, activities for which the demand for thought is the demand for language of a fairly sophisticated character.

On many occasions, we simply do not have to think, but can proceed immediately to the appropriate action. But what of those occasions when thought is necessary for action? To say that you do not have to think is to say that you know already what to do. Conversely, thought may be necessary to work things out, to arrive at a conclusion on which one might act. It is not that thought is necessary to action *tout court*, but it may be necessary to *rational* action, which often means: to action which stands a good chance of success. Once more the cherished necessity reveals itself as logical, not as causal. To return to an earlier point: of course the right decision matters; not for any causal virtues it may have, but because it initiates a disposition to do the right thing. The right thoughts and beliefs may matter for just the same reason.

But, surely, if it is only because *q* that I think that *p*, then, had *q* not been so, but everything else had been the same, I should not have thought that *p*. And is that not a causal matter? As before, we might counter: if it had not been that *q*, or anything comparable, then our thought that *p* would have been without reason or foundation. More accurately, that is all we are committed to with our claim that it is only because *q* that we thought that *p*. But perhaps even this is to concede too much. Consider: it was only because I bothered to check that I found that the key had been taken. Suppose that we have to do here with a genuinely necessary condition; that, in the circumstances, there would have been no other way of coming to this knowledge. So, if I had not checked, and if no one had told me, if I had had no other way of coming by the information, then I should not have found that the key had been taken. Quite right. Without any checking or the like it would not have been possible, logically, to speak of finding, or finding out. Learning, finding, finding out—these do not occur *in vacuo*, but as the upshot of certain activities, of preliminaries necessary to confer the very description. 'Think' too has, if to a lesser degree, a comparable implication. So, why do I not suddenly, with no basis, think that *p*? Because thinking here is a terminus of reasoning, so the usual preliminaries are absent. It is not just: I had the thought, the thought crossed my mind, but more: I reasoned, formed the opinion. But for *q* I should have been without the only premiss that, by hypothesis, would have been acceptable to me, in which case there would, of course, have been no reasoning to *p*. Contrast thoughts as questions. I find myself wondering whether today is the day I have to go to the dentist. Why do I have this thought? Very often, one will be able to do no more than conjecture: perhaps something I heard or saw prompted the question. A causal query, no doubt, but remote from the case of thoughts as the termini of reasonings—the most important in the contexts which present our main concern.

8

Reasons and Consciousness

Granted that a person's sincere declaration of his reason for acting is not open to contradiction, what does that tell us about the explanation it provides? Does such invulnerability perhaps reflect adversely upon its value? Again, if the honest agent is above challenge, there may none the less be circumstances in which we can say that his is not the whole story, so we should like to know how an explanation in terms of reasons can be supplemented. What of the appeal to the unconscious? Is this a route to a genuine mode of explanation? If so, does it compare with explanations by reasons or with explanations by causes? These are some of the questions which have been with us for some time and which we shall now pursue.

8.1 REASONS AND INCORRIGIBILITY

To say that reasons are not causes, though correct, is not altogether helpful. The respective grammars of the terms stand in the way of any identification—for example, you can speak of the reason why, but not of the cause why—but this need be of no great consequence. So, why is the engine racing? You give the reason when you point out that excessive oxygen is mixing with the fuel. That is, you give a reason or explanation with a propositional form, whereas a cause may be introduced differently—via the designation of an event, for instance. But, as mentioned at the outset, that does not mean that in stating a reason we are not at the same time specifying a cause. Clearly, however, any statement which involved such a specification would be corrigible, so would not amount to stating the kind of reason for doing something which we avow when giving the aim of our action.

It is, then, the authority of the subject that matters. If I sincerely declare R to be my reason for acting, then it just is my reason, and has nothing to fear from any rival. Why do I clean the windscreen of the car? So that I may see through it better. Why am I turning out my pockets? Because I want to find some change. What sense can be made of the suggestion that these may not be my reasons, given that I am speaking sincerely and with understanding? This is not to say that we can always confidently avow a reason; only that, when we do, our honest word is not subject to challenge.

The explanation of behaviour in terms of the agent's avowed reasons is sometimes treated as a *hypothesis*, a hypothesis which a more sophisticated approach to explanation can be expected to expose as misconceived. That cannot be right. I turn the tap on to get some water. Unless there are extraordinary circumstances, circumstances which mean that I cannot regard my actions as my own, I cannot sensibly say: I believe it is because I want some water that I am turning on the tap. The appeal to reasons simply *defines* a category of explanation, whatever other forms there may be. There are, of course, reasons of other kinds, as reasons why we slur our speech or tremble, but these are not reasons for acting. A more plausible observation would be that the incorrigibility which arises with reason-giving is bought at a price. We have remarked that such character makes for a gulf between (the concepts of) giving one's reason and assigning a cause. Perhaps, more generally, it shows that there is not much of depth to explanations in the former terms. Here, as elsewhere, the greater the immunity to error, the less substance there is to one's claim, any certainty one has being just the 'certainty' that comes when doubt makes no sense—not certainty that rests on eliminating grounds for doubt, on reassuring oneself that a genuine but conflicting possibility has not been realized. If, in contrast to causal explanations, it takes no more than our word to secure a reason as our reason, if there is no need to undertake any investigation of rival factors, in that there is nothing that would even count as a rival factor, how can avowing a reason, however sincerely, offer any kind of substantive explanation?

Certainly, any use we make of 'explanation' in relation to the giving of reasons must be geared to this lack of risk. But then is any other kind of explanation to the point, is any other able to do what we ask of an explanation in this context? Do we, can we, in fact ask for anything more that is not something utterly different, as with a physiological explanation? Consider, after all, the illumination that may dawn when, and only when, a person reveals the thoughts behind his otherwise unfathomable behaviour. If someone is standing on his head on the pavement we may wonder why. Unless we despair of getting a satisfactory answer, we shall not be concerned with the switch to a totally different level that comes when we consider how his bizarre stance might have followed on some series of neural happenings. We want to know what he thinks he is doing, what he hopes to achieve, and his honest word can give us enlightenment where reams of information about his physiology would be likely to leave us as perplexed as ever. Again, what is often of paramount importance to us is a person's state of mind: is he ill- or well-disposed to those who stand to be affected by what he does? Once more, reassurance on this vital concern is not to be secured by investigating the workings of the body—though, of course, the inferences we draw as to likely behaviour do not rest simply on what is avowed, but require the assistance of other (corrigible) ascriptions of tendencies to act. To be of consequence, the state of mind must continue into the future.

Compare causal and non-causal uses of words such as 'remind' and 'bring to mind'. If someone says that a certain melody brings to mind 'Auld Lang Syne', we may retort that it does not have that effect on us. But if it is said that the one is reminiscent of the other, in a way that requires no more than a suitable *likeness* to be established, the claim will not be vulnerable in the same way. The connection is now a formal one, not causal, and there is no pressure to reduce it to the latter; the two are not in conflict, but can happily exist side by side—though it might be said more generally that laying bare formal connections answers more to our real interests than does the pursuit of causal connections which the natural sciences encourage to obsession. (Cf. Wittgenstein (*LC*, *GB*) on aesthetic explanations and explanations of rituals.) Or again, compare 'That he is aggressive' and 'That he has exceptionally high levels of testosterone' as answers to the question 'What does it tell you about a man if he regularly behaves in that way?' The first purports to give a general characterization which holds just on the strength of a correct description of the behaviour. The second seeks to probe beneath the behaviour to a physical explanation. How could these answers conceivably conflict?

When first discussing explanations of action, we suggested that, for a reason to be as stated, the agent was not obliged to take a stand on what would have happened had his beliefs and/or desires been different. Since this is a major point on which our position is likely to be challenged, it is worth taking a second look at the argument. This occurs in the context of the claim that belief/desire explanations are required 'to support counterfactuals in ways that are familiar in causal explanation at large', and hence that it is reasonable to read the 'because' in such explanations as a causal 'because' (Fodor 1985: 77). As hinted in §1.1, however, queries about the role of counter-factual conditionals are possible even when there is no dispute that what is being spoken of is a cause. Consider such an example as 'Peter of Spain was killed by the collapse of a roof'. The author of *Summule Logicales* would not have died—certainly not just then— but for the collapse, there being, let us suppose, no other threats to his life at the time. But what has that observation to do with the causal truth? It surely looks *beyond* the cause to what was—or was not—to be found in the circumstances: supposing nothing else to have happened in lieu of the collapse, Peter of Spain would not have been killed. But that is just to say that *some* antecedent event was necessary for the death; or, perhaps, that this would not have occurred without a cause, and that the collapse of the roof was in fact sufficient for its occurrence.

We shall, of course, be in no hurry to allow that events should occur uncaused, but the important consideration is that this is an *independent* matter, not something that flows from the truth of the causal proposition. Moreover, when we have to do with an agent's reasons, there is no difficulty in allowing that what was done might have been done for no reason, since this means only that it was done thoughtlessly, that the agent was oblivious to what he was doing. There is no admission of an uncaused happening, precisely because 'without a reason' does not mean 'without a cause'. We can accordingly conclude, as before, that we are not threatened with having to accept a counterfactual proposition which might be inconsistent with the authority which the subject has as to his reasons for acting.

Would it not be fair to say that 'one's reason for acting' just *means* 'the reason one is sincerely prepared to avow or acknowledge', whence *of course* there is no question of error? But, as noted, the avowal can still tell you something of importance about the agent, something which may not otherwise be learned about him. True, it is in large measure the person's sincerity, something which we may have to take on trust, that is doing the work, but the particular words are none the less critical. Moreover, the sufficiency of the agent's honest avowal closes a gap which otherwise opens up to invite the introduction of extraneous factors. Thus Davidson (1963: 9), noting that 'a person can have a reason for an action, and perform the action, and yet this reason not be the reason why he did it', makes the further requirement that, to be the reason why, the reason must be a cause. As is sometimes said, the reason is to be a 'motivating' reason.

It is certainly true that one may do *x*, knowing or believing that it will lead to *y*, but not be doing *x* *because* it is believed to have this consequence. Once more, the shift from *reason* to *reasoning* better enables us to appreciate how a fuller account may proceed: it is not enough that the thought should occur to the agent, that he should be reminded of his belief; it is also required that the belief have a role in the agent's reasoning; such reasoning has a *structure*, and the connective 'because' is warranted if, and only if, the thought or belief has an appropriate place therein. If *A* has overlooked the fact that *p*, or failed to appreciate its relevance to his designs, then, despite his knowledge that *p*, no reason for his action is to be found in that direction. The knowledge or belief is not effective, in the sense that it plays no part in his plans, his calculations, not in the sense that it is causally impotent.

A possible distinction between 'intention' and 'motive' is relevant here—one somewhat at odds with the usage proposed for 'motivating reason'. *A* may have a motive for murdering *B*, but no intention of doing so, the reason given with the motive not being part of the reasoning that culminates in a decision to act—a decision which might issue in an intention, but not, of course, in a motive. We tend to run 'motive' and 'intention' together so long as we seek to distinguish them in the context of asking what someone's motive or intention was in acting, but if action is not presupposed the difference is plain. You have a motive for Ving in so far as there is, to your mind, something you stand to gain from Ving, but that does not mean that you have formed the intention to V. To specify an intention is to specify an end aimed at, but without necessarily any indication of the interest which it is thought to serve. In introducing a motive, however, we introduce a consideration which ostensibly makes sense of the particular aim, relating this to a desire, often given in general terms, as a desire for revenge or power. A decision can be a decision to adopt a means, but it cannot be a decision to have an interest or desire.

Appeals to incorrigibility are sometimes suspect because of the inappropriate model on which they are based. Not only is awareness of mental states and operations thought of on the analogy of visual perception, but it is a superior form of perception, to the point of delivering infallible verdicts about its objects. As already observed, disowning this picture need not mean rejecting all talk of *reporting*, and the notion of incorrigibility, as here interpreted, would also appear to survive unscathed. If expressive forms were neither true nor false, they would fail to qualify either as corrigible or incorrigible, and, if genuine reports had to be corrigible, then incorrigibility would be an illusory feature quite generally. But these are no more than ifs. An expression of belief can have a truth value without prejudice to its character as an expression, and reports of how things seem are paradigmatically incorrigible. True, talk of incorrigibility does tend to put the matter in the wrong light—as if it were a question of an investigative technique which could be counted upon to turn up only truths, and not of, simply, the senselessness of an expression of uncertainty. We might accordingly prefer to lay emphasis on another notion mentioned at the outset—namely, that of the agent's reason as what he is prepared, at some point, to *acknowledge* as such. This is also better suited to those circumstances where there can be consciousness of one's reasons to a greater or lesser degree, where full consciousness dawns only after some time has elapsed. We shall make something of this possibility shortly.

It was because he considered incorrigibility to go hand in hand with a misconceived model that Ryle refused to grant such character where we are discerning it. Hence the distinctive feature of his conception of human beings as essentially as transparent to others as they are to themselves. We are not embracing the misguided account which Ryle rejected, but it is none the less worth pausing to look at what he has to say on what he styles 'motive explanations' (1949: ch. IV).

Ryle is anxious to differentiate motive from causal explanations, but he sees the former as involving an appeal to a disposition, a motive being akin to the brittleness of the glass which breaks rather than to the blow which shatters the glass. However, although Ryle with some reason disallows the title of *cause* to dispositions, it is not improper to call them causal *conditions*. Consider again our stringed instrument. It is by plucking the strings that we produce a sound, but the character of the sound is determined by such factors as the length, tension, and constitution of the strings, and this can be reckoned a species of causal determination.

Whether or not dispositions qualify as causal conditions, it seems that the agent is not beyond challenge in their regard. None the less, there is a way, albeit of limited application, in which attributions of a motive can conform to Ryle's scheme without contradicting the present analysis. In saying, in the face of Harvey's protestations to the contrary, that he acted out of greed, ambition, or vanity, we need not be undermining Harvey's more specific statement of his reason for doing what he did. Rather, we may say that, in the circumstances, acting as Harvey did *counts* as seeking to advance an ambition or as a manifestation of vanity or greed. So long as this is the point of dispute, it is not one on which the agent's authority is final. If the person protests, 'I wasn't being greedy', he may be challenged: 'greedy', we say, is just the word for that sort of behaviour. Such an analysis is perhaps only exceptionally possible, considerations of motive more commonly taking us straight to the agent's reason, but when it does apply there is no more question of offering a cause than when, to take another of Ryle's examples, we answer the question, 'Why is the bird flying south?' with 'It is migrating' (Ryle 1949: 142). What Ryle has drawn attention to is a further way in which the agent's explanation can be supplemented.

If *R* is to be our reason, must *R* itself be beyond challenge? Suppose that Harvey is asked why he is buying avocado pears. He replies that he is fond of guacamole and that Kate has promised to make some if he can deliver the ingredients. This may be, as it stands, quite wrong. The supposed fondness for guacamole may not be borne out by past behaviour, and Kate may have promised nothing of the sort. None the less, despite such a comprehensive misconception, we can still salvage the basic pattern of explanation: Harvey is buying avocados to give to Kate to make guacamole. That is not for him a matter of conjecture, though considerations on which it is based, which give the activity point, are not as he supposes. The pertinent question is whether that is in truth how he reasoned, or a pattern of reasoning which he would sincerely acknowledge. Misconceptions which his reasons harbour are of no account.

But in this example it is at least true, we are supposing, that Harvey thinks he is fond of guacamole. What if we should allow that there are occasions when a person decides on reflection that he did not really think that *p* when he said, sincerely, that he did? When, after all, 'I think (believe) that *p*' is a report, it is likely to be corrigible in so far as it purports to report more than the state of mind of the moment. Certainly, we might say, what the person states does not square with a lot of things he has said or done in the past. And, surely, if the agent did not think that *p*, then it will not be true that his reason for doing what he did was that he thought that *p*. However, to reinstate the belief as his reason requires only that he in fact subscribed to it. It does not need, in addition, a causal link: if he thought that *p* and declares that that is why he acted, then that *is* his reason.

How do matters stand if it is the genuineness of the desire that comes into question? Kate may insist that she wants to go to the ballet, yet have second thoughts when presented with the opportunity to do so. It may be said that her expression of desire will at least reflect the feelings of the moment, but that is surely worth little if the moment never lasts long enough for her ostensible desire to be put to the test. So, Kate sincerely claims that she wants to be helpful, or that she wants to give to a charity, but if these declarations have to stand the test of actual helpfulness, actual generosity, what becomes of the incorrigibility of an avowed reason for action?

We note, first, that, if there is a failure to act to fulfil a desire, there will by the same token be no question of the desire's being offered in explanation of an action. Again, if at a later time we should misremember our desire, that is likewise not to the point; it does not expose one's sincere avowal to challenge at the time of acting. It is true that, if it is possible sincerely to avow a desire yet not have that desire, the declared reason will be no reason, but once more there would appear to be no more of a problem with 'I am Ving *because* I want *x*' than there is with 'I want *x*'. The 'because' does not reflect an attempt at diagnosing or deciphering one's action or motivation; if there is any uncertainty, it will be in making up our mind what we want. It is not that a causal hypothesis has yet to be verified, but to concede a degree of corrigibility is here too of no account so long as causation remains out of consideration.

Kate is waving to attract someone's attention. That is what she wants, what she is aiming at, but what makes it so? She could, after all, be doing something which she believes has had or will have a certain outcome without that outcome's defining an aim of hers. For instance, she knows that waving her arms will cast shadows, alarm nearby birds, draw attention to herself generally. In many cases, certain outcomes which could be the agent's goal will, as indicated, be disqualified through having had no place in the reasoning about means to attain the true goal. Kate gives some thought as to how she might catch someone's attention, but no thought at all as to how she might frighten the birds. Since it could be said that she is frightening the birds intentionally if she is knowingly frightening them, we have to look elsewhere for a more restricted way in which intention may enter, and this is what we get with the intention before it was put into effect, assuming that this consequence had not been foreseen.

This last qualification is necessary. Suppose I shatter the peace on a Sunday afternoon with my lawnmowing. As already intimated, a neighbour can rightly protest that I am making a noise intentionally. Could it be said that the noise had been intended, or that it had been my intention to make a noise, if I had known it would come about when I decided to mow the lawn? On the one hand, making the noise is something I can be said to be doing for a reason. If asked why I am making the noise, I need not reject the question, but I should allow that I am making the noise because I must do so if I am to mow the lawn. Given the requisite knowledge, consequences and side effects are perhaps comparable with known necessary means to the given end. I intend to take the various steps I know I must take to mow the lawn, but I also intend what I knowingly bring about in the belief that it *has* to take place if my end is to be achieved, even if, like making a noise, it is not necessary as a means. On the other hand, because it will make no difference to my plans if I learn that in fact there will be no noise, this is reason for saying that production of this effect lies outside anything intended. The question of usage is not insignificant, but more important is the consideration that we are not without resources to differentiate the relevantly different aspects of the state of affairs brought about, even if intention lets us down as a concept with which to do so. We can still couple the admission of intentionality with the claim that making a noise is not the point, purpose, goal, or aim of our action. It is what is aimed at for itself that matters, or any means adopted to such an end, rather than any inseparable side effects that attainment of either necessitates.

A similar issue arises with respect to the claim that action gives proof of wanting, though here the means also fall into the area of dispute. Harvey says that he didn't want to stay for dinner, and we consider this belied by his doing just that when he could have refused. So long as he did what he did knowingly, it can be said only that 'ideally' he did not want to. That is, he would have preferred not to, only circumstances made that course of action unavoidable. Again, however, since 'want' may mean much the same as 'ideally want', we have more than one possibility.

To return to our main theme, if there is no need to work out a strategy, nothing that could realistically be reckoned reasoning, then what is aimed at will be what is acknowledged as such by the agent. However, a further possibility is, of course, that the agent is not ready with a reason, has not made the goal clear to himself. So, why did Harvey agree to write the letter? He wanted to oblige; he wanted to give Kate a pleasant surprise; he thought it would be a good thing anyway; he felt he would look mean if he did not. And so on. Perhaps he cannot say that one rather than another was his reason; perhaps any would do, so there is no decision for him to have to take. If there is uncertainty here, it is not because the agent is unsure what is causing him to act. He may not know what to say—may not know why he is behaving as he is—but such 'ignorance' compares with not knowing what one wants more generally, where it is not as if one wanted something but awaited learning what that was. The outstanding question is whether the person may be deceiving himself. He claims, in all sincerity, not to find x a desirable consequence, but must this claim be accepted? The question of self-deception is one we shall take up shortly.

But suppose that, while confidently citing an anticipated benefit to another as the reason for my action, I also know that I shall find it hard to live with myself if I do not act to that end. How do I know that the former, rather than the desire to avoid feelings of guilt, gives my true reason? One obvious reply is that this is not in any event a context in which we can speak of knowing, so the question is wrongly put. Certainly, there can be no question of finding out, and, while there is such a thing as not knowing why one acts, as just indicated, the supposition is that the reason is confidently given. But could there not be states of mind which made it doubtful whether avowals of a reason made by one in such a state were to be accorded their usual significance? And if so, might it not be that having accompanying thoughts of the kind envisaged could be one such? There are failures of understanding and sincerity, and there is uncertainty as to one's reasons, but if the thought envisaged does not occur in these or perhaps other related conditions, it does not seem that we have any ground for not according the avowal its usual significance unless, despite appearances, what we have to do with is not an *action*. This, too, is a possibility to which we shall return.

8.2 UNCONSCIOUS THOUGHT

To the extent that we cannot go wrong with our avowals, we cannot go wrong, it would appear, through deceiving ourselves. Yet is not self-deception a familiar human failing? The condition that the avowal be sincere offers some protection to incorrigibility, but the issue calls for further discussion.

A man claims to be acting from a desire to serve his country, but all the evidence of his past behaviour suggests a person whose overriding concern is his own self-advancement. Might he not simply be deceiving himself as to his true motive? Once more, I should wish to say that the person's honest avowal can be allowed to stand, however justifiably sceptical we may be of a lasting conversion to other-regarding aims. To fail to challenge his reason is not to acknowledge more than a passing deviation from a single-minded pursuit of his selfish ends. He can, of course, be deceiving himself about the permanence of this change in attitude. How might he deceive himself about his present state of mind?

I might *intentionally* deceive myself. I put on paper a false account of an incident which I know I am likely to read and accept as true at a much later date; and indeed this could be an eventuality that I intend. Clearly, the lapse in time is essential, since it allows me to lose sight of the falsity of what I have written, so makes it possible for me to accept it as true. I cannot deceive myself *now* in a way that involves the aim of persuading myself of the truth of something that I believe to be false. None the less, the closer it approximates to what is possible with interpersonal deception, the more interesting ostensible self-deception becomes. As this example uninterestingly shows, cases of both believing *p* and not believing *p* are not invariably paradoxical; even less those of both believing *p* and believing not-*p*. The element of *deception* need have no place in either, whether a time lapse is exploited, whether different criteria—verbal and behavioural—are associated with the inconsistent beliefs, or whether, even, the subject's mind is supposed somehow partitioned. This last perhaps takes us nearest to matching deception practised by one person on another, but at the cost of endorsing an even more paradoxical account of consciousness. It is similar to treatments of blindsight which seek to accommodate the strange behaviour which its subjects exhibit by supposing them possessed of two streams of consciousness, when all that is needed is to acknowledge that the impaired brain function in question has as a consequence that certain acts which normally fall within consciousness are removed from that sphere.

There are various forms that self-deception can take, but the basic variety can perhaps be thought of along the following lines. Sometimes we can (logically) accept *p* as true because we have refused to entertain, to dwell on, considerations which, we suspect, would rule it out. Or, we close our eyes to a possibility for fear of what we might have to admit. Such a refusal introduces the element of will, the point at which there may be dishonesty, but it does not confront us with anything as incoherent as an acceptance of something we plainly know to be false. We can truthfully say 'I did not know . . .', but appealing to the letter rather than the spirit of the law, as it were. Here it would seem we have a spectrum of cases, but it is again only to the extent that the person's self-deception borders on insincerity that we have grounds to challenge his declared reason.

As well as giving a wide berth to sources of unwelcome news, we may also give disproportionate attention to evidence of a more agreeable turn of events. Once more, the element of will comes in with the selectivity shown, and the uncertainty in evidential relations makes it possible to avoid incoherence: what is known may not flatly rule out the hoped-for possibility, and the unlikely does sometimes prove true. A relevant pattern of practical reasoning could take the following form: if I do not pursue such and such a line of enquiry, my grounds for the possibility which I wish to see supported will not be impugned; I shall therefore not pursue that line of enquiry. Of course, the more the agent makes explicit to himself such a pattern of reasoning, the more irrational he is seen to be, but he is still not irrational to the point of inconsistency. To repeat, he does not *know* that the area to which he is closing his eyes harbours refuting considerations. We accordingly are not obliged to think of such reasoning as unconscious, or as farmed out among homunculi. Note that such wishful thinking is not a matter of a desire's causing a belief. It is simply that someone who wants to believe that *p* can *ipso facto* be expected to take steps which result in having or preserving that belief. Of course, while there can be intention in the way indicated, this is not inevitable: the agent might simply fail to take account of the threatening considerations rather than purposely ignore them. However, if there is no more an element of intention than when the relevant considerations are simply inaccessible to the subject, it is hardly in place to speak of self-deception.

One kind of example which may involve self-deception—which certainly gives a prima facie reason for discounting the agent's avowal—is provided by behaviour consequent upon post-hypnotic suggestion:

Spurious reasons (rationalizations) for post-hypnotic acts may often follow as a sequel to post-hypnotic behaviour, especially if the individual has had no memory of the suggestion's origin. This occurs in all probability because we prefer to think of our behaviour as being the result of fully conscious motives. For example, if a person is required post-hypnotically to take off his shoe, he may explain this behaviour by saying that his sock was bunched up and uncomfortable, or if required to take a drink, that he was thirsty. Such rationalizations are important in the study of personality, showing as they do the difference between real reasons and stated reasons in accounting for behaviour. (Marcuse 1959: 75–6)

Suppose that the subject has been told under hypnosis that, at some time after he is out of the trance, someone will cough in his presence, at which point he will take off a shoe. This comes to pass, and on being asked why he acted thus he tells us that his sock was bunched up and uncomfortable. This presents us with more than one possibility. First, it may be that, before producing this as his reason, the person should have felt bewildered, not know why he took his shoe off, but just be aware of an extraordinary urge to do so. If that was his state of mind, then, however briefly it endured, so long as it persisted he would not have honestly ventured the reason given. If, after a fleeting realization that he had no acceptable reason—none that would not make him look foolish—he comes up with the reason suggested, there is no problem, since it was the first reaction that revealed the man's state of mind at a time most relevant to giving his true reason.

And, indeed, it may be difficult to reconcile the declaration of a reason with the admission of an overwhelming desire to act in the way in question. A person is given the post-hypnotic suggestion that he will select an umbrella and put it up, and on carrying this out he explains that he wanted to show thereby that he was not superstitious (Eysenck 1958: 41–2). But, since, presumably, any urge he felt was simply to put up the umbrella, not an urge to dissociate himself from the superstition about the misfortune awaiting those who do so indoors, it would be difficult to accept that both the avowal of such an urge and the stated reason could be given sincerely. He is, after all, seized with an *urge*. It is not, that is, a matter of a reasoned want, the kind of want to which a change in belief may put an end.

Secondly, if there is no suppression of the momentary awareness which the agent had had of the true situation, but he genuinely does think it would be desirable to act for the reason avowed, then I see no grounds for disallowing his explanation. This is indeed how he reasoned, and remains so whatever the part played by the hypnotist. The aetiology of the thoughts, whether normal or exceptional, does not figure in an analysis of what *counts* as the person's reason. We simply have, with hypnotic suggestion, an unusual way of inducing discomfort, or of making it feel as if one's sock were bunched up.

But suppose that, as a result of hypnotism, the person is unable to desist from what he does. For instance, he takes hold of an object and finds himself unable to let go of it. I am assuming that we are dealing with an action. If we are not, then the agent's avowed reason does not have its usual significance. If he could not prevent his arms and hands from engaging in the movements involved in taking off his shoe, then, whatever he declared, it would not be the explanation of an *action*. Similarly, when I duck a missile thrown my way, it may be true that I know or think that I can thus escape being struck, but this will not count as the reason if the movement was involuntary. For the ducking to be voluntary, it has to be that, had we chosen not to duck, we should not have done so; the movement must have been under our control. Just as we can have excellent reasons for affirming the directly verifiable possibility—if we choose not to duck, we shall not do so—so, too, we can have such reasons for the counterfactual form, though we are not, of course, above challenge with respect to either. Our explanation is accordingly incorrigible only against the presumption that we have to do with an action, but a causal role for the reason is not required to ensure incorrigibility. Just what these crucial conditionals involve will be considered in the next chapter.

For Freud, post-hypnotic suggestion is one of the phenomena which testify to the reality of the unconscious. Commenting on the case of a person responding to an order previously given him under hypnosis, he writes: 'It seems impossible to give any other description of the phenomenon than to say that the order had been present in the mind of the person in a condition of latency, or had been present unconsciously, until the given moment came, and then had become conscious. But not the whole of it emerged into consciousness: only the conception of the act to be executed' (1912: 261). Given that the order is subsequently brought to mind, it could be said to have been 'in a condition of latency' in so far as the subject had a *capacity* to recall it. To go further than this, as Freud does with 'present unconsciously', is unwarranted, and in no way needed for an explanation: the order ostensibly takes effect at the time it is issued, the subject forming, in response, the intention to act as ordered when the signal is given. There seems to be no reason why the consequent readiness to act on that signal should not persist, even though the subject has no more than a capacity, temporally inhibited, to bring the order to mind. Recall the example of action in accordance with an abandoned intention, where the usual mental accompaniments are absent. Freud (ibid. 260) envisages the objection that a physical disposition for the recurrence of a mental happening might be all that the latency of the mental involves, but he dismisses this alternative as overstepping the bounds of psychology proper. It is true that in postulating a physical state associated with a latent ability to recall or a disposition to act we go beyond what, more minimally, the demand for an explanation obliges us to acknowledge, but so too does the supposition of an enduring mental item. All that postulation of this contributes is unnecessary paradox; it does not enable us to explain more than we should had we stayed with the ability or disposition. Note, too, that, if we do postulate an underlying physiological state, this does not have to merit the description 'unconscious order' or 'unconscious memory' in order to explain the subsequent behaviour, the subsequent recall. The persistence of a capacity does not have to be understood as the storage of an item which the capacity is a capacity to produce.

While the unconscious is not convincingly established by appeal to post-hypnotic suggestion, the question remains whether we can find a place for it on other grounds. The fact that one's honest say-so *suffices* to make R one's reason does not imply, it would appear, that there could not be reasons which we have not acknowledged. The question is whether, or to what extent, detachment from consciousness is consistent with our concept of a reason for action. Prima facie, there is some incongruity in linking 'unconscious' to terms which denominate something in the domain of the mental—as though one could be turning over in one's mind thoughts about the causes of the French Revolution, say, without having the remotest idea that one was thus occupied. If, on the other hand, it is simply a matter of thought in the sense of *belief*, then, of course, we can say even of someone dead to the world that he thinks that *p*. Such a thought is unconscious so long as it is not brought to consciousness.

With these two possibilities we swing from the absurd to the commonplace. Is there room for an intermediate position? We may note that there need be nothing in the least remarkable about the unconscious if this is simply a domain in which *causes* of behaviour are to be found. The notion of cause comes under no pressure through the factors which it would characterize being outside the agent's awareness, but the applicability of 'unconscious' to causes of which we have no knowledge, as with internal states of our body, is too easily secured to be of interest here. In claiming that certain pathological phenomena oblige us to acknowledge the existence of unconscious mental causes, Freud is in effect calling upon empirical findings to resolve a grammatical issue. Whether any relevant cause can be mental and unconscious is problematic on both counts; there is no question of the evidence being overwhelmingly in favour of such status, but it remains to be decided whether any cause which we may infer could warrant either description. The example of causes just heightens the contrast with the family of terms currently in question, as 'think', 'want', 'try', and 'intend', terms which may have to be radically reinterpreted if disconnected from all awareness. Thus, if it is a question of a thought which has never been in consciousness, yet can be regarded as fully formed, with as much determinacy as its verbal counterpart, we remain closer to the absurd than to the commonplace. And it is true that some speak of unconscious thoughts in just this way—as if, as far as the character of thought is concerned, it were all one whether there were any connection with consciousness or not. Such a view, which Freud explicitly endorses, is natural enough if, as he also thought, we know the contents of our mind by a form of inner perception; after all, with objects of perception generally, things are as they are whether perceived or not. Why not with our thoughts as well? (Cf. 1915: 171; 1925: 216.) However, while this conception invites prompt dismissal, it is not the only possibility, and there is a less mystifying approach which allows some scope to speaking of the unconscious without going back on what we have said concerning reasons; indeed, it simply requires that we extend further the general approach which we have been developing.

When a person gives a reason for acting, his sincerity is, of course, critical as a precondition for the truth of what he says. However, although his avowal is not then open to challenge, a sincere avowal represents only one point on the relevant scale. Whether we are talking of thoughts which give a reason for action, or thoughts more generally, they are not always brought to this state of explicitness. For it to be true that you think that *p*, it is not necessary that you should have addressed the question whether *p* and delivered your verdict. Belief as a state of mind may exist prior to the time when we actually acknowledge the belief. The thought that something in what another has said was not quite right may fleetingly cross our mind, but we may not have time to dwell on the matter and get clear about what had half caught our attention; or again, the thought that such and such would be desirable may have just begun to form when other matters distract us.

Here is an analogous, and equally familiar, circumstance. Suppose that, interrupted in mid-sentence, we later state, 'I was going on to say . . .', a disclosure we may make with full confidence even though there has been no further advance, at the time or subsequently, towards formulating the thought which we had been on the point of divulging. We are entitled to such confidence so long as we can now take up where we left off; so long, that is, as the earlier surroundings of our thought, the various things that had occasioned it, are still alive for us—a question of what had caught our attention, what other thoughts had crossed our mind, what inclinations we had experienced, and so on. With the passage of time we may, of course, find it difficult to recapture anything relevant, and so be uncertain just what we had been going on to say, but, this aside, there is nothing more puzzling than when the expression of our thought proceeds unchecked. Of course, there may not be much of relevance for us to bring to mind, but then there may equally be very little that we have in mind when we continue without interruption. But how can we be so sure that, for instance, we should not have got sidetracked onto some other line of thought? It would certainly be presumptuous to rule on what might have unfolded with a change of circumstances, but then it is only a matter of 'I was going on to say . . .'. A matter, that is, of the intention at the time of the interruption, not of the more vulnerable claim, 'I should have said . . .'. Nor is it a matter of an *interpretation* which best fits what is remembered. We are not here saying what we say as a *hypothesis*.

Think, too, of the experience of being unable to bring a word to mind but having it 'on the tip of one's tongue'. Sometimes the identity of the word in question may be determinable by another party—for example, when you announce that you are trying to think of the French for 'sky'—but with the usual invocations of this idiom any external criterion is out of place. However, while the individual's sincere declaration that a word suggested is indeed the word sought may settle it as such for his present state of mind, when some time has elapsed between the initial search and eventual suggestion there could be grounds for not reckoning the word hailed as incontrovertibly the word which had eluded him. But is this really the only basis possible for querying the person's declaration? Suppose he changes his mind. Might he not then say that he had got it wrong with the word which had first struck him as right? That is not impossible. The first word could be recognized as one he had somehow confused with the second. What is still operative, however, is the subject's acknowledgement. This cannot be dispensed with if there is no question of misremembering, no question of seeking an accord with an earlier identification.

In so far as the notion of an unconscious reason has a place, it is to be found towards the end of the scale on which an avowed reason is located; not at a point where the agent has no inclination whatsoever to accept that this was his reason. It compares, then, with the notion of *going on to say* when our declaration that we were going on to say that *p* can stand so long as we are able to resume the state of mind we were in when interrupted. Here, as with the present case, the wrong model is that of having to cast our mind back to a thought which we had articulated at the earlier time.

So long as we remain on this scale, a connection with consciousness is preserved. Is there a place for a more definitive detachment consistent with retaining talk of thought? Behaviour provides the most likely domain in which this possibility might be realized, a possibility for which we have already seen precedents. Recall the example of lifting a suitcase which we declare to be much lighter than we had thought. Given that the thought was not consciously entertained prior to lifting the case, and given too that we may none the less speak in these terms, it would seem we have just what is needed for a notion of unconscious thought to apply. More generally, if thought can take shape both in words, spoken or unspoken, and in behaviour, there would seem to be no reason why the former should not on occasion lag behind the latter. True, the drift of earlier discussions has been towards letting behaviour testify to a mental state only so long as a verbal expression is also possible, but this does not require one ordering rather than another of the two conditions.

Again, consider those cases where it is so apparent how things stand, we do not even need to think; once more, in one sense we may not think—we do not address an issue, answer a question posed—but simply act, yet our action is describable using 'thought', as when we say we thought we could overtake another vehicle safely. We may not be altogether happy to speak of unconscious thought—as though there were something which took place at the time but of which we were unaware—but, if we choose to do so in such cases, this does not appear to be a way of speaking that brings any problems with it. Thus, in the example of lifting the suitcase, the existence of an unconscious thought can be affirmed with as much assurance as our avowal: I thought it would be heavier than it was. Such an avowal is not a hypothesis, as if we could say that we *must* have had that thought, but that final verification waited upon some further identification of it—as I say, there is nothing relevant which took place at the earlier time and which escaped our attention. For the same reason, there is no question of having to envisage the thought as having the status of a theoretical construct.

It was noted earlier that an invocation of 'thought' may sometimes be felt to overstate the degree to which something intrudes into our consciousness. Rather than say that a thought struck us, or crossed our minds, we might prefer to say that, for instance, we took something to be so and so, that we took the figure on the lawn to be a child; or we saw, though did not actually notice, that the deckchair was in the shade. Indeed, that this registered with us may be appreciated only retrospectively. But if 'thought' thus tends to repel a characterization as 'unconscious', such episodes none the less present us with close relations of thinking which are not fully conscious, so may be enlisted in plotting further points on the scale which peters off in the truly unconscious.

It is unfortunate that the notion of the unconscious has been appropriated to such an extent by psychoanalytical theory. As a result of focusing on examples where there is some reluctance to admit to a thought, it is made to seem as though such reluctance is somehow definitive of the whole phenomenon, and leaves us overlooking the extent to which the idea of a half-formed thought, or a thought which fleetingly crosses our mind, is a familiar phenomenon, not at all something which it might not have occurred to us to acknowledge had it not been for our exposure to Freudian theory. But surely, without relying on behaviour, we should wish to allow for the possibility of thoughts which a person could never admit to, which could never be brought to consciousness at all. Is not that where Freud had something truly novel to say? Why should not something which is often difficult become in some cases quite impossible, so successful is the repressive mechanism? Indeed, have we not been talking merely about the *preconscious*, not about the truly *unconscious*? But, however strong the repressive forces, there is no question of a *logical* barrier to becoming conscious, and no such barrier is erected by invoking the unconscious rather than the preconscious. Our only warrant for speaking of a thought lies in the chance that we hold out of its taking shape, if not in our minds then at least in our behaviour.

The idea of a totally successful repressive mechanism is likely to be taken to make for the suggested possibility only because it is associated with the picture of a fully formed thought knocking on the door of consciousness but being barred entry, when it should be conceived of as something which stands in the way of the very formation of the thought. That is, as intimated above, we go wrong if we think of the subject's awareness of his reasons as allowing of degrees in a way that parallels his awareness of the conversations going on around him. Such a comparison suggests an unchanging object of awareness, the variability residing in the subject's relation to it, when it is more apposite to think of the reason as not having taken shape so long as the subject is unaware, and as fully formed once he is fully aware— with all the matching degrees in between. If it is insisted that right *could* be on the side of one who claims the reality of the thought, notwithstanding its permanent repression, what has then to be justified is a particular way of speaking. We are not divided on an empirical issue—no one is going to show, contrary to what I say, that in such a case the thought will have been there all along.

The conception of an unchanging object of awareness which has just been found wanting is, as indicated, one which applies readily enough to perceptible objects or happenings, as with the shiverings, blushings, and tremblings of which the subject may or may not be conscious. However, it is worth considering further how the model they provide fails us with the philosophically more interesting episodes which may be held to occur in either mode. That is, the question whether working out a problem, say, is something that can occur both consciously and unconsciously is not, or not necessarily, the question whether what takes place in the latter case is something of which we may on other occasions be conscious. Presented with a riddle, a mathematical question, or a problem of recall, we may find ourselves unable to provide an answer, yet come up with one at a later stage despite having given no further thought to the matter over the intervening period. Various neural happenings will presumably lead up to the production of the answer, but these are not happenings of which we become aware in the conscious case, where we reason our way to the answer in steps which we can disclose.

It is incidental to trembling whether or not the subject is aware of it; conscious trembling is not the form which the trembling takes, in the way that consciously working out is a species of working out. But can we not say that, when we consciously solve a problem and when we solve it unconsciously, the same thing occurs, only now with our awareness, now without it? Even to speak of being aware of one's thoughts has its dangers, drawing us uncomfortably close to the false perceptual model—as if a thought were something one might come across, something which might catch and hold one's attention. Still, we may agree that this question has an affirmative answer in the sense that solving or working out can be said to occur in either case. However, that is more: both activities count as such because of what they issue in—the answer. That does not imply that the conscious case is a matter of awareness of just what takes place when the working-out is unconscious. The former case could, as a neural happening, *take in* the processes which lead to the same outcome when consciousness is lacking, but that does not make these processes the object of consciousness. It could equally well be said that in the unconscious case we come up with the answer *without* working it out. Certainly, it is not that some of the brain's workings are accessible to the subject's consciousness, whereas others of them are not.

There is a more general moral to be drawn from this example. We might, I say, speak of working out the answer subconsciously, or of producing the answer without working it out. Confronted with choices of this kind, Freud in effect insists on opting for the former style of description, making it look as though we were obliged to accept a certain form of words, along with its attendant difficulties. If we see these as insuperable, we should remind ourselves that we have a choice: we should not let ourselves be browbeaten into accepting this way of speaking; nothing forces it upon us; indeed, there is good reason to avoid it. And, therewith, the self-inflicted difficulties.

8.3 UNCONSCIOUS DESIRE AND INTENTION

We have concentrated so far on unconscious thought. What of desire and intention? Suppose it is said, 'Harvey wants to take out girls who look like his mother.' May not the person in question be less than fully conscious of the character of his desire? A behavioural interpretation of the desire would appear possible; otherwise, the reading then appropriate is as with 'The girls Harvey wants to take out look like his mother.' This is all we are entitled to say if the desire as first formulated has not entered the man's head, just as 'The woman Oedipus intended to marry was his mother' is all 'Oedipus intended to marry his mother' comes to when Oedipus is ignorant of his beloved's true identity.

Recall too the different ways in which a why-question may sometimes be taken, as with the query 'Why do you wish to make him look foolish?' This may be an enquiry as to the end aimed at—what do you hope to gain by that?—but it may also be an enquiry as to the source or origin of the desire; often, though not invariably, a causal matter, with accordingly no difficulty in citing in explanation factors of which the subject has no inkling. As noted, many of the queries which might be raised about our likes and dislikes also show this twofold character.

The thought that might be unconscious is not an interlude in an interior monologue, but a state of mind which might come to be articulated *sotto voce*, or out loud, or which is manifested in behaviour. This is where we might also expect to find the desire that qualifies as unconscious, rather than in the domain of urges, impulses and cravings. It is perhaps because we think in terms of desires of this latter sort that we are inclined to consider the notion of an unconscious desire a nonsense, but there is also the more general notion of wanting, where there need be no felt desire, where the wanting may be revealed in behaviour, and this might be considered more congenial to an unconscious realization.

Even here, however, there are countervailing considerations. In the absence of appropriate thought, a behavioural act may not, once more, have the significance we should otherwise attribute to it. This obvious truth seems applicable in the present instance with respect to the requirement that the subject have at least some glimmering of the putative desire. If this condition is allowed to lapse, we shall be left with desire in a derivative sense only, I should say, but, more importantly, without this condition there is no question of a desire which might *explain* the behaviour, given that nothing beyond the latter is required for its attribution.

That consciousness is not easily set aside seems particularly clear with respect to intentions. So, although he had not made his intention explicit to himself at the time, Harvey comes round to agreeing that in doing what he did he had been trying to impress. How is this to be understood? We may think in terms of the gradual dawning of a realization by Harvey that this is what he was doing. If so, then 'trying to impress' will be interpretable in such a way that the behaviour is not the manifestation of a mental state to which the person might also have given verbal expression. Rather, the subject's relation to his behaviour is much as to that of another person: reflecting on its character he can appreciate the justice of such a description, as he might come to see that the level of his performance at some task had been falling off, even though this had escaped him at the time. This gives a sense to the notion of an unconscious intention, but in a severely behaviouristic way, the mental being nowhere in sight. Once more, the more interesting case is one which does not make such a sharp divide, but where the intention had at least started to take shape at the earlier time. If there is not even the beginnings of a readiness to avow an intention, desire, or inclination—enough, however slight, to give a foothold to dishonesty or deception—it becomes difficult to justify speaking of *trying* to impress as anything more than an essentially mindless activity. Either way, we note, we are not concerned with a causal hypothesis.

Again, there are occasions when we have to be reminded of an intention, and occasions when, performing some habitual act, the intentionality makes itself known only when things go wrong, but, if it comes as complete news to the agent that he 'intends' to V, then the quotes have to stay. Even if an act is one that might be performed in furtherance of a general aim which the subject has, that is no guarantee that the act is intentional—a point that is particularly clear with respect to examples which might be used to mark the possible distinction between 'aim' and 'intention' indicated in §2.5. The point also has some bearing on Freud's analysis of parapraxes (1916: pt I). Consider a slip of the tongue which results in a proper name's being supplanted by a similar, but insulting, verbal form. Words which we thus let slip can testify to a preoccupation, a dislike, a fear, and so forth, without there having to be any intention behind their utterance. After all, not only is there no deliberate choice, but their production would be considered by the speaker to be an involuntary error even when he allowed that they reflected something he felt. Freud's confusion of reasons with causes, coupled with his adherence to a thoroughgoing psychic determinism, lead him to assimilate the claim that everything in one's mental life has a cause with the claim that every such thing has a meaning. It is then a short step for him to discern intention where it has no business to be (cf. Bouveresse 1995: 105).

Are there any other ways in which a behavioural embodiment of intention might be defended once all links with consciousness have been severed? One large category of behaviour we might look to is that of so-called 'body language'. Consider this account of a 'critical evaluation gesture cluster':

The main one is the hand-to-face gesture, with the index finger pointing up the cheek while another finger covers the mouth and the thumb supports the chin. Further evidence that this listener is critical of the speaker is seen by the fact that the legs are tightly crossed and the arm crosses the body (defensive) while the head and chin are down (hostility). This non-verbal 'sentence' says something like, 'I don't like what you are saying and I disagree with you.' (Pease 1984: 14)

It is of interest that the behaviour described—gestures made, posture adopted—is in the sphere of the voluntary, as also with gestures indicative of impatience, loss of interest, deceit, and lack of self-confidence. These are not like a blush, say, which is likewise a sign of the subject's mental state. On the other hand, while it is a matter of movements which the subject presumably could control, it may well be that he is not fully aware of making them, let alone making them with an end in view. If that is so, then here too we have to do with signs or symptoms of the attitude in question—supposing, that is, it is possible to confirm the attitude more directly. Certainly, to be told that one was *aiming* at such and such with one's gestures is again more difficult to make sense of when we cannot honestly avow any such aim.

There is a spectrum of cases here. As well as gestures which are straightforwardly intentional, we have those which, with varying degrees of plausibility, we could contemplate performing intentionally: self-ingratiating movements may be considered better geared to attaining their end than movements made to conceal the fact that one is lying, as covering one's mouth with one's hand. If the subject contests some such account of the point of his behaviour, an intention in line with that account is ruled out, and, even when its possible efficacy is acknowledged, that only removes an obstacle to intentionality. There is still the threat of the subject's sincere denial. If that threat is realized, then, if the behaviour can none the less be regarded as purposive, that will be in accordance with some more primitive scheme, some broad notion of functionality: the significance of the acts may be lost on those who perform them, but they can still be vestiges of a response, the occurrence of which is explicable in terms of its consequences in the past. Once more, there is no loss in refusing to speak of intention in such a case. On the contrary, once the constraint of consciousness has been lifted, the notion of intention is deprived of its usual explanatory power, whereas the more primitive form provides an explanatory scheme which is not similarly vulnerable. It would accordingly be a backward step to persist in ascribing an intention at the cost of making it unconscious, perhaps even at the cost of finding some sub-agent or homunculus to be what has the intention.

If the thought component in intention cannot be dispensed with, it is none the less at a minimum when known side effects of one's actions are at issue. These, we noted, could be regarded as intentionally produced, even if they were no part of the end aimed at or the means taken to achieve it. Take a person whose remarks are causing his audience some hurt, some embarrassment. If this consequence has not escaped him, it is clearly something that he is at least prepared to tolerate, and, if he takes no steps to avoid or minimize the discomfort, we can say without further ado that he is intentionally making the person uncomfortable. The ascription of intention does not require us to probe beneath the surface, as it were, but on this minimal conception the alternatives are stark and simple: either the person has no knowledge of the effect of his remarks, in which case the desire to hurt did not move him, or he did, in which case he was hurting his victim intentionally. Moreover, even if the effect formed no part of his purpose, 'intentionally' remains appropriate in light of the responsibility which the speaker none the less bears for the consequences of his act.

The claim that a person's reason for acting just *is* the reason he is prepared to avow or acknowledge is, of course, consistent with his having nothing to contribute on this score, and, even when we come up with a reason, it may leave much unanswered. Recall the familiar problem posed by practical reasoning: an adequate reason why a person had a drink—he was thirsty—may not extend to the choice of means to relieve his thirst—with lemonade rather than orange juice. This is a common pattern with much verbal 'behaviour'. Our speech will take place within a general framework of reasons—to exchange pleasantries, to answer questions, to while away the time—but we may not know why one thing comes to mind, as a way of keeping the conversation going, say, rather than another. There may thus be patterns within our speech which are not of our choosing. What we say may betray an overriding preoccupation with our own concerns; contrariwise, it may reveal a tendency to belittle one's own achievements. Without querying the general reasons for speaking, there may be ample room for wondering why someone says what he says. Why is *A* always so self-deprecatory? Could it be because, if he plays down his achievements, he does not then have to live up to the higher standards otherwise set? Why is he so unfailingly honest? Is he perhaps frightened that he will be found out if he deviates from the truth? The interesting question is how, if at all, we can make sense of such conjectures against the supposition that the subject's sincere word will not necessarily provide the answer.

Suppose *A* says, 'You won't have to put up with me much longer; I'll be gone by the end of the week.' We might reasonably suspect that the reason behind this sad declaration is to elicit a reassuring denial of the attitude which *A* is ascribing to his audience. He wants to hear something like: but we *like* having you around. Couldn't this indeed be the reason, despite *A*'s sincere denials? When asked why he says this, *A* may simply reply, 'Well, it's *true*.' That, clearly, is some sort of answer to the question, but it will hardly put an end to our queries. After all, there are all manner of truths which might have been uttered; why this one? Again, however, the question is one as to the kind of explanation which takes shape. As before, if *A* genuinely has no awareness whatsoever of any such motivation, then we have to forsake any explanation in terms of his reasons. The trouble is, the explanation we have surmised is of such a form that, if it can be made out to apply, it is difficult to see how it could be safely lodged with any permanence anywhere outside this category. The language used is patently intentional: *A* is looking for reassurance, we conjecture. Indeed, do we have any justification for such language if we are not thinking in terms of an explanation which awaits the subject's acknowledgement for its eventual validation?

So long as the explanation makes use of intentional notions, it always makes sense to suppose that we shall end up with an explanation in terms of the agent's reasons, but not every explanation need take this form. A strategy may have been learned, but its rationale been long forgotten. Or, as with the Skinner scheme, there may be no rationale which occurred to the agent at any point. Again, the suggestion that such and such is sought may be rephrased as a claim about what would in fact be found desirable. And, of course, some explanations may amount to no more than redescriptions: an unremitting use of the first-person pronoun may warrant a charge that someone is self-centred without this being by way of a hypothesis.

Could an explanation in terms of the unconscious clash with one in terms of the conscious? The possibility is of interest, since on my account the two explanations are in the relevant sense in the same category: even if they relate to very different points on a scale of awareness, both involve reasons rather than causes. Wittgenstein gives such an example when he imagines someone pushing him into a river while ostensibly concerned only to point out a church spire (*LC* 22–3). Could the honestly avowed reason cohere with the psychoanalytical explanation—namely, that the person subconsciously hated Wittgenstein? The example is a useful one, in that we are being invited to link the subconscious desire to *actual* behaviour—the crucial case if, when there is full consciousness, the desire is to be sufficiently firm as to survive the test of action.

We have two ways of making sense of an ascription of hatred in such a case. Either the person's behaviour qualifies as a manifestation of this attitude, whatever he should own to, or he can be brought around to acknowledging such an attitude. The former would require far more by way of relevant behaviour than is provided by this isolated incident, and it is in any event not of great interest unless the further condition—that there is something which it should be possible to bring to consciousness—is presumed, since it is only then that we have any warrant for speaking in terms of a subconscious *motive*, in any defensible use of this term. Given this presumption, there is in principle no difficulty in allowing that the conscious and the subconscious motives should coexist. There is, of course, the appearance of conflict in so far as the person pointing might vehemently deny any hostile intent, opposing the more friendly explanation in its stead, but this could be accompanied by a dim awareness of the truth in what he was denying—much as with the examples of post-hypnotic suggestion discussed above—an awareness which on reflection might become less dim, thus aligning the case with less emotionally charged occasions when the agent has more than one reason for his action. Anything which made for irreconcilability would do so just as much if both were conscious as if only one were. And this does not appear to be so: in the circumstances, pointing out a church spire offers a useful opportunity for, at the same time, pushing someone disliked into the river, just as travelling by bicycle may enable one both to avoid the traffic and to get exercise. In so far as the present, more intriguing, example presents a special problem, it lies with the temporal conditions needed for joint reasons. That is, if one started to point to the spire with no thought whatsoever of pushing Wittgenstein into the river, and this possibility suddenly struck one, and struck one as being not altogether a bad thing, then to qualify as an actual reason for what was done it would have to account for something further about the action already under way—a sudden shift in movement, or added vigour in its execution. Circumstances in which this reason might have equal weight in explaining precisely what the other reason explains are less easy to describe than those in which we have overdetermination of reasons for riding a bicycle.

From the very outset, the place has been prepared for an acceptance of reasons of which the subject is less than fully conscious, our initial account encompassing (i) reasons as arise with reasoning, in a more or less articulate train of thought, and (ii) reasons which are shown to be such by the subject's acknowledgement. If we can have (ii) as well as (i), the unconscious can be accommodated, but were we right to accept (ii) so readily? Is there not, indeed, a tension between (i) and (ii)? If we acknowledge that R *was* our reason, then it presumably was our reason at the earlier time, but, since that was a time at which we had no awareness of R, what does it *mean* to say that it was then our reason?

In dismissing a parallel between reasons of which we are not fully conscious, and conversations of which we likewise are not, we appeared to be repudiating any view of the former as having a real-ity at the time of acting, but being all or partially hidden. A reason that is beginning to take shape is not a determinate item which has so far revealed only a part of itself. Compare Wittgenstein's obser-vation, as reported by Moore, about the psychoanalytic explanation of a person's reason for laughing at a joke: 'He explained that the patient who agrees did not think of this reason at the moment when he laughed, and that to say that he thought of it "subconsciously" "tells you nothing as to what was happening at the moment when he laughed" ' (Moore 1959: 317). If acknowledging *R* as our reason fol-lows this pattern, we shall be inclined to regard the retrospective attribution of a reason as at best misleading, yet this seems at odds with the way we view quite mundane cases, cases where we think of ourselves as making explicit a reason which we did indeed have at the earlier time.

Here we may note that in the situations which concern us, situa-tions in which we are said not to have been (fully) conscious of our reason, there will at least have been an *action*. And just as we may have only the faintest awareness of a perceptible object, so there may be no more than an inchoate awareness of what we were aiming at with our action. So, even though in one sense I gave no thought to what I saw, the scene registered with me sufficiently for me to recall what was there and to appraise as correct or otherwise a description fuller than anything that had passed through my head. A description of an action may be handled in a comparable way. I sit down to eat, and, although I do not give it a thought, I am aware that there is a cloth on the table and a salt cellar on that. I extend my hand to pick up the latter and am aware to a comparable degree that that is what I am doing. But, if we can speak of acting for a reason when habit and familiarity dispense us from having to think, it would also appear that without such dispensation there is no such action if the appro-priate thought, let alone behaviour which might manifest the inten-tionality, is lacking.

But talk of the unconscious does not always arise against the back-drop of action. The claim that a person's dreams reveal a desire to kill his father may be made even though there is no relevant behav-iour on which such an interpretation is placed. Could we make sense of such a claim? I do not see how. It could be conjectured that the person would be pleased if his father died. That is a verifiable con-jecture, and one which might prove true even though, in advance of its realization, it is hotly disputed by the subject. But its eventual truth does not justify the retrospective ascription of a desire. Nor, finally, will it do to say that such an ascription is warranted as part of a *theory*. We are at a loss to know what to make of a desire when all recognized criteria for it are lacking, and the appeal to theory does nothing to make good what is lacking in point of intelligibility.

8.4 REASONS AND CAUSES

The possibilities of explanation are in no way diminished by my insistence that the agent has a special authority when anything in the domain of his reasons for acting is at issue. It simply means that forms of explanation for which this is not so are to be differently classified. And there is no shortage of alternative forms.

Suppose that, after a meal in a restaurant, a man leaves an exceptionally generous tip. He gives as his reason that the meal and service warranted this largesse, but we suspect that he wished to impress his friends, or that he did not have the nerve to present the waiter, a rather forbidding figure, with a lesser sum. Do we need to impute insincerity to the diner in order to have a chance of attributing such reasons to him? The answer is Yes, if we are talking about *his* reason, but, while accepting what is advanced in this capacity, we may wish to take the matter further: his thoughts took the form avowed, but it was also true, we surmise, that he would not have given the large tip if the eyes of his friends, or of the waiter, had not been upon him when he did so. Suppose we confront the person with our supposition. Can he agree to this yet still maintain that he acted for the reason given? The answer is again Yes. The person can be adamant, yet sincere, in reiterating the reason given, but his authority does not extend to the question of what would have come about had circumstances been different. There is no more than a presumption that, knowing himself as he does, his views will then be nearer the truth than another's.

If we can plausibly say that the man would not have been so generous had the circumstances been as envisaged, are we not in effect discounting his explanation of his action? I think not. Rather, by pooling the two considerations we build up a more comprehensive picture of the kind of person he is: on the one hand generous, on the other hand a person whose behaviour is subject to certain influences.

It may be that we see the supplementary observation as telling us more about his character, but not, we may note, by revealing the causal determinants of his conduct. Or at least not in the first instance. We claim that he would not have Ved had he not thought that *p*. Why? Because, with him, Ving can be counted on not to occur in the absence of that thought. That is the sort of person he is, someone who reveals, by word and deed, this state of mind, does this sort of thing in these circumstances. The supposition 'He would not have . . .' clearly cries out for supporting reasons, and these are naturally sought in a generalization which cites an established pattern of speech and behaviour.

Supposing, that is, that we aim at an explanation with such a generalization, a supposition which we have seen reason to question. However, while, whether explanatory or not, the generalization does not present us with a putative cause, one causal hypothesis it suggests is that the reason which the person gave would not have taken shape but for the circumstance which we have fastened upon. We may even have grounds for saying that, had the given reason not been available, the person would have been sure to find another. This possibility—looking beyond the avowed reasons to the factors which explain why they count as such for the agent—is of some importance in giving a comprehensive explanation of action, and is a familiar feature of biological or evolutionary explanations of patterns of behaviour, as with choice of a mate, which appear to have nothing whatsoever to do with the explanation which the individual would offer.

Consider, too, the kind of debate which often arises when there is a spate of criminal or delinquent behaviour, some insisting that the perpetrators be punished, others countering that they are to be pitied, the victims of deprivation, poverty, and other adverse social conditions. In the first case, the presumed ill will or lack of consideration evidenced by the agents' *reasons* is likely to underlie the response, whereas the latter is perhaps thought of as identifying *causes* to be tackled—a social rather than a moral problem. However, there is no reason why both forms of explanation should not stand, and indeed stand in a complementary relation. Once more, it could be that the causal factors have a part to play in explaining why certain reasons count as such for the miscreants. If someone has been brought up without worldly goods which he should like to have had, this may explain why the belief that another enjoys such benefits is considered a reason for trying to dispossess that person of them. Again, if asked why he broke into someone's house, a person's honest explanation would tell us, we may suppose, what he hoped to get thereby. A knowing criminal, one versed in sociology, might explain that he suffered serious abuse as a child, but this does not even pretend to tell us the *reason* with which he acted on the occasion in question.

The distinction between reasons and causes allows us to make room for very different kinds of explanatory considerations. For instance, it may be that self-regarding factors are prominent in the latter style of explanation, but that other-regarding considerations can be accepted as such with the former. Perhaps the training which tempered the child's self-centred concerns exploited his self-interest. None the less, the other-regarding reasons which, as an adult, he now offers for his actions can still be genuinely such, and not a cloak for selfishness. Or again, despite our protests to the contrary, it is insisted that we did what we did only for the pleasure it offered us, or to avoid the guilt we knew we should feel if we didn't; it wasn't the unselfish act which our explanation represents it as—helping out the victim of a disaster, let us say. Once more, there is nothing to such a charge if it fails to strike a responsive chord with the agent. There is no difficulty in envisaging spontaneous behaviour of an altruistic kind: you park your car that much closer to the car in front in order to make room for anyone who might wish to park behind you; you rearrange the objects on the cupboard shelf so that they do not risk falling on the next person who opens the door. And so on with countless familiar occasions when someone other than the agent stands to gain from the action. At the same time, there is no doubt a reason why certain considerations weigh with the agent, why someone's plight will be considered a compelling reason for action by one person but not by another. Here the explanation may well lie in the agent's education; perhaps it has taken rewards and punishments to bring him to a state where he responds as he does; perhaps the only way that a sense of duty can come to hold sway is by being inculcated with these methods. However, that does not mean that the avowed reason is in error, that the person is in some sense deceiving himself as to his true reason.

None of this, we might add, of itself settles questions of desert in favour of a particular moral standpoint. It is sometimes supposed that the possibility of explanations which call upon genetic, environmental, or other causal factors to supplement an explanation in terms of the agent's reasons militates against an ascription of freedom or responsibility and makes punishment unwarranted; or, conversely, that to acknowledge our freedom of action is thereby to sanction some medieval doctrine of punishment. As will be argued in the next chapter, what counts as free action is to be decided independently of any moral considerations.

The special place which our analysis assigns to an agent's honest declaration of his reason for acting has had to meet a number of objections. First, such a declaration may present us with undoubted falsehoods, falsehoods which have to be recast in terms of belief, say, to render invulnerable the explanation which embraces them. Secondly, a person may be blind to the character of his actions, failing to see that what he is doing falls fairly and squarely in, say, the category of inconsiderate behaviour, though this does not make an honestly avowed reason suspect unless it takes us to an instance of the third case, where the agent has a fleeting awareness of a reason other than the one declared. Our frequent suspicion that we are confronted with such a possibility is probably one of the main considerations that lie behind a readiness to query incorrigibility. In the typical example mentioned, where self-advancement is strongly suggested as the agent's overriding aim, we may feel that the person could not have been entirely deaf to a voice from within declaring his true motive. Or again, someone who tells the truth when there is much to be gained from lying may, we surmise, be conveniently ignoring the thought that he risks getting caught out if he lies, and hastily putting a more respectable reason for truth-telling in its place. Such cases come close to the fourth category, that of self-deception, where there is a refusal to dwell on a possibility for fear of where it might lead. This is to be distinguished from the case where there is actual awareness, however brief, of a reason other than the one avowed, though the line between them may become blurred. Fifthly, there is the possibility of unconscious reasons. However, in any sense in which there would be an opposition with incorrigibility, we have not had to acknowledge that anything which would count as a reason is to be met with which falls quite outside consciousness, but once that point has been reached we have moved to the realm of causes rather than reasons. Sixthly, there is no necessity to deny that known effects of one's actions are intentional on the grounds that they fall outside anything planned. As known outcomes of calculated acts, they can be admitted to the sphere of the intentional, even if they are excluded from the agent's intention as formulated before the act.

Finally, accepting the agent's special position *vis-à-vis* the reasons for his current action does not extend to the matter of how he would have acted in other circumstances, but this, like questions concerning the origins of his likes, dislikes, skills, and talents, is a question over the answer to which he has no final authority.

9

Freedom

If it is as much as granted that we have to do with an action, then the agent's freedom is not something additional to be ascertained. That this is so, at least on one way of linking these concepts, is already clear from our discussion, even if the emphasis, and the problems, are somewhat different when this aspect is to the fore. Bringing out this involvement will allow us to profit further from the distinction we have noted between two uses of 'want', and to take in more of the network of relations into which our concept of action enters. The area is yet another where causation may be wrongly invoked in elucidating reason-involving notions—as with that of a compelling choice or an irresistible course of action—and indeed where freedom may be denied because of a supposed conflict with universal causation. Whatever the chinks in determinism, they do not let in any light on free will, but nor, it will be argued, is there any call to defend our freedom at the expense of this doctrine.

9.1 FREEDOM AS DOING AS ONE PLEASES

Discussions of freedom commonly centre around two characterizations: to act freely is to act as one pleases, to do what one wants to do; alternatively, though perhaps equivalently, a person can be said to have acted freely if he could have done something other than what he in fact did. As anything more than starting-points, these are patently unsatisfactory. In digesting a heavy dinner, a person may be doing what he wants to do, but he is not 'doing' anything in the requisite sense, and pinpointing that sense is really just what is required, the explanation of 'action' and 'free action' being much the same task. Again, you may want to inherit a fortune, shake off a bad cold, lose weight, or recover your appetite, but, while these may be things you want to *do*, that does not mean that they are things you can do *freely*. Similarly with being able to do otherwise. You crossed the room, but you claim that you could have done something else. You mean you could have tripped on the carpet, slipped on the polished floor? No, clearly; we are concerned again only with *actions*. This is not to reject these characterizations as pointless. Since we are confident that the term 'action' bears a sense in which the qualification 'free' is redundant, we may rest assured that sometimes at least we act freely, that character as voluntary does not make for an intractable addition to our commonplace notion of action. If it is sometimes made to seem otherwise, that is largely because, I suspect, it is wrongly supposed that only a metaphysical notion of some profundity could be commensurate with the importance which freedom has for attributions of praise and blame. However, there is a question as to the significance of the freedom we enjoy supposing that our universe is deterministic, at least in the regions that concern us, a question we shall work towards with our analysis.

The relation between *free* and *action* just indicated is not the only one conceivable, but another possibility may lie behind the use of such locutions as 'I did not do it of my own free will'. The intention here may not be to claim that what was engaged in was not even an action, but the implied contrast could be one between doing what, quite generally, one wants to do—this being associated with freedom—and what one reluctantly feels obliged or constrained to do in the circumstances—part with one's money under duress, for instance. The contrast is of obvious importance, but my chief interest is in the broader category under which both possibilities are subsumed: despite the duress, handing over one's money can still be reckoned an action; it remains under the agent's control, something he may choose to do, unwelcome though it is, not something he cannot help doing.

I am not concerned that freedom of action, so understood, is in no way a prerogative of adult human beings. A child is acting freely if it is doing exactly as it pleases. An animal, too, can be said to be acting freely—if the dog wants to sniff this tree, it can sniff this tree; no obstacles are laid in its way. In a figurative sense, the same idea may extend even to inanimate subjects: the traffic is moving freely if it proceeds without let or hindrance. Of course, neither child nor dog need be considered responsible for what it freely does, but then the two notions do not invariably come hand in hand, responsibility requiring an awareness of the significance of what one is doing that may well be denied the child and is certainly denied the animal.

Even with human behaviour, the notion of freedom here favoured takes in more than many would allow. Certainly, we should be wary of making the familiar concessions: 'There are special cases, where I do what I want but am still unfree. These are cases of desires I cannot help having or cannot resist. Drug addicts, alcoholics, compulsive hand-washers and others have such desires' (Glover 1972: 156). Notoriously, the reasoning which finds room for these exceptions may make it difficult to avoid enlarging the range of special cases until the area of freedom contracts to vanishing point.

Consider the plight of the obsessional neurotic who feels he must wash his hands several times every hour, the man of whom it is said: 'He does not choose—he is impelled by inner drives' (Benn 1976: 113). Is it so evident that such a person is not acting freely? He will certainly wish he were free of his destructive desire, but that is a different question from that of his freedom to act, or in acting. By and large we have no say in our desires, but will inevitably want to eat, sleep, and so forth. If I take steps to quench my thirst, I am doing just what I want to do, my freedom in this respect being in no way diminished by the consideration that I at no time chose to have such a desire. As should be apparent from earlier discussion, it is the broader *want* rather than the narrower *desire* that is inseparable from acting freely. Suppose that the obsessional hand-washer finds himself in a situation in which there is some embarrassment to be suffered in going off and washing his hands, something to be weighed up against the relief that this will bring. He may decide he would rather put up with the physical discomfort than the social malaise, and act to relieve the former. He may decide and act the other way. If what takes place conforms to this scheme, then it follows the usual pattern of human action: we make up our minds what we most want, or least dislike, and act accordingly. For freedom to be wanting, a departure from this pattern is needed, but the only departure from the norm that we have so far lies in the unusual character of the man's desires, and that is not enough.

Behaviour that is unfree, but not physically constrained, is not easily come by. True, when an act becomes automatic, unthinking, we might decline to call it free, but, although its stereotyped character may take it in the direction of a reflex act, such character does not make for constraint. Is it more that the free/constrained contrast is ill-suited to such behaviour? Think, for instance, of the way one shifts one's gaze from speaker to speaker in a conversational group.

There is no compulsion here, but it may well be felt that if this qualifies as free action then it is too easily earned to count for much. Once more, the significance of freedom lies more in the consideration that movements of this character can fall within the sphere of the deliberate as well as in that of the unthinking, that we can desist from, initiate, or vary what we are doing, if we choose. As has been argued, whether something we do is intentional is further to the question of its character as an action, the latter calling for no more than the possibility of intentionality.

As a type of behaviour that is more challenging for our account, consider that of the alcoholic or other such 'addict', someone often said to be acting under a compulsion when indulging his habit. The alcoholic knows that, if he accepts the drink offered him, it is likely to lead to more drinks, drinks which he can ill afford and which will result in his ending up in a sorry state, a disgrace to himself and to his family. On the other hand, to set against the familiar litany of drawbacks is one very powerful consideration: he desperately wants a drink, and will feel wretched, on edge, unless he has it. His problem is one of deciding what he wants most. If he reaches a decision and acts in accordance with it, there is no difficulty; the sequence of events remains within the familiar pattern of free action. And what would the opposite look like? Suppose he decides not to drink, and that his resolution is shown in steps taken to remove himself from the source of temptation, yet he suddenly finds his hand straying towards the glass, closing around it and lifting it to his lips; his head tilts back at just the right angle, his mouth opens at just the right moment, and down the liquid goes. Could we have any grounds for believing a claim that he was not acting freely in behaving thus? When do we find such a series of purposive, coordinated actions to be out of our control, forced upon us against our wishes? Given the closeness of *wanting* and *acting*, there is good reason here for scepticism: we are simply looking at behaviour which can plausibly be described as the expression of a desire.

But what of behaviour as irrational as the kleptomaniac's? Such behaviour is commonly thought of as requiring us to recognize something akin to an illness in its aetiology, being often associated with hormonal changes which befall a woman in mid-life. May this not be sufficient to take away all freedom and responsibility? The irrationality of the kleptomaniac's thefts is a matter of the apparent disproportion between the value of what is stolen—often a mere bauble—and the social stigma, and possible punishment, consequent upon being apprehended. I say *apparent* disproportion, since presumably, while the article stolen may be in itself of little value, monetary worth is not the scale on which the kleptomaniac's evaluation is made, but what is attractive is the idea of taking a forbidden object, something belonging to another, kleptomaniacs often being found to have ample funds to purchase the article in question. Also, while our natural response is to regard such thefts as irrational, it is worth considering whether a person given to such behaviour actually goes into shops well aware of what is likely to occur, whether she takes care not to pick up objects and secrete them on her person when a shop assistant is watching, and so forth. If the strategy adopted is aimed at minimizing the risk to the agent, then, foolish though it may be to gamble one's good name in this way, there is none the less rationality in the steps taken. However damaging the consequences may be, and be appreciated to be, by the kleptomaniac, there may be all the marks of free action. Such a person chooses to steal rather than to pay. What is different is the way the prospect of stealing something exerts such a strange and powerful attraction. Such attraction explains why getting the object in the right circumstances is reckoned a reason for acting, as far as the kleptomaniac is concerned, and it may also be possible to bring in reference to an illness, or something similar, in explaining further why the reasoning goes the way it does, why the theft of a trifling object is found so alluring. Once more, that is, causal considerations may complement an explanation in terms of reasons; and once more there is no call to see them contradicting such an explanation. Some have feared that one day all behaviour will somehow be revealed to be comparable to the kleptomaniac's; if there is any assimilation, it is, surely, in the other direction.

But it is one thing if the desire is one the agent is content to have; if it is something that is against her true will, something to which she is not reconciled, something which indeed she may fight against, then action in accordance with that desire is surely not to be reckoned free (cf. Frankfurt 1971).

It is here that the distinction between uses of 'want' or 'desire' comes into play. As remarked above, there are desires that assail one, as an urge to scratch oneself or to sneeze, even to make a bad pun, desires we can often speak of feeling or experiencing. In avowing such a desire we need not be indicating how we are minded to act, not be expressing a decision taken. Such desires are just further items to be taken into account in arriving at a decision. But, if we do take that step, if saying 'I want to V' expresses a genuine decision, then, even if our will is to satisfy an unwelcome desire, it genuinely is none the less our will, an expression of our overall preference, just as much as if the desire had been one we had welcomed. We have not simply acknowledged a desire, we have assented to action. But may we not struggle unsuccessfully against a craving to which we do not want to succumb? (cf. Frankfurt 1975: 114). If what we do is then not what, all things considered, we want to do, then our action is not free. But, if that is so, it is not just in virtue of the fact that the desire is one we did not want to have. It has to be that we are helpless in the face of that desire, quite unable to act otherwise than we do. Whether a desire can render us thus impotent is not a familiar fact of experience, but a fact, clearly, is what it has to be for our freedom to be put at risk—in which event, of course, we shall have to do not with an *action*, but with something like a cough or a sneeze.

However, I say that the action engaged in as the result of a decision *can* be reckoned an expression of the agent's will. I do not wish to claim that we could not associate the notion of one's true will with that of what *ideally* one would wish to do. The issue is akin to one touched upon earlier when a notion of acting freely was acknowledged which made just such a connection, so would reckon as unfree an act of handing over money in order to avoid the unwelcome consequences of non-compliance. An acceptable use of 'unfree', but not the use that is central when our concern is with action which is under the agent's control, which he can engage in, or not, as he pleases. Moreover, this is not a case where one wishes one had different desires; it is other circumstances, circumstances which call for action, which one wishes were different.

It is the pressures of unwanted situations rather than those of unwanted desires that are, I suggest, the more important when questions of freedom and responsibility are at stake, the former being more likely to present extenuating circumstances, to be the kind of situation in which the agent may be said to have had no choice—as when a failure to cooperate means that the person's life is under threat.

Suppose someone has the choice of being shot, or of driving a van loaded with explosives into a densely populated area. It is asking a lot of a person to agree to be shot, even though the alternative may be far greater loss of life. The question is a moral one, concerning the proper attitude to such choices; questions of freedom arise only when, for instance, it is suggested that the person could not act because he was paralysed with fear. Even when it is said that the person could not bring himself to do something, physical powers are usually not at issue. You declare that you could not bring yourself to fire an employee. It is not that your ability is in doubt, that you try and are thwarted, but it is more an emphatic affirmation of an evaluation: the consequences were so repugnant, you were not prepared to go ahead and do it. Once more, the difficult question concerns the appropriate attitude—which might be different with this example as against 'I could not bring myself to break off the affair'. Again, someone confesses that he could not resist pointing out some pompous fellow's mistake. 'Resist' finds its way in because there were considerations to be weighed up relating to a questionable aspect of the act, and which the person decided to discount. He may have acted against his better judgement, but that is not to act against one's will.

9.2 FREEDOM AS BEING ABLE TO DO OTHERWISE

Our discussion of freedom began with the observation that, while to act freely is to do as one pleases, this characterization depends for its cogency on a somewhat damaging presupposition: the use of 'do' must be one in which involuntary doings are not admitted. Suppose that the verb is taken to embrace both the voluntary and the involuntary. Then doing as one pleases becomes acting freely when the further condition is added that the agent should have been able to refrain from the act in question. This gives us freedom in the sense in which Hume thought the notion compatible with determinism, his 'liberty of spontaneity', though the way we have explicated the notion of action has gone against Hume's construal, on which acting 'according to the determinations of the will' is made out to be explicable as action which is caused by one's will (desires). With this notion of freedom, rightly understood, in view, the usual problem of free will looks to be somewhat contrived. Try describing someone engaged in a complex series of operations, as those involved in dismantling an engine, and add that it was all done involuntarily. Involuntarily, mark, not unwillingly or reluctantly. The former goes with reactions, not actions.

But we have still to elucidate the notion which this characterization presupposes, and which recurs in Hume's 'liberty of indifference', a form which he thought could not be reconciled with determinism. The suggestion is that a man will have acted voluntarily to the extent that he had control over what he did, and that what he did will have been under his control to the extent that, within certain limits, he could have varied his actions at will; in particular, he will have had to be able to desist from what he was engaged in, and to refrain from the act in the first place. The counterfactual character of the proposition 'A could have done otherwise', with its apparent difficulties of verification, may seem to point to an ineradicable uncertainty at the heart of claims to freedom, but on one reading what is advanced can readily be granted. To declare, for instance, 'I could have cooked a better meal than I did' is to make a claim of substance, and one that may be hard to vindicate, but if trying and failing counts as doing otherwise, the demands on one's powers and skills are at a minimum. So, I in fact produced an edible meal, but, it goes without saying that I could have done otherwise. It is success that is difficult to ensure; failure is all too easy. Or is this to take the formula the wrong way? Should we appeal to the very real possibility of failure to make good a claim that we could have *done* otherwise? Surely we want to hold that alternative *actions* were within our power, not failure; that is more: something else could have happened.

That something else could have happened is just what the determinist is intent on denying, but in any case, would it not be absurd to say of someone who had succeeded in a project demanding great resources of skill, knowledge, and strength that there is none the less no other feat, no *lesser* feat, that he could have performed? As though we could happily accept that someone had designed and developed a large garden, yet claim that he would inevitably have come to grief had he sought merely to plant a row of beans. Anyone who can propose this as a serious possibility has lost his grip on the notion of being able to do otherwise and the kinds of consideration which warrant such a pronouncement. And even this sort of claim is more than the truth of 'I could have done otherwise' needs. As implied, for that nothing more is demanded than that the agent should have been able to desist or refrain from what he did; no more elaborate range of alternative actions has to be within his capacity. So what precisely does this involve?

My cough, I claim, was voluntary, something I could have refrained from. That, it might again be insisted, poses no problem. Mere not doing is minimal in what it demands, requiring nothing by way of skill or power; such voluntariness is easily achieved, and elucidated, if it needs no more than an ability not to act. Or is 'refrain' too restricted, suggesting not doing something which one might realistically think to do? We, as it were, say No to an action to which we are to some degree drawn, at least enough to have to decide one way or the other.

In the more interesting cases, certainly, to refrain from coughing is not merely to fail to cough but to choose not to cough, and not cough. Not: I shouldn't have coughed if I hadn't wanted to, but: I shouldn't have coughed had I wanted, or chosen, not to. I wasn't forced; it was the kind of cough over which one exercises control. But now, something which one can do or forbear from, thus understood, is nothing more than an action *tout court*, as we have defined it. The two definitions of free action reduce to the notion of action, and therewith to one another, as has been apparent for some time. And this is hardly surprising. Liberty of spontaneity is glossed by Hume in the following way: if we choose to remain at rest, we may; if we choose to move, we also may (*An Enquiry Concerning Human Understanding*, VIII. i). How, given that both possibilities are granted, could it be maintained that, when you opted for action, you could not have done otherwise? The two characterizations have been made to seem further apart than they are by our concentration on acting freely rather than on being free to act. In saying merely that freedom consists in doing what one wants to do, we leave it to the notion of action to supply the further condition concerning refraining, whereas, if we consider the agent prior to his engagement in action, we may bring in reference to the alternatives open to him at that point: he can V if he chooses to, refrain if he chooses not to V.

What of Locke's example of the person who mistakenly believes himself able to leave a room, but chooses to stay put (*Essay*, II. xxi. 10)? Does he act freely? If it is acting, that is so only in a diminished sense, but it seems reasonable to keep to our characterization and to withhold 'freely'. The person is under the illusion that he is acting freely, though it remains true that he chose to stay where he is, and that he did so choose may tell you something about his state of mind, about his good or ill will, often the consideration of importance to us. More difficult to specify are examples of action as opposed to inaction where the person mistakenly believes that an alternative was open to him. This would in all likelihood be a matter of a mistaken belief about an act that was usually voluntary. An out-of-the-way event, but we noted a relevant possibility with respect to behaviour under hypnosis.

You could have refrained from coughing. That is, you would not have coughed had you wanted (chosen) not to. We have still to get to grips with the counterfactual conditional which this analysis presents us. However, with coughing as an action, the conditional must be granted, action being behaviour of just the kind to which 'refrain' applies. We may be able to *check* an involuntary act, but such checking will itself be a voluntary act, not an instance of refraining. What of the more substantive claim that without the desire there would have been no cough, where an involuntary cough is now allowed? This is not something we may be able to deny categorically, but there could be good reason to regard such a denial as a presumptive truth. The cough that comes unbidden may have recognizably different marks, to such a point that it can be reckoned a different kind of cough—and what grounds have we for saying that, if the given cough had not occurred, a cough of a different kind would have? No more than we have for saying that, if that cough had not come to pass, a sneeze would have. And without grounds in favour, the presumption is surely that there would have been no cough.

Consider now the converse possibility: you choose not to cough, but insist that you could have done so. Once more there is a possibility that has to be allowed—that you should have gone to cough, but have failed to bring it off—and once more, against the assumption that no attempt at coughing was made, the conditional can enjoy no more than indirect support, not direct verification. Such support may be weak, but it may also be strong; it depends on what happens to be known, not on resolving some omnipresent difficulty. When you go to sing a high note, you seldom succeed, so your claim that you could have produced such a note on this occasion is far from assured; on the other hand, when it comes to coughing, your ability has been proven often enough, perhaps to the point that you have known no failures.

If saying 'You could have refrained' just emphasizes that it was a voluntary act, it might seem to be an observation with little point. Not necessarily, I should say, but it is true that the relevant considerations are often somewhat different from our present concern.

First, in saying that someone could have refrained from Ving, we are not usually concerned to affirm a bare physical possibility, a power or ability that a person might show himself to lack if he tried and failed, but the issue is closer to one introduced in the preceding section. It is more 'You didn't have to do that', where the 'compulsion' envisaged relates to reasons, not to physical force. Similarly with 'I couldn't have done otherwise', or 'I couldn't have done anything else', which generally come to claiming that any other course of action would have been unreasonable, or have disqualified itself in some other such way; it would be unlikely to mean that one had been powerless to act differently.

Likewise with 'I had no choice', which may be an observation on the character of the available alternatives as much as on one's powers: you may be said to have no choice if there are only two alternatives and one is beyond you; we may also say that there was no real choice when a particular goal is overwhelmingly attractive, or its rivals overwhelmingly unappealing, but that represents an evaluation of one's aims, not an observation that one's ability to act was impaired. When the action bears the hallmarks of voluntary character, we have to have a compelling reason to accept 'He can't help doing it' as a warranted observation, rather than simply conclude that nothing more desirable has been put the agent's way. These various possibilities arise with respect to kleptomaniacs, pyromaniacs, and inveterate gamblers, but not in such a way as to make for a significant difference with choices which arise for everyone. They do not offer any general basis on which such people might be exculpated for their deeds, any basis for removing them from the category of responsible agents. If there is any consideration which comes to their aid, it lies more with the sympathy which their plight may evoke.

9.3 ABILITY AND POSSIBILITY

Determinism may be challenged by showing that there are areas in which it does not hold, but for our purposes a more relevant response is to follow the many writers who have emphasized the detachment of determinism from the concept which genuinely does stand opposed to that of freedom, namely, that of *constraint* (cf. Ayer 1956; Schlick 1962: ch. VII). Constraint *against the will* is, of course, the operative notion, but we may also query the conception of natural laws as constraining, or even determining, the behaviour of bodies generally, a picture likely to rest on an improper analogy with legal or moral laws, as talk of bodies *obeying* laws suggests. Nature does not act with one eye on what is, as it were, permissible under the law; a natural law does not limit the behaviour of anything, but it is the behaviour of the things falling under the law that has priority, any laws simply having to adjust to that behaviour. It may be objected that this is so only for a *putative* law; a genuine law is not thus at the mercy of particular happenings. However, that observation does not detract from the priority of such happenings, since it is these that determine what *counts* as a genuine law. No more is being said than: whatever happens, we shall find a lawlike description for it; and, of course, if indeterminism has to be conceded, even that may be to say too much.

According to Elizabeth Anscombe, 'My actions are mostly physical movements; if these physical movements are physically predetermined by processes which I do not control, then my freedom is perfectly illusory. The truth of physical indeterminism is thus indispensable if we are to make anything of the claim to freedom' (1971: 146). Indeterminism is somehow to make room for freedom. Will it be a convenient matter of empirical fact that comes to freedom's rescue, or is it grammar that is to perform this service? That is, does it just so happen that relevant events are not predetermined, or does it not even make sense to suppose that they should be?

If it can be sustained, the grammatical thesis will make for a more secure, and seemingly less arbitrary, basis for an escape. And, indeed, that possibility is not without support, the effect of our analysis of acting for a reason being to take the notion outside the area where determinism holds sway, in that it is never a possibility, given the grammar of 'reason', that a reason will prove to be a cause of behaviour. Furthermore, the issues which have come up in relation to freedom—issues concerning choice, compulsion, and the like—have maintained this focus on reasons, any causal considerations tending to relate to a different range of questions.

But perhaps this does not take us far. First, it cannot be said that we have seen off psychological determinism, precisely because, for example, a belief that *p* is not something psychological, this epithet belonging with the state of belief or believing. Moreover, even if believing, desiring, choosing, and so forth are disqualified as causes of action, this is not to deny that something else has this role. We

have already tried to meet the argument based on the uncontrolla-
bility of neural happenings, but, while 'A could have done otherwise'
and 'A could have refrained' have been represented as in general easy
to support when ability is at issue, it would be useful to see in more
detail how these measure up to the determinist's challenge.

One of the most celebrated and contested attempts to defuse the
threat to freedom from determinism is due to G. E. Moore, who suggested that to say that an agent could have done something he did
not do is to say that he could (or should) have done that thing if he
had chosen (1912: ch. VI). Since a difference in choice would have
made for a difference in the antecedents of the action, there is, on this
analysis, no conflict with determinism, and, since the analysis offers
a grammatical rather than an empirical resolution of the issue, it is
worth seeing whether it is defensible.

On the determinist's view, it is intolerable to suppose that someone who acted in a certain way might do something different were
the circumstances of his action to be repeated without relevant deviation. Determinism is often held to be insufficiently well defined to
be worth taking seriously—or, if well defined, then no more than an
article of faith—but dissatisfaction with the possibility advanced by
the anti-determinist is eminently understandable, and it would be a
desperate man who sought to establish freedom by endorsing it—not
only as a real, but as a recurrent possibility, supposing our usual
belief as to our freedom is to be upheld. There are areas in which
determinism comes into question, but the general movement of
empirical investigation is inexorably in the direction of tracing different events back to different antecedent conditions. But in any
event, we might suggest, freedom does not for a moment require this
heroic step. When I say that I could have done something other than
what I have been doing for the past five minutes, I do not envisage
an exact repetition of the circumstances which have just unfolded;
rather, I imagine a difference in my behaviour appropriate to a different train of thought. As it happens, I did not even contemplate the
possibility, but I could have turned the wireless on if I had wanted
to, if the prospect had appealed to me sufficiently. It is difficult to see
why anyone should be interested in the kind of possibility that would
be at odds with determinism: just the thoughts the agent then had but
a difference in behaviour with nothing to account for it; not merely
no difference in his thoughts, but no difference at any level! What
kind of superstition is that?

However, attractive as this compatibilist argument may appear, it is not beyond challenge. In particular, it has been queried whether the circumstances in which we might truly say 'I could have done otherwise' can always be redescribed by a conditional or its equivalent, as 'I could have done otherwise if I had wanted (tried, chosen)'. Nor, moreover, is it clear that what has just been called a superstition deserves that label. Is it not precisely one of the striking features about choice that, faced with the same alternatives, we sometimes go this way, sometimes that? Indeed, it is not merely that we do not know of any relevant difference; so long as we are in the realm of reasons, the differences will be only as the agent acknowledges, and that means that the possibility of no difference at all is a real one. But, if it has to be allowed that, in the same state of mind, I might have opted for the alternative which I in fact declined, what becomes of Moore's strategy for deflecting the threat from determinism?

Let us begin with the problem posed by the conditional analysis. The supposition is, of course, that we are speaking of possible actions, or intended effects of one's actions, so are not concerned with such propositions as 'He could have started a fire', supposing this to be detached from intention, and meaning simply that the person's activities could have had that consequence. If, on the other hand, it is a matter of a conjectured achievement, if we are saying there is something the person could have succeeded in doing, then our claim is that, had he embarked upon some action, it would have had a certain upshot. In this, as opposed to the unintentional case, he should, in general, have had to do something he did not do, and here 'try' offers itself as a suitably general antecedent to any such achievement. What, then, are we to say to Austin's objection: 'Consider the case where I miss a very short putt and kick myself because I could have holed it. It is not that I should have holed it if I had tried: I did try, and missed. It is not that I should have holed it if conditions had been different: that might of course be so, but I am talking about conditions as they precisely were, and asserting that I could have holed it' (1979: 218)? There are familiar uses of 'could have' in which no expansion to a conditional is in the offing. So, wondering about Kate's whereabouts, we venture the suggestion: she could have gone to visit her cousin. Kate's abilities need be in no way in question, but it is a matter of possible courses of action consistent with what is known about her movements, and with no conditionality implied. Again, if 'I could have holed it' is like 'I could have started a fire', no intention implied, then Austin is right to refuse the proposed expansion. It is also true that relevant conditions may comprise just those conditions which the agent had to cope with. In that case, however, it surely must be supposed that *he* might have proceeded differently. Not a difference to be indicated by 'if he had tried', given that an attempt has already been acknowledged, but it must be thought that something would have made the difference between success and failure: if he had hit the ball harder, if he had hit it a little to the left, or whatever.

On the other hand, not only does it seem incorrect to describe 'I could have holed that putt' as *incomplete*, but there appears to be no scope at all for relevant additions to the variant given with 'I had the ability to hole that putt'. Happily, the least contentious view, which is to grant that both positions are, in their own way, correct, is also a possibility: there is a use of ability words in which there is no question of a grammatical or semantic incompleteness, but another use which requires an if-clause or equivalent, and which can always be invoked in paraphrasing the former use. Perhaps 'always' is too strong, but there are countless contexts in which the paraphrase appears to capture the intended sense.

To see these two uses at work, consider the statement 'I was able to reach the vase'. This could be understood as implying success on the part of the speaker in reaching the vase, and not mere possession of an ability that went unexercised on that occasion—as would be conveyed by 'I could have reached that vase'. Similarly, 'I was able to hear their conversation', or 'I could hear their conversation', is likely to contradict 'I failed to hear their conversation', and 'I was able to hit the target three times' is more than likely to report three successful accomplishments. Again, 'He would have been a hero if he had been able to stop the robber' might be true, but only if a successful exercise of an ability is being envisaged, not merely its possession. On the other hand, 'I came as soon as I could' means 'I came as soon as it was possible for me to do so', not 'I came as soon as I succeeded in coming'.

To the extent that it compares with 'I had the ability to hole that putt', 'I could have holed that putt' reports an unexercised ability, and is in no way in need of completion. However, it can be recast, depending on circumstances, in a form which introduces a suitable if-clause, as, for example, 'I could have holed that putt if I had allowed for the borrow', where 'could have holed' means 'should have succeeded in holing', now specifying an exercised ability, and in a way that demands the associated if-clause to complete it. Of course, someone who claims that he could have holed the putt may not be able to provide any such expansion, but it would seem reasonable to hold that the truth of his claim would depend on the kind of possibility which such an expansion provides. We might agree with Austin that there may be inexplicable failures (ibid. 218), failures which do not oblige us to deny an ability, but there must be circumstances in which one would have managed to bring the act off if the claim to have had the ability means anything.

In so far as Austin refuses to accept that an elaboration in terms of an if-clause is to the point, he is in effect aligning statements of ability with more general statements of possibility in which actions are not distinguished from other happenings. The model here would be 'I could have missed that putt'—that is, that could have happened—rather than the achievement envisaged with 'I could have holed that putt'. And that is a legitimate reading. In saying 'You could have lived in China', we may simply be advancing a possibility in which no exercise of an ability is envisaged, not claiming that, in the right circumstances, you would have succeeded in living in China. But, if your ability is in question, it is the latter construal that is our concern. Note that, because 'could' implies success in this use, it makes little difference which of 'could' and 'should' or 'would' we enlist in our expanded form. Similarly, of course, with 'can'. In saying, 'She can be quite charming', it may be that mere possibility is at issue: that is how it sometimes is with her. On the other hand, if we are thinking of a voluntary exercise of charm, a conditional expansion is now to the point: she can be quite charming if she wants to, if she is so minded.

Even now, however, there are at least three possible objections to the proposal. First, on my reading, 'I can reach the top shelf' may paraphrase as 'I shall manage to reach the top shelf if I try', but this latter is consistent with each of 'I can't reach the top shelf if I don't try' and 'I'm not going to try', and so with their consequence, 'I can't reach the top shelf'. Our initial equivalence cannot, accordingly, be sustained (cf. Lehrer 1968). However, this apparent predicament simply points up the difference in the uses of 'can' which we have distinguished. 'I can't reach the top shelf if I don't try' is not 'In the absence of any attempt on my part to reach the top shelf I lack the ability', but simply 'I shall not succeed in reaching the top shelf if I don't try'. The conclusion 'I can't reach the top shelf' retains this latter reading of the main clause, so there is no clash with the initial statement of ability.

However, straightforward though this solution may be, there is still room for doubt whether it is to be achieved by distinguishing different readings of 'can'. Is it really allowable to associate the modal with the notion of a successful achievement, as opposed to the more general ability to do something? Consider the following from Irving Thalberg: 'A person whose hands are crippled with arthritis visits Lourdes. He dips his hands in the holy water of the grotto, and his fingers begin to move. Has he regained the ability to lift his fingers? Surely we need more than one display to be convinced' (1969: 190). There can be doubt whether the person was able to move his fingers on this occasion, rather than that his fingers simply moved, but, if it is right to say that he *succeeded* in moving them, then there certainly is a sense in which he then had the ability, was then able, to do what he did. However, there is obviously room for a distinction between an ability proven by a single successful performance and a more lasting ability, as with: I was able to touch my toes right up until adulthood. It is a matter not of different senses of 'ability', but of abilities which differ in duration. True, if our concern is with what is possible for an agent on a single occasion only, then 'was then able to V' is more appropriate than 'then had the ability to V', but it is only the former that our purposes call for. The same observation applies with Kenny's example (1975: 136) of being able to spell 'seize' correctly on some occasions only. In his view, the cases of failure make it incorrect to say that he *can* spell the word correctly: *ab esse ad posse non valet consequentia*. But, if a temporally unrestricted 'can' is unwarranted, it is also true that he *was* able to spell the word correctly on those occasions on which he actually did so, and this is all that we are committed to in saying that performance gives proof of ability. A triviality, but failure to see it as such can have far-reaching consequences; in Kenny's case, a demand to revise the very logic of possibility as one might think to apply it in this area.

However, there is yet a third objection to answer. Consider the sentence 'He could have mended the puncture if he had wanted to'. If this is a conditional, then it would appear that a hypothesized desire is being said to be sufficient for an ability. And this seems wrong. How might a mere desire have it in itself to ensure an ability or a power? In the event that he should have wanted to mend the puncture, he could have done so. Certainly, but is this not more a matter of specifying circumstances in which the question of the person's ability would have arisen, would have been of some relevance, rather than a claim that he would have had the ability inasmuch as he had had the desire? Compare 'I can mend the puncture if you want me to', where I am surely not crediting your desires with any causal powers over my actions, as if you need but have the desire and I shall have the ability. Rather, the ability is something I take myself to have irrespective of your desires, the role of the if-clause being merely to indicate the point of making this known. Compare 'There's a recital on Wednesday, if you're interested'. Or again, take 'You can bring your brother along if you want to (wish, like)'. Not a conditional, but here too the interest of the person addressed is thought to give point to what is said with the main clause. Contrast 'I shall mend the puncture if you want me to'. In this case the possibility of contraposing attests to genuine conditionality—'If I do not mend the puncture, you will not have wanted me to'—a move that is blocked by the replacement of 'shall' by 'can': we cannot proceed to 'If I cannot mend the puncture, you will not have wanted me to'.

It is certainly possible to find a model for a non-conditional reading of the relevant forms, but, as an argument to show that this is the reading appropriate to the if-sentences which concern us, the preceding considerations are far from conclusive. Indeed, there is some doubt whether we are even addressing a relevant form with such an example as 'You can bring your brother along if you want to (wish, like)', where 'can' is used in granting permission, not in ascribing an ability. At all events, when the latter role is at issue, it seems we can realistically entertain a conditional reading. Consider 'There will be biscuits on the sideboard if you want them'—a variant of Austin's celebrated example. Here the speaker may be saying that he will be arranging for biscuits to be on the sideboard provided that they are wanted, or he may be stating that they will be there anyhow. Despite the possibility of the latter reading, the former, conditional, interpretation is not ruled out.

Moreover, the parsing which would have the speaker claiming that the desire to V is sufficient for the ability to V misrepresents the words in respects already considered—as if it were the ability quite generally, rather than simply success on the particular occasion, and as if it were a matter of a desire which compares with an urge, rather than the wanting which involves a commitment to action. The relevance of the appropriate readings to 'He could have mended the puncture if he had wanted to' is clear. We can take the consequent here as equivalent to 'He would have been able to mend the puncture' and interpret this in a way that implies success: he would have succeeded in mending the puncture if he had wanted to. Taken as 'would have succeeded', 'could have' demands completion in a way the if-clause provides, and there appears to be no bar to such completion: if he had wanted to mend the puncture he would have tried to, and if he had tried he would have been successful. The conditional might be advanced by way of countering a defence of the person's failure to deal with the puncture, on the grounds that the task was beyond him, the point of adding 'if he had wanted to' being to indicate that, while the task was within his capacities, he just couldn't be bothered, was not prepared to make the effort. He'd have succeeded if he'd been sufficiently well disposed, if he'd made the effort that wanting implies. If we overlook this relatively simple construal, this may be in part because of the unfortunate choice of the term 'ability' in paraphrasing the sentence, 'He could have mended the puncture if he had wanted to.' To say of this that it affirms an ability conditional upon a desire may well suggest that an ability—or power or skill—would have somehow developed from the mere desire, whereas saying that he would have succeeded if he had wanted to presents the success as conditional upon the wanting, it is true, but without implying that a desire is a means to an ability, something which generates it.

To discourage the incongruous suggestion that an ability might flow from a choice, we might follow Kenny (1975: 141) in relocating the if-clause so as to block this reading. Not 'If I choose, I have the ability to charm snakes', but 'I have the ability to charm snakes if I choose', where the structure here matches that of 'It is my intention to protest if he is elected'. Just as the if-clause in the latter enters into the specification of what is intended, so 'if I choose' joins with 'to charm snakes' so as to define a restriction of the ability which this verbal phrase specifies. However, there is no need for this strategy if the conditional involves the success use of 'can' invoked in our analysis of the ability statement. 'I can charm snakes if I choose' then compares with 'I succeed in charming snakes if I choose', each affirming an unproblematic dependence of the success on the choosing.

With the statements of ability so far considered, we envisage a task carried through to a successful conclusion. While the ability is thus verified at this latter point, it might be objected that this scheme takes for granted an ability at the other end, an ability to set about the action, to get it under way. At the back of this objection may lie the idea that, for 'getting V under way' to apply, there must be an act which is performed *before* anything takes place which could be described as the initial phase of Ving. But, if nothing is done *to* get one's hand moving, or whatever, then there is no room for any such act. Setting about writing one's name or sharpening a pencil, say, is just performing the first stages of the writing or sharpening, the same activity as is involved in the completed act, only not carried through to its conclusion. Here we may recall that 'A could have tried' simply credits A with the ability to perform the first stages of the relevant act—or something A takes to be such—had he thought that the most desirable option, and trying to try will in turn involve the early stages of an act that counts as trying. Obviously, if we try to try, we shall succeed in trying. It is only if nothing counts as trying for us that we cannot try to try.

These observations indicate where we are to look for an answer to the objection that a difference in behaviour might not be accompanied by a different train of thought. Suppose that I do not V. It may be true none the less that I could have Ved if I had wanted to, even if the wanting does not constitute an antecedent state, different from what in fact occurred, but comes only with the acting. What we then have is: if I had set about Ving, I should have seen it through to a successful conclusion. My wanting would be shown by the first stages of the Ving, and my ability would be revealed in its final accomplishment—a different initial state, occurring now at a later point, but still antecedent to the completed act.

However, there are still ability statements which appear to fall outside our scheme. When 'You could have done it' interchanges with 'You could have done it if you had wanted to', a very minimal condition for success is being imposed. It is not as with 'You could have done it if you had been a surgeon', or 'if you had been 8 foot tall'. The trying that comes with wanting continues to be minimal in its demands, but there appear to be cases where it none the less lacks application. With 'She could have stopped fidgeting if she'd wanted to', the point of 'if she'd wanted to' need not be to indicate that there are steps the person could have taken if only she could have been bothered, or tried hard enough. It is not like 'She could have stopped the engine if she had wanted to'. Rather, we are saying: that is the sort of activity it was, one which comes about only in so far as the agent wants it to. If she had wanted not to fidget, she would not have continued. If it is asked *how* she might have stopped, there is nothing to answer. It is simply: she might have failed to keep it up. In such a case not Ving or refraining from Ving does not represent the exercise of an ability, but we are saying no more than that the person might not have Ved—a more general statement of possibility. However, this is not the full story. Perhaps the person might have wanted to stop, but found that the fidgeting continued. To exclude this we need to add that she could have put a stop to the fidgeting, could have checked any unwanted continuation, and with this condition the more positive ability makes a return.

A conditional reading of the relevant forms has emerged as a real possibility, but the particular expansion given with 'want' is not invariably to the point. We may be happy to pass from 'He could have had the contract altered' to 'He could have had the contract altered if he'd really wanted to', since our claim may be as just indicated: the eventuality in question would have come about if the person had made the effort that wanting implies. The if-clause is in place if there is a question of a possible failure of will, or of a lack of goodwill, whereas sometimes our concern in saying '*A* could have Ved' is merely to deny that there were any obstacles to Ving, or to affirm that Ving was a possible strategy for attaining the end desired. Consider 'You could have counted them on the fingers of one hand'. It is hardly in place to add 'if you had wanted to', and even less 'if you had tried'. Nobody's ability is in question, but it is a matter of what the relevant number makes possible. On the other hand, once ability is at issue, a conditional rendering appears natural. Take 'I could have danced all night'. This does not necessarily equate to 'I could have danced all night if I had wanted to'—perhaps the person did want to, as things were—but it would not be unreasonable to seek an expansion in terms of some enabling condition which, as things were, went unfulfilled.

Since the ability to act is just what is at issue in the debate with the determinist, it would seem that we have, with the relevant conditionals, a ready means of circumventing his objections. If he is alleging that, while Kate did indeed comb her hair, if she had tried to do anything else, such as brush her teeth, all her efforts would have come to nought, he may be arguing in the face of Kate's well-attested ability to carry through just such a task, with not the

slightest reason for supposing that her efforts would have been frustrated on the occasion contemplated. This, of course, just emphasizes
the irrelevance of determinism to these attributions of ability: what
we begin by envisaging—the person setting about brushing her
teeth—was not part of history on the occasion in question, so the
determinist is himself at liberty to imagine it continuing in whatever
way experience shows to be the most likely.

The conditionals here defended are plainly not causal—no more
than is 'If I start I shall finish'—but they have no need to be so in
order to do what we are asking of them. Their non-causal character
is worth a brief word. Contrast 'I can lift the chest if I want to' with
a form where the antecedent does not make such an immediate connection with action, as may be the case with 'If I have a wish to lift
the chest, I can do so'. If, as far as implications for action go, having a wish is on a par with making a wish, the subsequent deed
remains unexplained. As though: 'The prospect of lifting the chest
strikes me as highly desirable and, hey presto, I am able to lift it!'
The success implied by 'am able' requires action to have been
embarked upon, an attempt to have been made, and mere wishing is
quite detached from that. We might, it is true, live in a world where
wishes came true with greater regularity, in which case we should no
doubt surmise, as parapsychologists now dream, that wishing was
instrumental in bringing about the happenings wished for. As things
are, we do not need a causal hypothesis, let alone a parapsychologi-
cal theory, to understand how wanting is bound up with acting.
Compare 'You could have lent a hand if you'd wanted to'. This is
not 'You could have lent a hand if you'd felt the urge'—where the
relation between antecedent and consequent is again quite opaque—
but a matter of: if you'd had the good will, been well disposed, prepared to make the effort.

To sum up this discussion, we have a range of possibilities to which
appeal might be made in explaining how success in Ving might have
been expected by one who insists that he could have Ved. Sometimes
the appeal will be to some further action, sometimes to the satisfaction of some external condition; sometimes it will be simply: if he had
tried; more generally, and less problematically, if he had wanted or
chosen. Not causal conditionals, when the verbs are psychological
verbs, but not conditionals to which determinism poses any threat.

Admittedly, the failure of the conditionals to be causal does cast
the argument in a less familiar light, most obviously when we have

to do with instances of V*ing* and refraining from V*ing* which are accompanied by identical states of mind. We argued that this could be made to fit in with Moore's reconciling strategy, but we did not do so by showing that the different behaviour would have different causal antecedents. No doubt it does, but different reasons do not establish that the acting and the refraining proceed from different causes, and identical antecedent reasons followed by different behaviour does not mean that any causal principle has been violated. What is important is simply that, in the relevant reading, 'A could have done otherwise' can well be true, irrespective of the standing of determinism.

Sometimes, the condition for action which we have in mind in saying 'A could have V*ed* if he'd wanted to' is not at all negligible; if, for instance, it is a matter of: if A had really wanted to, if he had been prepared to go to the lengths needed. However, when the conditional reduces to 'If A sets about V*ing*, he succeeds', no real qualification is being placed on A's ability to succeed, the wanting then being only as is required for it to be possible to speak of an action embarked upon. Given that truth of the consequent logically implies that the antecedent is fulfilled, there is plainly no significant departure from the bare 'A can V'. This—a condition which is guaranteed satisfaction by the very beginnings of action—is, I suspect, what is glimpsed when it is said that we do not really have to do with a conditional, and where it is proposed that 'If he wants to V, A can' is to be parsed as 'A can V-if-he-wants-to'.

The remoteness of our conditionals from causal propositions is particularly evident when the condition imposed with 'want' is thus minimal. This is not to dismiss the analysis. There is a contrast with forms which resist it—with, for example, 'A can appreciate that p', the inappropriateness of adding 'if he wants to' reflects the consideration that appreciating is not an action—and the reduced form is still sufficient to allow us to circumvent determinism. However, perhaps the main point to emerge is that statements of ability fall outside the class of possibility statements to which the determinist challenge is offered. Moore's strategy does not involve taking the statement of possibility which determinism condemns as false, adding an if-clause, and passing off the result as a now harmless conditional. A conditional does indeed serve to formulate claims about our powers which we should not wish to abandon, but it is essentially the difference in the kind of possibility affirmed that enables us to neutralize deterministic considerations. Whether or not determinism is correct, the belief that a different historical development was possible can with some reason be held to rest largely on ignorance: we know of nothing that rules out such a departure. But when we say we could have acted differently, or specify an actual alternative, our claim is one for which our experience may well provide a more positive backing: we know what we are capable of, what actions we can carry off. Both kinds of possibility may be advanced as hypotheses, but there is a great difference in the support that each commands.

9.4 DETERMINISM AND RESPONSIBILITY

The problem of free will is of interest in that the worry which the prospect of a fully deterministic universe generates is of a kind suited to the making of an alarming discovery about oneself—much as if one came to a realization that one had been practising self-deception on a grand scale and for a considerable time—yet we do not expect anything different to come to our attention depending on whether or not determinism is true. On the other hand, hypotheses about the degree of control we enjoy are another, and a more importantly relevant, matter. Here there is room for unpleasant surprises, and so for real concern. The fact that such surprises are so rare—cf. the example of acting under hypnosis—can accordingly be regarded as genuinely reassuring.

However, if our actions are dependent on our desires, they are dependent on something over which we have no control, something which, for the determinist, could not have been other than it was. It is not that 'I could have done otherwise', or any other more specific forms, are implied to be false, but there is the risk that they lose their significance under the supposition that there was no real question of our having had the relevant desire. We have still to get to grips with this familiar objection.

In one variant, the objection seemingly takes a more damaging turn: with the given supposition, it just is not true that an alternative action is possible. If you will do x only if that is your desire, and if it is impossible that it should be your desire, then it is surely impossible that you should do x (cf. Chisholm 1964). That is correct, and it may well be that there are many actions which, given your psychological make-up, you could never be tempted to perform. This, however, does not show that you are lacking in the relevant ability, that you would meet with certain failure were you to take it into your head to embark upon the action, which is what the denial of ability involves. So, we say, Kate could (or would) have married Harvey if only she had chosen to do so, but that she should ever have taken such a choice is quite out of the question. That she should have married Harvey is thus ruled out, but the 'failure' thereby acknowledged is not one that contradicts 'Kate could have married Harvey', rightly construed; it is not a failure that proves inability. I could take up angling if I wanted to; it is just that I cannot imagine myself so possessed. That is not worrying, not a threat to my freedom, but there would be such a threat, would be failure in the relevant sense, only if I wanted to take up angling but was unable to do so. That is, the real obstacles to freedom come from obstacles which threaten to thwart the will; whether, and in what circumstances, our will might have been different is not a question which has to be answered one way rather than another for our freedom to be secured.

Similar considerations apply with respect to the predictability of human conduct. Imagine a device which, fed in enough details about us and our circumstances, could accurately foretell our next action. We naturally regard this as a challenge to refute the device by acting in a way at odds with its prediction, a challenge we feel confident we should win. We are on safe ground here, since our claim is to have the ability to do the opposite to what is forecast, and there is no reason to suppose that we should find our efforts frustrated. All that is entailed by the unfailing accuracy of the device is that this will not be something we want to do, and, if that is disturbing, it is so for reasons independent of determinism. It is not disturbing if, when it comes to making our choice, we can truthfully say we see no point in going against the course of action predicted: it is predicted that I shall make certain investments, and indeed I consider I should be a fool not to, there being more to be said for easing my financial situation than for refuting this device. It would be disturbing if we found ourselves acting against our better judgement, or even against our will, but determinism gives no particular support to this possibility, does not favour one class of action over another. Once more, there is no obvious advantage to be found in life under a non-deterministic regime; certainly, there is no reason to suppose that the opportunities for fulfilling our aims are less extensive than they would be in such a world.

In similar vein, we may note that, even if, in deterministic terms, some event could not have happened otherwise than it did, we are not left acknowledging its inescapability or inevitability, since these concepts are to be elucidated in terms of the 'could haves' to which determinism poses no challenge. To be a source of concern, determinism has to come hand in hand with some notion of inevitability, and that it does not do. The fire was inevitable. It does not matter what you might have done, it could not have been prevented. The truth or falsity of the conditionals implicit here is independent of determinism: whether, if you had acted, you could have averted the fire depends on how late it was left for action to be taken. Determinism does not imply our powerlessness; that would mean that any efforts to bring about a different outcome would have been unavailing, and there is no reason to suppose that, if we had drenched the fire in its first moments, it would none the less have carried on unchecked. The counterfactual endorsed is as good as the generalization stating the efficacy of putting out small fires with water.

Recall the example of the person who succeeds in designing and developing a large garden, but whose very success is alleged by the determinist to imply that the man would assuredly have failed had he sought merely to plant a row of beans. It is perhaps unfair to saddle the determinist with this view, since he too can acknowledge the two readings now under consideration, but, whether or not there is, as the determinist claims, a sense in which the lesser feat could not have been performed, there surely is a sense in which it could have been. On the one hand, we have been concerned merely to indicate a reading suited to the kind of impossibility which the determinist wishes to affirm; we have not made out a case for the actual truth of his affirmations. On the other hand, if our position is as good as the claim that the person who succeeded at the more demanding task could also have managed the lesser feat, it has little to fear.

In seeking to counter the determinist's argument, we have had recourse to a point made with respect to liberty of spontaneity. Being free to act in accordance with one's desires is one thing; being free to have or not to have those desires in the first place is another matter altogether. However, because it runs together desire with the broader wanting, this reply makes for a less emphatic rejection of the objection than is possible. We have, normally, no say in our desires, where this is a matter of desires found towards the physical end of the scale, desires which we may speak of feeling or experiencing. But we do have a say in what we want to do, in how we are prepared to act. You decide that you want to make someone's acquaintance. That is not deciding that you are experiencing a certain desire to meet the person, but deciding that you will try to do so. Sometimes you decide you simply will V, but, if you foresee problems, you may have to content yourself with deciding that you want to V. With the same reading, I may say that I cannot blame you for wanting to change your job; in the circumstances, that is a perfectly reasonable aim. If, on the other hand, I should say that I cannot blame you for having an urge to start a forest fire, I mean not that it is reasonable for you to seek to start a fire, but that blame is not warranted just on the strength of your experiencing such an impulse. Perhaps the pyromaniac has the misfortune to have been born with his incendiary urges, but it hardly makes sense to say the same of your wanting to meet someone or your desire to change your job.

Suppose there is some psychological condition which for you is inescapable. That is worrying if it means being obliged to live with something unwanted, something which is forced upon you and which cannot be shaken off. A fear of heights, let us say, or perhaps even a desire to smoke. But, if some desires have this character, others as surely do not. You want to invest in mining shares. It is not that you have experienced a sudden inexplicable urge to embark on this course of action, but it is something you wish to pursue because, after giving thought to various possibilities, you conclude that this is the best way of using your savings. Your favourable disposition to this alternative, your readiness to do what it involves, is not something, like a craving, which you might speak of giving in to, not something, as a desire to smoke might be, that you have against your will. On the contrary, in taking the relevant steps you are giving expression to your will. And, of course, for this to be your will, it does not have to be *chosen*; that can be required of the action, but it makes no sense with respect to the will.

If a person's 'action' stems from an uncontrollable urge, then perhaps we have something describable as causal determination of behaviour by desire; no doubt what we have is not describable as free. However, with the more general sense of 'want'—the sense in which, if you choose to V, it follows that you want to V—to say that our actions depend on our wants is not to advance a causal truth. On the contrary, the relevant desires—what we want most—

are determined by the way we act. The same point might be made in response to the following objection. It is in no way my fault that I want to eat, or even that I want to eat above all else. But, if there is something I want to do above all else, then, if ability and opportunity allow, I shall assuredly act. But then how can I be held responsible, be blamed for thus acting?

It is again true that we may have had no say as to what desires we have, but, in the relevant sense, what we want most is not given along with whatever desires happen to be thrust upon us, but it remains for the agent to decide what that is, i.e. to decide how to act. In saying that it is not my fault that I want to eat, we shall be alluding to the kind of desire which we can be said to experience, even to be born with. When I say that it is not my fault that I want to eat above all else, 'want' now has a role in expressing an evaluation: I rate eating more highly than any other pursuit. This does not necessarily embody a commitment to action, since 'want' may still be opposed to what one thinks one ought to do, but, if there is this commitment, we can hardly disown responsibility: I am prepared to make eating my overriding aim, to do what I must do to that end, but I know full well that I do not have to.

But there are other psychological conditions on which our actions may be dependent, and which lie outside anything we can control. I claim that I could have Ved if I had thought it worth the trouble to do so, but suppose that I have no say about the occurrence of such a thought. Does the conditional somehow lose its point under this supposition? In particular, if it is impossible that I should have thought it worth the trouble to V, is the truth of the conditional of any significance?

Once more, the condition we have to do with here can be understood in more than one way. On the one hand, it may be that the thought occurs to me that it would be worth the trouble to act, where this is a matter simply of a possibility which I entertain. On the other hand, 'thinking it worth the trouble to act' is a description that may characterize my state of mind in the sense of being a characterization which my commitment to action, or my actual behaviour, licenses. This is the case where it makes sense to hold me responsible; not when the thought merely occurs to me. On this approach, freedom to *act* remains the crucial consideration, any psychological antecedents being of relevance only in so far as they reach right up to the act, as it were—as a decision may relate to the action decided upon.

However, granted that we have free action, in the sense of action that accords with the agent's choice, that is of little account, it may be said, so long as the choice itself is not free, and this might well be doubted with kleptomania, bulimia, Münchhausen's syndrome, and other disorders of this ilk. Wanting to V above all else may not be a matter of having a desire imposed upon one, but what of the decision or choice? Is freedom to be discerned in one's commitment to action?

Telling someone that he has a free choice may be like saying that he can choose what, or as, he likes, where the choosing is a matter of selecting, taking, or accepting, so in the sphere of action, in which case we have to do simply with a particular instance of what has already been discussed. When choosing is not a behavioural act, is freedom of choice none the less to be understood on the pattern of free, albeit mental, acts? Those who insist on freedom of choice as necessary to underpin any worthwhile freedom of action might well wish to detach it from this pattern; certainly, a regress threatens if every free act demands its antecedent choice or decision. On the other hand, if 'A can choose to V' presents us with a 'can' of mere possibility rather than ability, the determinist will once more have us in his sights. Kate did not speak, but, we maintain, she none the less could have chosen to. If this is simply 'That might have happened', we are faced with the kind of possibility which determinism relegates to the realm of the unreal.

Consider making up one's mind. This, as indeed choosing or deciding, is a task one can set about, engage in; or indeed put off—and earn a rebuke for doing so. One can also be said to make up one's mind freely, in the sense that one is not subjected to pressures in reaching a decision. On the other hand, it is the steps which lead to one's mind's being made up, to a decision's being taken, that are in our control rather than the actual deciding. To say 'I could have made up my mind to stay' is to make a claim about what might have happened, it is true, but not a claim about one's ability to do something. We may elaborate this point in terms of the distinction between choosing to decide and choosing to decide that *p*. The latter is surely ruled out: I do not choose to decide to return a compliment, say. But I can make up my mind to reach a decision, unspecified; I can in this sense choose to decide, but this is choosing to engage in activities which will in all likelihood have a decision as outcome.

Compare thinking. I decide it is time I gave some thought to a particular matter, and start doing so, but the thoughts that then come into my head come unbidden. There is a limit to what is within our control here. Or again, our position *vis-à-vis* our freedom to decide can be compared to our ability to avoid losing at chess against a far superior player, something we can contrive only by avoiding playing. The latter may be within our power, but, once committed to the game, our fate is sealed; we cannot choose not to lose. Choosing itself, like deciding, has a similar standing if it compares with concluding or realizing that something is so. Thus, a decision to act may be at one with a judgement that such and such is best, which in turn may be a matter of a realization which dawns upon us.

So, a person may decide to speak, but one does not decide, or choose, to decide to speak. The latter is accordingly not a free act. A regress is thus forestalled, but are there unwelcome consequences in the opposite direction, casting doubt on the freedom of the actions which flow from the decision? It would not be right to speak of the person as being compelled. That is in place primarily when *action* is thwarted, when one might try to resist and fail. Compulsion presupposes freedom. Certainly, it seems to have no place when, as with a decision, what takes place is not against the subject's will. In any case, I suggest that the relevant considerations take us away from the point of decision. With his decision, the person has become prepared to harm another, but it does not matter that he *becomes* prepared, that his preparedness, his attitude, dates from a particular moment. The fact is, he *is* prepared, prepared to do something which he knows to be injurious and from which he can refrain. What is of relevance is not that he experiences a desire to do wrong, but that he is prepared to act on that desire; perhaps, that he actually acts on it. It does not seem that our failure to choose to decide detracts from our freedom in acting, but what remains critical is whether, having made up our mind what course of action we wish to pursue, we are able both to go ahead and pursue it, and to desist from such action.

However, even if the antecedents of such an ability are irrelevant to our freedom, it may still be wondered whether enough has been said to justify holding people responsible for their actions. More generally, we may be uncertain as to what attitudes towards a person's deeds remain appropriate so long as it is granted that a belief that alternative happenings were possible may have no firmer basis than our ignorance.

Suppose that you fail to take action when doing so would have had highly desirable consequences for you, and consider what subsequent responses, as of anger, regret, or self-reproach, could be considered rational on your part. You say you could kick yourself for not selling those shares at their peak, for not troubling to lock the house when you left. The determinist is likely to discern irrationality in such everyday responses. Not simply on the grounds that what is done is done, so that it is pointless to lament the past, to agonize over what might have been. Rather, he would say, while we may dearly wish that we had acted differently, it is only an illusion to suppose that we had a genuine alternative.

The first stage of a reply seems clear. Self-reproach is at least a coherent response, precisely because it is not an illusion to suppose that we could have acted differently; we know only too well that a real opportunity was missed. But this fails to address the question of the involuntary springs of our action. You berate yourself for not having sold shares when you seriously considered doing so. But when, at the time, you came to the conclusion, now so bitterly regretted, that the time was not right, this was not something chosen; it simply struck you that holding onto the shares was the most reasonable thing to do. And this, the determinist will say, is something which could not but have come about as it did.

The question is, what is it precisely that you regret? If your anguish stems from the realization that there was something which you could have done but did not do, it does not seem that determinism offers any relief. If you knew that any attempt on your part at acting would have been bound to fail, that you would have been frustrated at every turn, you could gain some solace from the fact that you did not even try, but determinism has nothing to say about this possibility. Contrast those occasions when what you grieve for was not within your power to bring about. Regret is likely to be more keenly felt, self-reproach more unforgiving, the nearer one was to doing what in retrospect is seen to have been so desirable. 'I could so easily have . . .', we lament. Even without indulging in deterministic considerations, the extension of this way of speaking to the more general sense of possibility is questionable. With this species there are perhaps no degrees, the simple steps being as remote from any real possibility as the more difficult ones. At all events, when the possibility is not in our hands, as 'I could so easily have had that bright idea', it is not clear that we are entitled to treat it as we might treat a failure to take a real opportunity. What irks us here is the fact that we did not do something which was within our power, and this is no less of a fact if determinism is true.

Parallel considerations apply on the matter of what one should or ought to have done. Even for the determinist, a future-directed prescription, as 'You should see a doctor', remains good advice if there is something to be gained from complying with it; once more, nothing in his position implies that one's best efforts to comply must be unavailing. But if it makes sense to say, for example, 'You should report that accident', it seemingly also makes sense to say 'You should have reported that accident', and this is more likely to be queried. The idea of its making sense might, in the former context, be understood in terms of the possible point such a judgement might have *qua* injunction; something can conceivably be achieved if the person is able to act, but, if he cannot, it is pointless to urge that he should (supposing the inability not one he can remedy). But, if this is how we gloss 'making sense' in this connection, the transposition to the past is dubious. With the time for action now gone, constructive urging becomes pointless harping on what might have been.

However, this approach suffers through ascribing priority to the action-guiding aspect of *should*—a priority which, while commonly granted, is unmerited. Compare the questions 'Should I *V*?' and 'Should I have *V*ed?'. The pragmatic dimension of the corresponding assertions is no longer there to distract us with these forms, but we are left to confront directly the more central issue of the advisability or morality of the act, the issue which is so evidently in focus with the kinds of consideration which would be adduced in answer to the question or in support of the corresponding judgement. The question of the point, understood in terms of a possible action-guiding use, is a secondary consideration, of relevance in circumstances where action is possible, but no more. True, one who constantly insists, 'You should have *V*ed', may well irritate precisely because it is too late for us to remedy our inaction, but if it is part of a repeated argument aimed at showing up the wrongness of our ways, then, while it will not undo anything, it may succeed in its point if this is to change our belief.

These considerations give some support to the intelligibility of 'You should have *V*ed' where, as with the present-tense use, no more than an ability is presupposed. What of more serious matters, as of punishment for misdeeds? How do matters stand with responsibility?

Responsibility is commonly explicated as amenability to persuasion, a matter of a readiness to hold back from a proposed course of action once its consequences have been more fully appreciated, once unsuspected alternatives have been drawn to the agent's attention. For instance, that a person in an advanced stage of (so-called) drug addiction is not responsible might be thought to be shown by his insistence on taking his drug even though he knows it to contain a poison that will result in a certain, and a painful, death. This approach appears to fit in well with the notion of wanting which connects with acting, the notion in which belief is implicated. The addict who is still open to rational persuasion will not lose his craving on being told of these dire consequences, but, if the persuasion is successful, he will no longer want to take the drug.

However, this notion of responsibility is largely secondary to our notion of free action. If not being amenable to rational persuasion involves being incapable of taking in the consequences of a proposed course of action, then it will be very much relevant to responsibility. But we have to leave room for the idea of something which a person wants to do above all else, so which he will continue to pursue whatever countervailing reasons are advanced. We may, depending on the case, consider such a person impervious to reason, but I should have thought that, unless it can be said that he has somehow been rendered incapable of refraining, we have as yet no ground for exculpating someone who has grasped the consequences of what he is about to do. It cannot be simply that argument with him is futile because his commitment to action is unwavering. Having an unshakeable desire, even to the point of irrationality, does not establish one's powerlessness, but, once more, it is the capacity to act and to refrain from acting rather than the character of one's desires that is all-important.

As an alternative to this approach, consider the following. A person is confronted with the problem of weighing up different choices, with various courses of action carrying both advantages and drawbacks. Opting for his final choice is a matter of being prepared to accept attendant drawbacks for the sake of the anticipated advantages, drawbacks which might include the risk that he should be censured, or even punished, for his act. If such a risk is then realized, the person has in one sense no cause for complaint; the risk was chosen, something bargained for. His predicament is of his own making. Whether or not wanting the risk-laden alternative is something the person can be said to choose, the fact is, this *is* what he wants, and the opposition to his will, should he be unable to have his way, is in either case just as real, just as unwelcome to him.

In going into the situation with his eyes open, the person can be said to have brought upon himself any ensuing punishment, but this is perhaps as far as we can go with non-moral observations. Thus, whether there is any moral justification for making the person pay for his misdeed is not answered simply by observing that the man had indeed chosen to expose himself to this fate. Our concern is with the background non-moral matters: that the person should know what he is doing, be capable of refraining from the action, and be prepared to take the risk which his choice entails—these would appear to furnish a prerequisite for any system of punishment, as far as concerns conditions on the side of the subject and his psychological state, conditions which might be held to define the notion of responsibility. However, it is important to recognize the independence of this notion, and of that of the freedom involved. What is to count as free action, as responsibility, should not be dictated by preconceptions about desert, about punishment and its justification; as if, insisting that an agent was acting freely, that he was responsible for what he did, we thereby condoned at least some form of punishment for his offence; in particular, as if we endorsed a retributivist theory which regarded punishment as unquestionably warranted so long as the action was voluntary. That we are supposedly giving *carte blanche* to the champions of such a doctrine is possibly a reason why there is such reluctance to accept that those who suffer from phobias or who act under duress can for all that be free agents. We might well radically revise our notions about the propriety of punishing wrongdoers, but it is not because there are any general doubts about human freedom that there is scope for such revision.

REFERENCES

Anscombe, G. E. M. (1971), 'Causality and Determination', repr. in *Metaphysics and the Philosophy of Mind: Collected Philosophical Papers*, ii (Oxford: Blackwell, 1981), 133–47.

Aristotle, *De Motu Animalium*.

—— *Nicomachean Ethics*.

Austin, J. L. (1979), 'Ifs and Cans', in *Philosophical Papers* (3rd edn., Oxford: Oxford University Press), 205–32.

Ayer, A. J. (1956), 'Freedom and Necessity', repr. in Watson (1982), 15–23.

Benn, S. I. (1976), 'Freedom, Autonomy and the Concept of a Person', *Proceedings of the Aristotelian Society*, 76: 109–30.

Berkeley, G. (1713), *Three Dialogues between Hylas and Philonous*.

Bouveresse, J. (1995), *Wittgenstein Reads Freud: The Myth of the Unconscious*, trans. C. Cosman (Princeton: Princeton University Press).

Burge, T. (1993), 'Mind–Body Causation and Explanatory Practice', in Heil and Mele (1993), 97–120.

Cheney, D. L., and Seyfarth, R. M. (1990), *How Monkeys See the World* (Chicago: Chicago University Press).

Chisholm, R. M. (1964), 'Human Freedom and the Self', repr. in Watson (1982), 24–35.

Churchland, P. M. (1989), *The Neurocomputational Perspective: The Nature of Mind and the Structure of Science* (Cambridge, Mass.: MIT Press).

Davidson, D. (1963), 'Actions, Reasons, and Causes', repr. in *Essays on Actions and Events* (Oxford: Clarendon Press, 1980), 3–19.

—— (1982), 'Paradoxes of Irrationality', in R. Wollheim and J. Hopkins (eds.), *Philosophical Essays on Freud* (Cambridge: Cambridge University Press), 289–305.

—— (1985), 'Rational Animals', repr. in E. LePore and B. P. McLaughlin (eds.), *Actions and Events: Perspectives on the Philosophy of Donald Davidson* (Oxford: Blackwell), 473–80.

Davis, R. T., Leary, R. W., Stevens, D. A., and Thompson, R. F. (1967), 'Learning and Perception of Oddity Problems by Lemurs and Seven Species of Monkey', *Primates*, 8: 311–22.

Dawkins, M. S. (1993), *Through Our Eyes Only? The Search for Animal Consciousness* (Oxford: W. H. Freeman).

Dretske, F. (1988), *Explaining Behaviour: Reasons in a World of Causes* (Cambridge, Mass.: MIT Press).

Eysenck, H. J. (1958), *Sense and Nonsense in Psychology* (Harmondsworth: Penguin Books).

Fodor, J. A. (1985), 'Fodor's Guide to Mental Representation: The Intelligent Auntie's Vade-Mecum', *Mind*, 94: 76–100.

—— (1990), 'Making Mind Matter More', repr. in *A Theory of Content and Other Essays* (Cambridge, Mass.: MIT Press), 137–59.

Frankfurt, H. G. (1971), 'Freedom of the Will and the Concept of a Person', repr. in Watson (1982), 81–95.

—— (1975), 'Three Concepts of Free Action', *Proceedings of the Aristotelian Society*, supp. vol. 49: 113–25.

Freud, S. (1912), 'A Note on the Unconscious in Psychoanalysis', *Collected Papers*, xii (London: Hogarth Press), 260–6.

—— (1915), 'The Unconscious', *Collected Papers*, xiv (London: Hogarth Press), 166–215.

—— (1916), 'Introductory Lectures on Psychoanalysis', *Collected Papers*, xv (London: Hogarth Press), 213–22.

—— (1925), 'The Resistances to Psycho-Analysis', *Collected Papers*, xix (London: Hogarth Press).

Glover, J. (1972), 'Freud, Morality and Responsibility', in J. Miller (ed.), *Freud, the Man, His World, His Influence* (London: Weidenfeld & Nicolson), 151–63.

Goldman, A. (1970), *A Theory of Human Action* (Princeton: Princeton University Press).

Greenfield, P. M., and Savage-Rumbaugh, E. S. (1984), 'Perceived Variability and Symbol Use: A Common Language-Cognition Interface in Children and Chimpanzees (*Pan Troglodytes*)', *Journal of Comparative Psychology*, 98: 201–18.

Grice, H. P. (1968), 'Utterer's Meaning, Sentence-Meaning, and Word-Meaning', repr. in *Studies in the Way of Words* (Cambridge, Mass.: Harvard University Press, 1989), 117–37.

Hacker, P. M. S. (1992), 'Malcolm and Searle on "Intentional Mental States"', *Philosophical Investigations*, 15: 245–75.

Harman, G. (1976), 'Practical Reasoning', *The Review of Metaphysics*, 29: 431–63.

Harth, E. (1982), *Windows on the Mind: Reflections on the Physical Basis of Consciousness* (Brighton: The Harvester Press).

Heil J., and Mele, A. (1993) (eds.), *Mental Causation* (Oxford: Clarendon Press).

Hume, D. (1777), *An Enquiry Concerning Human Understanding*.

Hunter, J. F. M. (1978), *Intending* (Halifax: Dalhousie University Press).

Kenny, A. (1975), *Will, Freedom and Power* (Oxford: Blackwell).

—— (1989), *The Metaphysics of Mind* (Oxford: Clarendon Press).

Kim, J. (1993), 'The Non-Reductivist's Troubles with Mental Causation', in Heil and Mele (1993), 189–210.

Köhler, W. (1927), *The Mentality of Apes* (2nd edn., London: Kegan Paul).

Kripke, S. (1980), *Naming and Necessity* (Oxford: Blackwell).

Lehrer, K. (1968), 'Cans without Ifs', repr. in Watson (1982), 41–5.

Locke, D. (1974), 'Reasons, Wants and Causes', *American Philosophical Quarterly*, 11: 169–79.

Locke, J. (1690), *An Essay Concerning Human Understanding*.

Lorenz, K. Z. (1954), *Man Meets Dog* (London: Methuen).

McCracken, D. J. (1952), 'Motives and Causes', *Proceedings of the Aristotelian Society*, supp. vol. 26: 163–78.

McGinn, C. (1991), *The Problem of Consciousness* (Oxford: Blackwell).

Malcolm, N. (1968), 'The Conceivability of Mechanism', repr. in Watson (1982), 127–49.

Marcuse, F. L. (1959), *Hypnosis: Fact and Fiction* (Harmondsworth: Penguin Books).

Melden, A. I. (1961), *Free Action* (London: Routledge & Kegan Paul).

Mellor, D. H. (1995), *The Facts of Causation* (London: Routledge).

Millikan, R. G. (1986), 'Thoughts Without Laws; Cognitive Science with Content', *Philosophical Review*, 95: 47–80.

Moore, G. E. (1912), *Ethics* (London: Oxford University Press).

—— (1959), 'Wittgenstein's Lectures in 1930–33', in *Philosophical Papers* (London: Allen & Unwin), 252–324.

Nagel, T. (1986), *The View from Nowhere* (New York: Oxford University Press).

Nisbett, R. E., and Wilson, T. D. (1977), 'Telling More than We Can Know: Verbal Reports on Mental Processes', *Psychological Review*, 84: 231–59.

O'Connor, D. J. (1968), 'Beliefs, Dispositions and Actions', *Proceedings of the Aristotelian Society*, 69: 1–16.

O'Connor, T. (1995) (ed.), *Agents, Causes, and Events: Essays on Indeterminism and Free Will* (New York: Oxford University Press).

Pease, A. (1984), *Body Language: How to Read Others' Thoughts by their Gestures* (London: Sheldon Press).

Pepperberg, I. (1987), 'Evidence for Conceptual Quantitative Abilities in the African Grey Parrot: Labelling of Cardinal Sets', *Ethology*, 75: 37–61.

Plato, *Sophist*.

—— *Theaetetus*.

Priestley, J. (1965), *Priestley's Writings on Philosophy, Science and Politics*, ed. J. A. Passmore (New York).

Putnam, H. (1975), 'The Meaning of "Meaning" ', repr. in *Mind, Language and Reality: Philosophical Papers*, ii (Cambridge: Cambridge University Press), 215–71.

Quine, W. v. O. (1992), *Pursuit of Truth* (rev. edn., Cambridge, Mass.: Harvard University Press).

Rundle, B. B. (1972), *Perception, Sensation, and Verification* (Oxford: Clarendon Press).

Rundle, B. B. (1979), *Grammar in Philosophy* (Oxford: Clarendon Press).

—— (1990), *Wittgenstein and Contemporary Philosophy of Language* (Oxford: Blackwell).

Ryle, G. (1949), *The Concept of Mind* (London: Hutchinson's University Library).

—— (1954), *Dilemmas: The Tarner Lectures 1953* (Cambridge: Cambridge University Press).

—— (1968), 'Thinking and Reflecting', in *The Human Agent* (Royal Institute of Philosophy Lectures, vol. 1, 1966/7; London: Macmillan), 210–26.

Savage-Rumbaugh, E. S. (1986), *Ape Language: From Conditioned Response to Symbol* (Oxford: Oxford University Press).

Schlick, M. (1962), *Problems of Ethics*, trans. D. Rynin (New York: Dover).

Searle, J. R. (1992), *The Rediscovery of the Mind* (Cambridge, Mass.: MIT Press).

Skinner, B. F. (1953), *Science and Human Behavior* (New York: The Free Press).

Terrace, H. (1987), 'Thoughts without Words', in C. Blakemore and S. Greenfield (eds.), *Mindwaves: Thoughts on Intelligence, Identity and Consciousness* (Oxford: Blackwell), 123–37.

Thalberg, I. (1969), 'Austin on Abilities', in K. T. Fann (ed.), *Symposium on J. L. Austin* (London: Routledge & Kegan Paul), 182–204.

Watson, G. (1982) (ed.), *Free Will* (Oxford: Oxford University Press).

White, A. R. (1972) 'What We Believe', in N. Rescher (ed.), *Studies in the Philosophy of Mind* (American Philosophical Quarterly Monograph Series, No. 6; Oxford: Blackwell), 69–84.

Wittgenstein, L. (1958), *The Blue and Brown Books* (*BB*) (Oxford: Blackwell).

—— (1958*b*), *Philosophical Investigations* (*PI*), ed. G. E. M. Anscombe and R. Rhees, trans. G. E. M. Anscombe (3rd edn., Oxford: Blackwell).

—— (1966), *Lectures and Conversations on Aesthetics, Psychology and Religious Belief* (*LC*), ed. C. Barrett (Oxford: Blackwell).

—— (1967), *Zettel* (*Z*), ed. G. E. M. Anscombe and G. H. von Wright, trans. G. E. M. Anscombe (Oxford: Blackwell).

—— (1979), *Notebooks 1914–1916* (*NB*), ed. G. E. M. Anscombe and G. H. von Wright, trans. G. E. M. Anscombe (2nd edn., Oxford: Blackwell).

—— (1980*a*), *Remarks on the Philosophy of Psychology*, vol. I (*RPP* I), ed. G. E. M. Anscombe and G. H. von Wright, trans. G. E. M. Anscombe (Oxford: Blackwell).

—— (1980*b*), *Remarks on the Philosophy of Psychology*, vol. II (*RPP* II), ed. G. H. von Wright and H. Nyman, trans. C. G. Luckhardt and M. A. E. Aue (Oxford: Blackwell).

—— (1988), *Wittgenstein's Lectures on Philosophical Psychology, 1946–47*, notes by P. T. Geach, K. J. Shah, and A. C. Jackson, ed. P. T. Geach (New York: Harvester-Wheatsheaf).

—— (1992), *Last Writings on the Philosophy of Psychology*, vol. II (*LW* II), ed. G. H. von Wright and H. Nyman, trans. C. G. Luckhardt and M. A. E. Aue (Oxford: Blackwell).

—— (1993), 'Remarks on Frazer's "Golden Bough"' (GB), in *Ludwig Wittgenstein: Philosophical Occasions 1912–1951*, ed. J. Klagge and A. Nordmann (Indianapolis: Hackett).

INDEX